THE MACHINE GUN

Patrick Stephens Limited, a member of the Haynes Publishing Group, has published authoritative, quality books for enthusiasts for more than twenty-five years. During that time the company has established a reputation as one of the world's leading publishers of books on aviation, maritime, military, model-making, motor cycling, motoring, motor racing, railway and railway modelling subjects. Readers or authors with suggestions for books they would like to see published are invited to write to: The Editorial Director, Patrick Stephens Limited, Sparkford, Nr Yeovil, Somerset, BA22 7JJ.

THE MACHINE GUN

GUN

A MODERN SURVEY

TERRY GANDER

Patrick Stephens Limited

First published in 1993

British Library Cataloguing in Publication Data:
A catalogue record for this book is available from the British Library

ISBN: 1-85260-356-9

Library of Congress catalog card no. 93-78065

Patrick Stephens Limited is a member of the Haynes Publishing Group PLC,
Sparkford, Nr Yeovil, Somerset, BA22 7JJ.
Typeset by BPCC Techset Exeter
Printed and bound in Great Britain by Butler & Tanner Ltd, Frome and London

CONTENTS

INTRODUCTION

FIREPOWER kills.

The implications of those two words have been among the most difficult of all rules for military commanders to accept ever since man passed the stage of throwing rocks and devised the first projectile weapons, such as bows and spears, light enough to be hurled. It was gradually noted that, other than at very short ranges, the chances of a single projectile weapon hitting a worthwhile target, let alone an individual target, were usually slim. Only by massing several projectile weapon users together was there any chance of inflicting significant damage on an enemy or quarry.

Thus groups of humans learned to band together for hunting and warfare. By co-ordinating their efforts and working out means of creating sufficient discipline to ensure that selected targets were engaged, the first successful hunters and soldiers grew to prominence and enjoyed the resulting spoils. Without realising it, they had discovered that the more projectiles that were directed through the air at a defined target, the better were the chances of hitting (and disabling) that target.

Over the centuries improved social cohesion and methods of organisation assisted in the formation of what were to become armies, armies with groupings that eventually evolved into specialist bodies such as cavalry or infantry. It was the latter that usually developed into the specialists who used some form of projectile weapon for their initial attacking or defensive measures (although the Central Asian cavalry achieved their conquests by using their bows from horseback); by the so-called Middle Ages the archer was a well-trained and effective man of war.

However, at that stage close order combat was still the main method of determining the outcome of any fight, and the cavalry, with its shock tactics and mobility, usually provided the determining factor in battle. Quite simply, the bow, for all the potential produced by its rate of fire and effectiveness when used en masse, was still a relatively puny weapon of limited range, accuracy and striking power (other than in highly trained hands) and one that could be rendered fairly ineffective by careful use of body armour.

For a while the crossbow seemed to offer a considerable advance on the longbow but it was a cumbersome weapon to use and had a low rate of fire – once fired it took time to reload. However, it was powerful, had a longer range, and its bolts could penetrate thick body armour. Gradually the days of the armoured soldier were approaching their end; but what really turned the tide was the advent of gunpowder.

The early gunpowder weapons were used as what we now regard as artillery. They were inaccurate, slow to serve in action and they were very expensive to manufacture and operate. But they had considerable potential, and gradually over the centuries the gun developed into a formidable weapon with enough striking power to cause the demise of the castle with its high defensive walls. Eventually the gun-maker's skills reached the point where hand guns could be manufactured and used by individual soldiers, to the extent that the resultant firepower alone could win battles. The cavalry gradually lost its overall ascendancy.

But the gun was and still is essentially a projectile delivery device. It must always be remembered that any gun, whatever its calibre or weight, is (in modern terminology) only a weapon delivery system. It is the projectile, in the form of the bullet or whatever else is fired, that is really the weapon that kills or injures. (Despite this, the gun in all its forms is still generally referred to as a weapon – so we will do the same.) As a delivery system, however, the gun, although it often has considerable potential in terms of accuracy and on-target effectiveness, is often wasted because it is operated by human beings who, under the stress of battle, aim it incorrectly or somehow do not operate it to its full effect.

When this human failing factor was allied with the inherent inaccuracy of nearly all the early gunpowder muskets, it was no wonder that throughout the first centuries of their employment, muskets and their like were regarded and treated as relatively ineffective weapons. They could not be relied upon to hit any target other than at very short ranges, usually well under 50 metres. To have any chance of hitting anything in excess of this close-quarter range – even a target as large as a horse and rider – numerous barrels had to be discharged simultaneously in a controlled manner.

Thus there were developed the various forms of 'organ guns' with several barrels arrayed on a single carriage and all discharged together. While these weapons could be effective, they took a considerable time to reload and were often cumbersome in action to the point of being 'one-shot' weapons. The alternative was to organise foot soldiers, each carefully drilled in the basic use of a musket, into lines from where they all fired on command.

The effectiveness of this combined, or volley, firing could be devastating to an enemy, and, often without realising it, commanders were beginning to appreciate that simple fact – firepower kills. Many battles were won simply by the shattering destructive power of the first controlled volley fired by whichever side was in position and ready first. For many years battles were fought in this manner and continued to be so even after the advent of the rifle.

By the mid-1800s technology and metallurgy had made the large-scale production of the rifle, with its enhanced range and accuracy, a viable and sought-after alternative to the earlier smooth-bore musket. Following the invention and introduction of the metallic cartridge, rifles were also easier to use effectively in action, especially as the 50-metre combat range of the smooth-bore musket had been replaced by potential effective ranges of 1,000 metres or more. Moreover, once the technologies of breech-loading were understood, rifles became easier to reload in a very short time compared to the lengthy smooth-bore muzzle-loading procedures. It was at around this stage that the 'firepower kills' dictum began to be misunderstood on a significant scale.

In simple terms it meant that the firepower produced by the massive armies that had been made possible by the social upheavals and reorganisation introduced following the Industrial Revolution, made any movement by armed forces within rifle range of each other virtually impossible. The American Civil War of 1861-65 demonstrated time and again that the time-honoured methods of manoeuvring and standing massed opposing forces opposite each other would no longer work. The art of defence advanced to such a peak that odds of the order of three to one in favour of the attackers became the very minimum required to ensure some measure of success. Attackers who attempted to move in the open within range of their enemy's rifles were quite simply swept away and casualty lists rose to totals that passed the comprehension of the time.

Yet all that commanders could do was to pile mass upon mass and attempt to force some form of breakthrough against defenders by the use of sheer weight of manpower and courage. It proved to be of no avail. Well before the end of the 19th century the military rifle had reached the point where it could produce enough firepower to stop any enemy and render them ineffective, either by killing or wounding or by forcing them to take some form of cover by going to ground and digging in.

Thus firepower came to rule the battle-field, but many soldiers were unable to find any method of overcoming or even accepting that situation. In war after war, from Gettysburg to the Great War via the battles of the Russo-Japanese War of 1905, attempts were repeatedly made to create massive formations that were supposed to overcome the enemy's firepower by courage, determination and sheer numbers. Only rarely did they succeed and then only at the cost of horrendous casualties.

By the time of the Great War the breech-loading rifle had been joined by two further weapons with enormous firepower potential. One was modern artillery, a weapon that deserves (and has received) study in its own right. But this book will concentrate on the second new weapon, the machine gun.

The machine gun was developed via the evolution of many factors, perhaps the most straightforward of which was simply that technology made it possible. By the end of the 19th century metallurgy and machine-tool skills had long since passed the point where complicated mechanisms could be mass-produced on an unremarked and regular basis. All manner of mechanised devices were coming into widespread use in all walks of life, from printing and public transport to agricultural machinery and load-handling systems. Tasks that once required hard manual labour or the sheer drudgery of repetition were gradually assumed by machinery of all kinds.

It was thus only a short step from continuous manual re-loading and operation of rifles or other small arms to the mechanical process of sustained automatic fire from a single weapon. The rifle itself was developed to the point where bolt action or similar mechanisms made the process of re-loading with metallic cartridges simple and rapid (by 1914, 15 rounds a minute was a training norm), and by the time of the Great War the first fully automatic rifle mechanisms were in being.

By then the machine gun was already a fully developed in-service weapon. The first successful attempts to produce mechanised firepower were made during the latter four decades of the 19th century and initially nearly all were manually operated. The Gatling gun was one of the most successful designs of that period to be produced on any scale. By using multiple barrels rotating horizontally around a central pivot, the Gatling gun's loading and firing operations could be continuously repeated for as long as a hand crank was turned. We need not concentrate on the Gatling gun too much at this point other than to note that it was one of the very first mechanised firepower weapons to pass the point of fantasy and become a viable weapon to be used in large numbers, albeit not usually in the tactical form that was to emerge after 1914.

The Gatling gun was but one of numerous other multiple-barrelled sustained-fire weapons such as the Nordenfelt and others; each used a differing barrel arrangement but all employed manual power to operate their repetitive and rapidly firing mechanisms. Yet it was only with the Maxim gun and all its numerous and various descendants that the true machine gun in its present form emerged, and it is the present-day descendants that we will deal with here.

The modern machine gun is the result of the many ingenious minds and skilled technicians who together produced the numerous complicated mechanisms which repeatedly operate faultlessly at high speeds and under great mechanical stresses. Nor should we forget the investment of capital, manufacturing and other resources (including human resources) that have combined to produce mechanised firepower in its modern form, a form that requires human intervention only to aim, load and initiate the entirely automatic firepower process by pulling a trigger or pressing a button – the machine gun does the rest. But the machine gun is not a wonder weapon. It has its tactical and other drawbacks and it imposes its own training, logistic and other loads on any military organisation.

Throughout this survey it must always be borne in mind that the machine gun is meant to produce firepower that kills, injures and maims. Indeed, it can produce so much firepower that the only counters to its deadly effectiveness are massed artillery (and plenty of it) and the resurrection of armour in the form of the tank and armoured personnel carrier. One of the greatest pities of the last few centuries is that so much human talent has been misdirected to such an end, and that fact is often put to one side when an observer witnesses the functional details and lines of any machine gun, or stands on a range and watches the weapons in action.

Yet it has to be remarked that the sheer destructive effectiveness of the machine gun has had such an impact on the way we live now that it is still worthy of a survey of the type presented here. From Port Arthur to Berlin and from the Somme battlefields to Korea, the machine gun has inflicted its ghastly negative impact on populations and the manner in which they think, react and behave. Without many of us realising it, the machine gun has altered the way we all live today and on a scale that can only be matched by the relatively recent introduction to warfare of air power and the nuclear weapon. Such a weapon has to be worthy of more than a passing consideration.

* * * *

It is with the completely automatic machine guns that we will mainly deal throughout this survey and it is with the models, variants and types that are in service or under development today that we will concern ourselves. Numerous magnificent tomes have been devoted to the history of the machine gun in all its forms, and to repeat those efforts, other than in a summarised form, will far outweigh the capacity of these pages to bear all the words that will be required to do the subject justice.

We will also have to limit the upper calibres of the machine guns involved. Fully automatic weapons are now in service in calibres that were once the undisputed realm of heavy artillery, so we will have to limit ourselves to 15 mm or thereabouts, and deal with the machine guns used by infantry or as light weapons on armoured vehicles and helicopters. Once past that 15 mm calibre the automatic cannon starts to proliferate and that weapon family, again, becomes worthy of a study in its own right.

Acknowledgements

A book of this nature cannot be written without substantial contributions in one form or another from many people. Although it is not possible to mention every contributing individual by name I would like to take the opportunity to express my thanks to Christopher Foss, Ian Hogg, Max Gunn, Herb Woodend, Chantalle Regibeau, Ed and Virginia Ezell, Lyn Haywood, and all the many others whose advice, assistance and guidance has been so valuable.

CHAPTER 1

BEGINNINGS – THE MAXIM GUN

THE need to produce amplified firepower from a single weapon had long been a gun-maker's dream, ever since the very early days of gunpowder weapons. Almost as soon as the very first gun barrels had been produced, far-sighted souls were busy placing two or more of those barrels on the same mounting, while others went further by producing arrays of barrels on a common bed with their barrels splayed out to cover a wide arc – the great Leonardo da Vinci produced drawings for such a weapon.

These multi-barrel weapons, usually known as organ or volley guns, were not machine guns in any sense but they did anticipate the requirement for firepower to dominate a tactical scene. All manner of refinements were introduced to the basic principle over the years, including the so-called Puckle gun which seemed to anticipate the modern revolver, but it is virtually certain that it was never actually manufactured other than in model form, despite all the attentions lavished on it in some automatic weapon histories.

The problem was that all the organ-type guns were virtually one-shot weapons that could be effective if fired, but took so much time to reload via their multiple muzzles that they were virtually useless after their first discharge. Many ended up as fortress defence guns, where they no doubt looked good and impressed the locals and (hopefully) any attackers. Even so, during the 14th and 15th centuries battles were fought with hundreds of organ guns on each side. Thereafter they gradually fell from use.

Most organ guns were really exotic forms of artillery, although multiple barrel muskets were not unknown; they were either arranged to fire all their barrels in one spectacular discharge or the various barrels were rotated by hand to align with a single lock that (at least in theory) allowed an individual firer to produce a short-lived but often useful degree of firepower. Again, however, these multi-barrel muskets took time to prepare for re-use after firing and, judging by the examples that have survived, must have been heavy and cumbersome things to handle, to say nothing of the considerable costs and pains required to manufacture them. Accordingly they were therefore mainly confined to use within fixed defences.

The development of the metallic cartridge during the mid-1800s at least provided an opportunity for some more advanced form of multiple-fire weapon to be produced with some expectation of success. It was not long before the inventors were coming up with what now seems to have been some outlandish schemes.

Designs such as the Billinghurst Requa gun of 1861 were little more than modernised organ guns. For example, this gun used no fewer than 25 0.58-calibre barrels laid side-by-side on a light metal frame and all fired at once. Re-loading was hastened by the use of special cartridges arranged in clips. In theory the weapon could fire as many as seven volleys in one minute, but it was little used other than a few located in fortifications during the American Civil War.

By contrast, the Ager gun, usually known as the 'Coffee Mill' gun, used a single barrel with cartridges being fed down into a revolver-type mechanism from a hopper under manual power and control. It apparently worked, but despite being offered to the Union Forces during the early years of the Civil War, it faded from view, mainly because the military powers-that-were of the time could see no requirement for such a weapon and had other things on their minds. They did, however, order small numbers, but they proved to be rather unreliable due to the ammunition employed. For once American salesmanship seems to have drawn a blank.

Yet still the inventors battled on, proposing and in some cases actually producing prototypes of a whole host of weapons that are now just names in ordnance history books. The Claxton, the Ripley, the Lillie battery gun, the Vandenbery volley gun, the Williams, the Gorgas, the Farwell and others all came and went without success, despite the fact that many employed ingenious mechanisms, both overall and in detail. Some of their features were to be 'rediscovered' in other and later weapon designs – for instance, the proposed Bailey gun of 1876 used a belt-feed mechanism, the first recorded instance of an ammunition feed system later to be widely adopted in much-modified forms.

In about 1851 the Belgians came up with their now-infamous Montigny *Mitrailleuse*

which was really nothing more than an advanced organ gun with 37 barrels arranged in a horizontal cluster all of which could be fired by the turning of a crank in less than one second. Fresh cartridges were pre-loaded into a plate ready to be aligned with the barrels and loaded in a single operation; removing the plate after firing also removed the spent cartridges and another ready-charged plate could then be loaded.

This principle was not unknown by other designers and was, for instance, used by the Confederates in limited numbers during the American Civil War. However, the main reasons for the infamy of the *Mitrailleuse* came after 1867 when the design was procured by the French Army and adapted to fire a special variant of their then-standard *Chassepot* rifle cartridge; the number of barrels involved was at the same time reduced to 25.

The resultant weapon looked like a field gun as all the barrels were arranged in a cluster resembling a conventional field artillery barrel and the whole arrangement was mounted on a wheeled field carriage weighing a considerable 2 tons in all. Unfortunately, although the French Army came to regard the *Mitrailleuse* as a 'wonder weapon' with which they could sweep their enemies away, they had no real idea of how to deploy and use it in action. Although the French authorities attempted to draw a dense veil of secrecy over the manufacture and deployment of the 190 or so weapons they had produced by 1870, by the time they used them during the Franco-Prussian War of that same year they had decided that they were some form of field artillery piece and deployed them accordingly, out in the open and exposed in the artillery fashion of the period. The Prussian gunners had a great time knocking them out from ranges of 4,000 metres or so while the poor *Mitrailleuse* crews were unable to engage targets at more than 400 metres and were rarely able to survive to produce any effective fire. That experience poisoned the minds of many contemporary military observers against the use of multiple-fire weapons for decades to come, despite the successes that the *Mitrailleuse* did achieve when it was sensibly handled, such as during the Battle of Gravelotte.

This was a great pity, for as early as 1862 a viable multiple-fire weapon was already in being. This was the Gatling gun which, despite being a manually operated design, proved to be the precursor of the notion of the machine gun proper. As with so many other world-changing ideas, the basic principle of the Gatling gun was simple.

A number of barrels, usually four or six, were arranged to revolve horizontally around a central pivot using power from a manually operated crank. Cartridges were fed one at a time from a magazine or hopper into the mechanism and into one of the barrels. As that barrel rotated, a cam system ensured that the cartridge was pushed into the barrel chamber, fired, and the empty case extracted ready for the re-loading process to start again as the barrel came back round to its original position.

After a start that was delayed once again by the reluctance of military minds to procure an entirely novel and unknown type of

weapon, the Gatling was a commercial and military success. The number of models grew and grew and were employed from such unlikely mountings as the humps of camels (if contemporary illustrations are to be believed) and from the maintops of sailing ships.

We will return to the Gatling gun later in this book (see chapter 20) but it has to be stressed that the Gatling was most important during its time for providing indications of the potential of multiple-fire weapons. All manner of armed forces procured examples for trials or service and they gave them their first experience of the degree of firepower that could be achieved by a fast-firing weapon. The usually conservative British Army had their first taste of the power of the Gatling at the Battle of Ulundi during the Zulu War of 1879 when attacking Zulu *impis* were unable to even reach an advancing British formation, but it has to be remarked that the guns involved in that action were manned by the Royal Navy after being dismounted from warships. The British Army thereby learned the value of the Gatling gun and used it in many campaigns thereafter. (Actually two were taken

Woolwich Arsenal, circa 1895, with a 0.303 Maxim gun (centre), a Gardner gun (left) and a Nordenfelt (right).

to West Africa by the British during the Ashanti War of 1874 but do not appear to have been used in action.)

Gatling guns were sold to Russia and Turkey as well as Great Britain but overall export sales were disappointing and most were sold and used within the United States – many armed forces procured small numbers for trials but did not place the anticipated orders. The US Army used the Gatling on a very limited basis during the Civil War although later models were used in greater numbers and a few were still in US Navy service as late as 1911. Some appear to have survived until at least 1914, by which time they were regarded as obsolete.

The Gatling gun had its contemporaries. A Hotchkiss design that appeared to owe much to the Gatling was produced in some numbers but actually used a differing operating mechanism. The American Gardner gun, with from two to five barrels, achieved some measure of approval from the Royal Navy and Italy but faded from the scene after the 1880s. The Nordenfeld was also used by the Royal and US Navies but only in limited numbers compared to the Gatling. A late rival, the Accles, was little more than a modified Gatling gun. All these manually operated weapons, no matter what degree of success they achieved, were, however, soon to become military dinosaurs following the inventive innovations of one man.

Hiram Maxim

Hiram Stevens Maxim was born in the backwoods of Maine in 1840 and died in England in 1916. During his lifetime he proved to be one of those men for whom the term polymath has to be something of an understatement, for his ingenious mind turned its attention to many things and he was able to devise not just totally original approaches to all manner of problems, but also to actually make money out of them. During his long life he turned his attention to electrical, civil and chemical engineering,

aviation and numerous other technical topics, and was able to invent artefacts as diverse as an automatic fire extinguishing sprinkler system (of the type still in use today) and a small arms silencer that is still acknowledged as one of the finest of its type. Yet the name Maxim is most often thought of regarding what was probably his finest and best-known achievement, the Maxim gun.

The Maxim gun had its origins in Maxim's youth when, in common with many others, he noted that the recoil produced when firing a hunting rifle was considerable yet it was energy that was wasted. He decided to put this potential energy to good use following a conscious decision to create a fully automatic machine gun.

By that stage of his life, the much-travelled Maxim had moved his base to Europe. There he commenced his self-appointed task by examining as many patents and examples as he could of the various attempts to produce what would eventually emerge as the machine gun. By so doing he recognised the inherent flaws in most of the then current approaches. Most used multiple-barrel arrangements and manual operation, both of which he decided to avoid. His first automatic weapon was actually a self-loading rifle on which the firing recoil was harnessed to drive the reloading mechanism. This device was patented in 1883 and from then onwards Maxim took the precaution of patenting every form of automatic weapon principle his fertile mind could devise, thereby laying the foundations of his future commercial prosperity.

From that first self-loading rifle it was a relatively short step to the machine gun, but it was a step that involved a great deal of development work and refinement before the first example, constructed in Maxim's workshop in Hatton Garden in London, was ready in 1884. It was a 0.45-inch calibre weapon with a cyclic rate of fire of about 600 rounds a minute and in essence it used the same operating principles that every following model of Maxim gun would employ.

The start of it all – Hiram Maxim and his first prototype Maxim gun.

When a chambered round was fired, the resultant recoil forces were harnessed to drive back the barrel and a hinged lock mechanism, both of which were mechanically connected at this stage. During the first part of the recoil the lock had all its elements in a straight line and was thus maintained in a rigid state. After a short travel the hinged lock was allowed to open downwards as a post was struck, and an 'accelerator' lever mechanism withdrew the lock body from the barrel as the union between the barrel and lock was broken. The lock took the spent cartridge case with it for subsequent removal from the weapon and at the same time the rearwards pressure applied tension to a fusee spring. By the time all that had happened, the residual pressure in the barrel chamber had fallen to a safe level and the barrel was returned to its original position. The fusee spring then used its tension to push the lock back to the firing position, loading another round in the process. Once back in the firing position, if trigger pressure was still applied the round

was fired and the entire process started all over again.

The heat produced by the many bullets passing through the one barrel was overcome by surrounding it with a water jacket. Air cooling was used on some later Maxim gun models but these were either lightened variants for special applications, such as the models produced for use on exploration expeditions in Africa and elsewhere, or for mountings on aircraft where the slipstream provided the necessary cooling.

Ammunition was fed into the gun on a fabric belt and the mechanism was so arranged that the recoil forces were used to drive this system as well as the automatic loading and firing; Maxim had experimented with drum and vertical feed arrangements before deciding that the belt was best. Most of his rifle-calibre guns used 333-round fabric belts.

The mechanisms involved in the seemingly straightforward Maxim gun process were ingenious in the extreme, but they were also sound and were to withstand the test of time and much hard use. By careful development of the various levers, ramps and cams, to say nothing of the arrangement of the fusee spring which returned the lock to its starting point, Maxim was, by his own efforts alone, able to produce the first machine gun that would not just act as a 'proof-of-principle' test bed but which could also be developed into an efficient military weapon.

Maxim was greatly assisted in his subsequent developments by one important factor, the introduction of smokeless propellants for rifle cartridges. Apart from the benefits of concealment when firing, these cartridges provided a much smoother pressure curve when ignited – the old black powder was rapidly consumed when ignited, providing a steep pressure curve which imparted almost all its energy rapidly, whereas the smokeless propellant took time to burn and released its energy relatively slowly, thereby creating the all-important gradual pressure curve. This gentle imparting of cartridge energy was exactly what the Maxim gun operating principle required to operate at its maximum efficiency and made the overall design of the Maxim mechanism that much more reliable and practical.

Feasibility trials with the 1884 prototype convinced Maxim that he was working along the right lines and from then on all development work was directed towards making the design lighter and more amenable to the mass production which Maxim was far-sighted enough to realise would follow. He also ensured that the design would be simple enough for the average soldier to be able to field strip, maintain and repair every part of the gun.

Mass production did indeed follow, not only in the United Kingdom but also in Russia, the United States, China and elsewhere. Just about every armed force throughout the world made use of the Maxim gun at some time or other. The vigorous and often spectacular sales tactics employed by Maxim, along with his aggressive defence of his patent rights, brought him honours, wealth and prestige, but his invention was also to bring misery to many as in war after war the Maxim gun exacted its lethal toll.

The British Maxims and the Vickers

Among the first Maxim gun users were the British, but it cannot be said that the gun met with much enthusiasm from the British military establishment. Maxim set up a manufacturing company with the British Vickers armament concern in late 1884 and it was not long before Maxim guns were in production in appreciable numbers and in a variety of forms and calibres. As early as 1887 the British Government was acquiring Maxims in 0.45-inch calibre, and later examples were produced for the long-lived 0.303-inch rifle cartridge. The 'British' Maxims were produced in many forms, from examples carried on field carriages to pedestal-mounted naval examples.

However, the British military authorities did not exactly seize upon the potential of their new weapon – most of the Army's officer corps seemed to ignore it entirely. At first there was a distinct lack of agreement as to who would use the Maxim. The Royal Navy adopted the weapon as an anti-torpedo craft weapon and more were arrayed in batteries as harbour defence weapons to counter small raiding craft, so there was little argument on that front. However, the Army were for many years undecided as to whether the Maxim gun was an infantry or artillery weapon, especially when the wheeled mountings involved looked very similar to field gun carriages – it was the French *Mitrailleuse* argument all over again. In the end the infantry were given the task, but many serving soldiers were reluctant to assume something they regarded as an irksome and unfamiliar duty and had no idea of how the Maxim was to be employed in war.

The Maxim gun was at first thought to be ideal for the colonial warfare at which the

The Maxim gun section of the 2nd Battalion the Royal Worcester Regiment presenting an excellent target during training on Malta in 1897.

British were so adept in the latter part of the 19th century, but for more conventional warfare the Maxim was thought of as an ungentlemanly device best suited to artisans and not quite the thing with which the officers of the day need concern themselves. Even the rough experiences of the South African wars did little to stir any acceptance of the machine gun, even when handfuls of Boer Maxims and 'Pom-Poms' (large Maxim guns with a calibre of 37 mm) wrought havoc with the tightly packed British formations during several battles. As late as 1914 the British infantry battalion still had an allotment of only two rarely used machine guns each, and the command of that small section was often given to the lowliest of subalterns who usually spent most of their time attempting to pass the job on to someone else, instead of learning how to use their charges. The result was that when the BEF went to war in 1914 there were few officers who had even the faintest idea of how to employ the machine gun in action.

A small cadre of far-sighted British officers did appreciate the firepower lessons of the American Civil War and Russo-

The 1st Battalion Princess of Wales's Own Yorkshire Regiment (The Green Howards) manning a defensive position at the Curragh in 1896.

Japanese War but could do little to alter the seemingly entrenched indifference of the British officer corps towards the machine gun. Instead, the firepower prophets had to concentrate on producing a controlled rifle firing rate that has never been surpassed – the officers could understand rifles! The pity was that the firepower produced by those rifles could have been produced far more easily and effectively by the machine gun.

After 1914 that all changed as the German Army pressed home the full impact of how machine guns could be used, as will be related later. By then the Maxim gun had all but passed from British service (the last were withdrawn from front-line service in 1917) as from 1912 onwards the Vickers became the 'British' machine gun.

Following the early period of association with Vickers, Maxim formed an alliance with the Nordenfeld concern, only to return to the Vickers fold again later; in time Maxim's interest was completely taken over by Vickers after the Maxim gun's patent rights expired. Vickers then felt free to enhance the original Maxim design and

devised their own variation of the Maxim lock. Basically the Vickers gun was still a Maxim but the lock mechanism was altered to open upwards, thereby making the entire receiver smaller and lighter. Yet the basic principle remained just as durable and reliable as before, if not more so.

By 1918 the Vickers machine gun was regarded so highly that every battalion was happy to use as many as they could get. A measure of the altered attitude to the machine gun generally was provided by the practice of modifying captured German machine guns to accommodate 0.303 ammunition and thus bolstering the number of weapons in the field. A Machine Gun Corps was formed to provide specialised machine gunners and numbers of machine gun batteries, so by 1918 the old pre-war British attitude to the machine gun had altered entirely.

The Vickers machine gun went on to become the standard British heavy machine gun for another 50 years. It was not withdrawn from the British armed forces' inventory until the 1970s and even at the opening

British machine gunners firing a captured German 7.92 mm MG 08 in 1918.

A Vickers 0.303 machine gun in use by Sudanese levies in 1935.

A 0.303 Vickers machine gun mounted in its travelling lock on a Universal Carrier, circa 1942.

of the 1990s it would be unsafe to state that the type had entirely passed from service with every nation in the world. Many old soldiers still regret its passing. At the end of its life the Vickers machine gun could provide indirect fire support at ranges of over 4,000 metres, was capable of producing sustained automatic fire for periods of time that no present-day air-cooled machine gun can match, and it could even fire armour-piercing ammunition that would still defeat light armoured vehicles at considerable ranges today.

During its long service career the Vickers machine gun was produced in many forms, but the vast bulk of them were 0.303-inch

The classic view of a two-man team manning a 0.303 Vickers machine gun.

A Royal Marine Commando manning a 0.303 Vickers machine gun during manoeuvres in Denmark in 1955. The Royal Marines were the last of the British armed forces to retain the Vickers.

weapons capable of firing 450 to 500 rounds a minute, often for hours on end and usually from a tripod mounting. Also produced were larger 0.50-inch models for light tanks and air-cooled versions for use on aircraft. There was a 40 mm 'Pom-Pom' version used by the Royal Navy on multiple-barrelled mountings before they were replaced by the Bofors gun.

The US Army used the Vickers machine gun during the Great War and went to the extent of manufacturing large numbers in the United States in their own 0.30-inch calibre. Other manufacturers included Portugal and Australia. Nearly all the old British colonial nations had the Vickers at one time or another, including India and Pakistan who were among the last known large-scale users. South Africa at one point during the 1960s even went to the extent of converting their stock of 0.303-inch guns to take 7.62 mm NATO ammunition, and was the only nation known to have done so.

With the Vickers machine gun the Maxim gun came to the end of the line in its country of origin, the United Kingdom. However, many other nations adopted the Maxim, usually by direct purchase from

whatever concern Maxim himself was associated with at any particular time. Others took out licences to produce their own Maxim guns and three of them are worthy of note – Germany, Russia and Switzerland.

The German Maxims

The first Maxim guns were sold to Germany in 1888 and were purchased by Kaiser Wilhelm II himself for his Dragoon Guard Regiments. In 1891 the Berlin-based firm of Ludwig Loewe (later to become the Deutsche Waffen und Munitions Fabriken, or DWM) signed a licence production agreement to manufacture Maxim guns. By 1894 the first examples of this arrangement were in production for the expanding German Navy. Austria-Hungary became an early DWM customer and more examples were sold to Russia by whom they were used to dreadful effect during the bloody battles of the Russo-Japanese War of 1905. The German Army adopted the Maxim gun in 1901 and thereafter became the most technically advanced and enthusiastic of all Maxim gun users.

Within the German Army the firepower

potential of the Maxim gun was appreciated and promoted to the utmost degree. Machine gunners were trained to attain high levels of technical expertise with their weapons and special tactics were developed to make the greatest use of the Maxim's potential ranges and rates of fire. Not surprisingly, German Army machine gunners came to regard themselves as a special force; they were even allowed to devise their own special mountings and other Maxim gun-associated equipment that would soon be put to good use.

During 1908 the 'definitive' German Maxim gun was introduced as the 7.92 mm *Maschinengewehr* '*08*', or MG08. It used the *Schlitten '08* sledge mount, a seemingly heavy and cumbersome mounting but one which was to prove durable and adaptable over many years. The gun could be dragged over rough ground folded on to the sledge arrangement and opened up to become a sturdy mounting providing steady fire for long periods. The mounting could even be used to accommodate tools and spare parts. Other MG08 accessories were legion and ranged from optical sights to shields for the crew and the cooling water jacket. The sledge mounting was eventually modified to allow it to be used for air defence.

All these measures were put to good use after 1914 and it was the MG08 that rammed home to the British Army the harsh message that firepower kills. It was the MG08 that forced the onset of trench warfare and it was the MG08 that drove horse-borne cavalry from warfare once and for all. The German machine gunners had many opportunities to demonstrate their prowess, with perhaps the best example of their lethal skills being provided during the Somme battles of 1916. Time and time again British soldiers attempting to attack German-held trenches were mown down in droves by small groups of machine gunners operating MG08s from carefully selected positions.

Good as the MG08 proved to be, it was a heavy weapon, weighing over 62 kg altogether, so it was something of a problem to move in a hurry. Consequently the German Army developed the MG08/15, a much lighter model with a smaller water cooling jacket and receiver, a rudimentary butt and a small bipod. In this form the Maxim gun became a one-man load that could be operated in action by a single soldier, but at 22 kg it was still too heavy for its intended role, ie what was to become known as the light machine gun. A lighter

German Army gunners manning an air defence 7.92 mm MG 08 in 1935.

air-cooled MG08/18 was developed too late to see action, but other air-cooled Maxims with their usual water-cooling jackets replaced by slimmer perforated sleeves and revised trigger and other firing systems were used in great numbers as aircraft and airship weapons.

Many of the German Great War Maxims were to see action again during the Second World War, not only in German hands but with nations such as Poland, Yugoslavia and Belgium (MG08/15s converted to the Belgian 7.65 mm calibre) to whom they were awarded after 1918. By 1940 the MG08 and MG08/15 had been relegated to garrison and second-line formations and none survived after 1945 other than as war trophies.

The Russian Maxims

The Russian Army had been introduced to sustained-fire automatic weapons by their acquisition of a number of Gatling guns in 1865, a number later boosted by the licence production of the Gatling in Russia after 1870. The Russians knew the Gatling as the Gorloff gun after the officer responsible for preparing the weapon for production in that country.

The Russians used their new weapons to tremendous effect at the Battle of Plevna in 1877 and provided the world with yet another dreadful indication of the lethal firepower of automatic weapons when used against attackers moving forward in the dense formations favoured at that period. The Russians' Turkish adversaries also had Gatling guns but were quite unable to use them properly, and suffered accordingly.

Russia was high on the list of nations to whom Maxim demonstrated his gun and he was duly rewarded with a few sales to the Russian Navy from 1897 onwards – Maxims for the Russian Army came from Germany via DWM. Experience with those weapons in Manchuria when used against the Japanese in 1905 prompted the Russian military authorities to negotiate a licence production agreement to establish a Maxim production facility in Russia. The first results of this agreement left the Tula Arsenal (just south of Moscow) during 1905.

By 1910 the Russians had decided to introduce some design enhancements of their own, mainly directed towards reducing unit cost and weight and achieved principally by the introduction of a steel water-cooling jacket in place of the former bronze component. The result was the 7.62 mm *Pulemet Maksima obrazets 1910*, usually known as the PM1910. This model was thereafter destined to be one of the most important of all Russian, and later Soviet, infantry weapons, being produced in numbers reaching hundreds of thousands (one source has calculated over 600,000), easily outstripping all other Maxim gun production totals.

The PM1910 was based on a late model of the Maxim known as the 'New Light Model' of 1906, which may be regarded as the ultimate Maxim version before the Vickers gun was introduced with its various design changes. The 1906 model and the PM1910 therefore had some modifications compared to earlier models, including a muzzle attachment which acted as a recoil booster to create a more positive lock action, an attachment later used on the Vickers machine gun.

Perhaps the main point to note regarding the PM1910 was its weight. Even with the lighter steel cooling jacket the gun alone weighed 23.8 kg. This was combined with what can only be described as a miniature field artillery carriage, complete with steel wheels, folding front legs, a U-shaped trail arrangement that doubled as a tow bar, and a shield. Known as the *Sokolov* mounting, it was so heavy and sturdy that the complete weapon weighed a hefty 74 kg. The *Sokolov* was a copy of a Vickers-Maxim proposal that never caught on elsewhere, but the Russians took to it with a will and it has to be said that the design withstood the test of time – some PM1910s were still being encountered in Vietnam during the 1970s, still on their *Sokolov* mountings. The shield on

Longest-lasting of all the Maxims, the Russian/Soviet 7.62 mm PM1910, seen here for once without its shield.

the carriage could be removed but was often retained, as much to protect the weapon as the gun crew. Experience from 1914 onwards demonstrated that just knocking out an enemy machine gunner by rifle fire did not remove the gun from action – only a well-aimed bullet through the mechanism could do that. The carriage wheels were also very useful, for to attempt to transport the weapon by any means other than towing it behind a mule or by a couple of men using drag ropes would have involved a great deal of labour and manpower.

There were numerous other mountings for the PM1910 including fortification, armoured train and sledge mountings of every size, as well as naval pedestal mountings. One rather romantic mode of use was on small horse-drawn four-wheeled carts known as *Tachankas* which will be forever associated with the sights and sounds of the Russian Revolution of 1917 and the later Civil War. Production of the PM1910 for the new Soviet Union continued after 1918 and, after a definite fall in output during the inter-war years, continued right through the Great Patriotic War of 1941-1945 until some unknown date after 1945. Even when the invading German Army took over the Tula Arsenal during 1942, production was

maintained at numerous improvised factories east of the Urals. The finish of some of these 'non Tula' PM1910s was often very rough but they still worked. During 1943 the PM1910 cooling jacket gained a petrol-type cap from a tractor production line – this was intended to assist the rapid filling of the water jacket and to permit snow to be packed into the jacket when winter temperatures precluded the use of water, and was a copy of a jacket filler method used on Finnish Army Maxims during the Winter War between Finland and the Soviet Union in 1939-1940.

The Great Patriotic War also saw the PM1910 in a new role, that of anti-aircraft gun. Single PM1910s could be mounted on tall anti-aircraft tripods, but the most spectacular application was on a mounting designed by Fedor Tokarev in 1931. This had four PM1910s side by side on a single tubular frame, each with its own ammunition box holding a 250-round belt; water pipes connected all four cooling jackets. A truck-borne version of this mounting was also produced. This hefty air defence arrangement apparently worked very well, to the extent that the Germans were happy to augment their own light anti-aircraft gun inventory with captured examples.

In fact, the Germans impressed into their own armoury any serviceable PM1910s that came their way, and that meant a considerable number. Most were issued to garrison or second-line units but others ended up along the Atlantic Wall or were issued to the various home defence units formed during the latter days of the war in Europe.

After 1945 the PM1910 appeared again during the Korean War of 1950-53, this time in the hands of the North Koreans. By that period the Soviet Union was divesting itself of much of its older weapons material stocks, mainly those produced by them before the end of 1945, in order to get more modern weapons into service. PM1910s were thus prominent among the military aid and other largesse handed out to many nations who were deemed to be within the Soviet sphere of influence. PM1910s could therefore be found all over South East Asia and parts of Africa, and examples still seemed to pop up here and there even at the start of the 1990s.

The PM1910 was used as an aircraft weapon during the Great War, usually with revised cooling jackets perforated for air cooling. An air-cooled version of the PM1910 intended for aircraft use was known as the PV-1. It was developed during the 1920s and produced during the 1930s, but was out of production by the start of the Great Patriotic War in 1941. Attempts to produce a light machine gun version of the PM1910 for Army service came to naught when the notion proved to be impracticable.

The PM1910 was the longest-lived of all the many Maxim variants and it was produced in by far the greatest numbers.

The Swiss Maxims

The Swiss Maxim guns are mentioned here to note their superb standards of manufacture. Production of Maxims in Switzerland did not commence until 1915, all Swiss Army requirements before then having been met either by one or other of the British-based Maxim concerns or by DWM in Germany. The Great War cut off both supply sources so the Swiss started their own production at the Waffenfabrik Bern.

Bern-produced Maxim production continued until 1946 by which time 10,269 had

Twin anti-aircraft 7.5 mm MG11 Maxim guns fitted with finned cooling jackets to improve cooling efficiency.

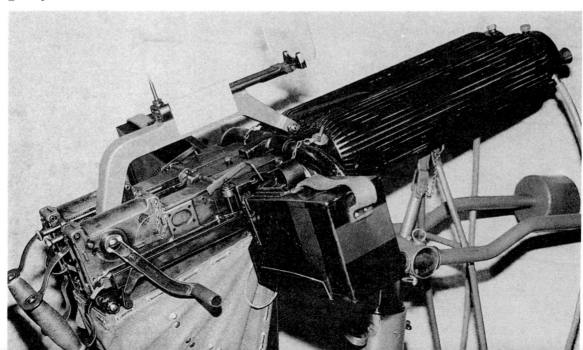

been made, 2,000 of them for export to Persia, plus a further 80 air-cooled versions for the Swiss Air Force. The model concerned was known as the *Maschinengewehr 1911* or MG11 and was produced in 7.5 mm calibre. Many variants were introduced such as fortification models and versions with special tripods for use by mountain troops.

At a time when many other nations had long since divested themselves of Maxim guns, the Swiss Army introduced various up-dating modifications during the mid-1930s. Modifications included the introduction of metal link ammunition belts in place of the more usual fabric, a revised trigger mechanism for operation by one hand, a new recoil booster and flash-hider muzzle attachment, and the introduction of an anti-aircraft mounting. Accessories such as optical sights were also introduced.

With these enhancements the MG11 soldiered on until well into the 1960s when it was finally replaced by more modern equipment. Even then the Swiss Maxims were still capable of many more years of service, for their standard of manufacture was of the very highest. Examination of museum spec-

Swiss 7.5 mm MG11 Maxim gun on a pintle mounting for use as an air defence weapon.

imens in Switzerland will still reveal that the Swiss just cannot resist the chance to demonstrate their superlative standards of metal machining, and to handle any Swiss-made small arm is a delight to anyone who appreciates the finer standards of gun-making. The Swiss MG11 Maxims were

A Swiss 7.5 mm MG11 Maxim gun in a fortification mounting – the tube over the gun is a sighting telescope, and note the heavy elevating arc.

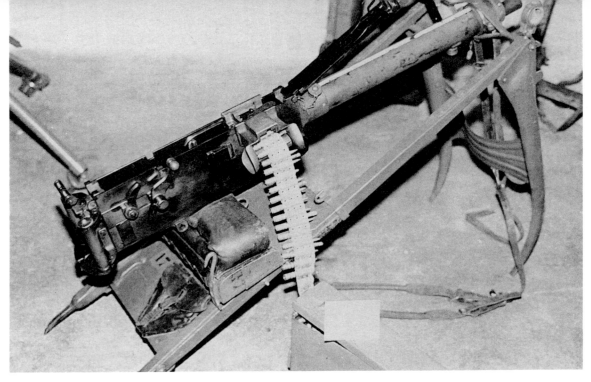

The Swiss 7.5 mm MG94 Maxim gun with its distinctive narrow water-cooling jacket and equally distinctive back-pack and quadruped mounting combination; this example is in a Swiss fortification museum.

among the very finest machine guns ever produced and have to be seen to be believed.

Other Users

The list of Maxim gun users is a long one, but top of the list must come China and the United States.

The first Maxim guns were shipped from the United Kingdom to China in 1892, and thereafter many ended up in the hands of one or other of the various government factions, but after the early 1900s the numbers imported were sporadic and mainly from the German DWM concern prior to 1914. There seems to have been no centralised military procurement system until Japan decided to move into Manchuria in 1931. By then China was in a state of political and social disarray as various warlords strove to use whatever local power they could obtain for their own ends.

A measure of central government was imposed by Chiang Kai-shek during the 1930s but the result of many years of bad government and upheaval meant that the so-called Nationalist Army was equipped with a quartermaster's nightmare of weapons and equipment. In order to impose some measure of standardisation it was decided to select an old Maxim design as a basis for future machine gun production.

Many of the machine guns then still in use were Model 1909 Maxims in 7.92 mm calibre that had been supplied by the old DWM and embodied many features of the MG08. It therefore made sense to standardise on that model, so the Type 24 was born; this was a slightly modified copy of the old DWM Model 1909, still in 7.92 mm, but the life of the production run was destined to be short.

The first examples were delivered in 1935 (the 24th year of the Nationalist dynasty that commenced in 1912), and by the end of 1937 over 36,000 had been produced. By that time the Japanese had resumed their campaign of mainland expansion and China itself was under invasion, so production was terminated. During the production run some air-cooled Type 24s were manufactured for aircraft roles.

The Type 24s that reached Nationalist

Army hands went on to give a good account of themselves. They proved to be reliable weapons that are still to be found around South East Asia in various hands – they were encountered in Communist Chinese service during the Korean War of 1950-53 and more were come across during the Vietnam campaigns, but by then most had been re-barrelled for the Soviet 7.62 mm × 54 cartridge.

The Chinese Type 24 was a remarkable off-shoot from the Maxim gun saga. The tale of the American Maxims was more familiar, and was once more a tale of the reluctance of military authorities to even accept the need for new types of weapon. The US Army had taken the Gatling into service only after a great deal of wrangling and was as happy as they could be with them. Besides, they had few funds to spare for new equipment. Thus, although US Army trials with the Maxim gun commenced as early as 1888, it took until 1903 before an order for 50 guns was placed; they were delivered the following year and became the Model 1904.

American production was undertaken by

Frontal view of a Chinese 7.92 mm Type 24.

Colt but the numbers involved did not come to much and were limited to 282. They were little used, although a special mule harness was devised to carry them during home-based cavalry operations such as the 1916

The Chinese 7.92 mm Type 24 Maxim machine gun.

campaign along the Mexican border. The Model 1904 was not among the weapons taken to France in 1917 with the result that when the US Army got there it was woefully short of machine guns and had to 'borrow' Vickers and other machine guns from its British and French allies. Even as the war ended the armed forces of the country that was the 'home' of the machine gun still had to go to the extent of re-barrelling captured German MG08s to fire American ammunition. Even so, most of the Maxim guns still retained as war trophies and collector's pieces in the US are MG08s and MG08/15s.

Maxim guns were sold throughout South America to nations such as Argentina, Chile and Peru, to Balkan nations such as Bulgaria and Serbia, and to European nations such as Spain, Portugal, Italy and Belgium – there were few corners of the world where the Maxim gun did not penetrate at some time or another.

Wherever it reached the gun changed or ended the lives of many, and the modern machine gun continues that sad process to this day. However, it must not be forgotten that it all started with the Maxim gun.

DATA

Model	Maxim	MG08
Calibre	0.303 in	7.92 mm
Weight (gun only)	18.15 kg	26.44 kg
Length	1.18 m	1.175 m
Length of barrel	717 mm	719 mm
Rate of fire	600 rpm	450 rpm
Feed	belt	belt
Muzzle velocity	838 m/s	892 m/s

Model	PM1910	Type 24
Calibre	7.62 mm	7.92 mm
Weight (gun only)	23.8 kg	23.81 kg
Length	1.107 m	1.22 m
Length of barrel	721 mm	n/a
Rate of fire	520-580 rpm	200-300 rpm
Feed	250-round belt	250-round belt
Muzzle velocity	863 m/s	approx 890 m/s

Model	Vickers
Calibre	0.303 in
Weight (gun only)	18.1 kg
Length	1.155 m
Length of barrel	723 mm
Rate of fire	450 rpm
Feed	250-round belt
Muzzle velocity	745 m/s

CHAPTER 2

THE BROWNING GUNS

THIS book is intended to be a survey of modern machine guns in use today, and while the previous chapter had necessarily to relate the early days of the machine gun and the part played in its development by Hiram Maxim, there was another man who played an equally important and long-lasting part in the development of the machine gun. That man was John Moses Browning.

John Browning occupies a unique niche in both the history of the machine gun and in its present-day account. The weapons he devised and developed have proved to be so good that just one of them, the 0.50/12.7 mm M2 machine gun, can lay claim to having been produced in far greater numbers than any other type – well over two million and still rising. Despite dating back to 1918 (or even earlier if the basic design concept is considered) the M2 remains in large-scale production to this day, virtually unchanged from the original.

Unlike Maxim, Browning was a gunsmith through and through. Whereas Maxim turned to the development of the machine gun as an outlet for his creative abilities, Browning was born into a family of gun-makers and learned his trade in family surroundings in Tennessee.

He learned his trade so well that it was not long before he was designing his own weapons, throughout his career following much the same line of action. He devised the mechanisms involved, constructed the prototypes himself and prepared the design for subsequent production. His expertise extended to automatic pistols, various types of self-loading and automatic rifles and even to large-calibre automatic anti-aircraft guns. The modern pump-action shotgun was but one of his innovations, but his greatest successes came with machine guns.

As mentioned in the previous chapter, Maxim had noted that the recoil produced when firing a rifle was wasted energy. Browning noted the same regarding the blast produced at the muzzle. By harnessing this muzzle energy, Browning devised his first machine gun from 1889 onwards. It was first produced by Colt in 1895, thus becoming the Model 1895, and it was the first of what are now known as gas-operated machine guns.

With gas operation, expanding gases behind the bullet moving along the barrel are tapped off from just below the muzzle to drive a piston system under the barrel which in turn drives the operating mechanism. On the Model 1895 the piston pushed a swinging arm that moved vertically down below the gun, which meant that the weapon could not be fired from a position too close to the ground; it was this swinging arm that gave the Model 1895 its nickname of 'potato digger'.

However, the Model 1895 proved to be much lighter than contemporary Maxim guns, mainly due to the adoption of an air-cooled barrel, thus doing away with the bulky and heavy barrel water-cooling jacket. The price for this lighter weight was that the gun could not fire the sustained bursts of the Maxim, but in its favour, its lightness made it handier and it was soon adopted by the US Marines and several South American nations.

Browning then demonstrated his pragmatic approach to gun-making by realising that, at that time (the 1890s), the recoil-based principle of machine gun operation had more to offer than gas operation. He therefore turned his attentions to what is now known as the short recoil principle which, in very general terms, was not too unlike that used on the Maxim gun.

The system as used by the Browning gun had a breech block locked to the barrel at the instant of firing a cartridge, so the two components recoiled together. After a short travel, during which time the gas pressures in the chamber fell to a safe level, a lug holding the barrel and breech block together was forced down and the breech block was then 'accelerated' to the rear while the barrel stopped. During this rearward travel, a cartridge was taken from the ammunition belt and positioned in a T-shaped slot in the breech block face, pushing out the old cartridge case in the process. The breech block then started to move forward again under recoil spring pressure and connected with the barrel, when the fresh round was fired. It should be noted that the round was fired as the block and barrel moved forward locked together. In this way some of the firing forces were absorbed by the energy of the forward movement, and the whole process then started again for as long as the trigger

remained pressed. To add to the overall simplicity and reliability of this mechanism, the gun was easy to field strip after only a minimum of training. Yet another virtue was that the Browning design proved to be relatively cheap to manufacture when mass production commenced.

This basic mechanism, much simplified in the above account, has remained virtually unchanged on every Browning machine gun ever since it was first devised by John Browning back in 1901. At that time the system went un-used, for the US Army had no funds for the procurement of new machine guns (it still had the Gatling and was in the prolonged process of adopting the Model 1904 Maxim gun). Browning thus had to concentrate on other things until it became obvious that the United States would become embroiled in the Great War.

In 1916 a count of all the machine guns available to the US Army revealed that they had only 1,100 or so in stock, nearly all of them obsolete and in need of replacement. Thus in early 1917 Browning, realising his moment, demonstrated his new machine gun to the military authorities, along with an odd offshoot of machine gun development history, the Browning Automatic Rifle or BAR. The BAR, which was really an early attempt at an assault rifle, went on to have a distinguished military career that did not end for the US Army until after the Korean War, but it need not concern us here.

The Browning machine gun was an immediate success. Early demonstrations were made involving the firing of thousands of rounds without stoppages or malfunctions, and so thorough was the Browning approach to detail design that the weapon was ready for mass production as soon as manufacturing facilities could be made available. Orders were immediately placed for no fewer than 45,000 examples, and the Browning machine gun saga commenced.

The Model 1917

The Browning Model 1917, or M1917, was

The Browning 0.30 M1917A1 water-cooled machine gun.

a 0.30-inch water-cooled machine gun having a rate of fire of around 500 rounds a minute with the ammunition fed into the weapon in 250-round belts. It was fired from a tripod but many other mountings, including mobile carriages, were eventually employed.

It was not long before Model 1917s were pouring from the production lines, and by end of 1918 a total of 56,608 had been manufactured. However, only a handful of those had actually reached the Western Front by the time that the November 1918 Armistice was signed, although masses were on their way. Perhaps it was just as well, for the rush to production had forced the use of some unsatisfactory materials and the base plate of the receiver proved to be prone to cracking. Post-war modifications to this drawback and other slight changes resulted in the Model 1917A1; existing M1917s were later brought up to M1917A1 standard.

Thereafter the M1917A1 remained virtually unchanged as the US Army's standard heavy machine gun until after the Korean War. During the Second World War a further 53,854 M1917A1s were made, although with some changes such as steel water jackets in place of the former bronze.

The M1917A1 was also produced under licence by Fabrique Nationale (FN) of Herstal-Liege, Belgium. John Browning had formed an association with this concern after falling out with Winchester earlier in his gun-making career and many of his subsequent designs, including the widely-used 9 mm Model 1935 Hi-Power automatic pistol and the pump-action shotgun, were produced in Belgium. FN produced some M1917A1s for export to nations in South America (and elsewhere), where many remain in service to this day.

The M1919 Series

The Browning M1919 series of air-cooled machine guns grew out of a Great War requirement for such weapons to arm the

US Army's new tanks. The result was an M1917 with an air-cooled barrel which was heavier than the standard item. By the time the US Army had finished testing the design it was 1919, so the new machine gun became the Model 1919, or M1919. Few, however, were destined to be fitted into tanks, for the American tank production programme was severely curtailed during that year.

Most of the 2,500 or so M1919 guns were produced by converting M1917 water-cooled weapons, thereby commencing the practice of interchanging parts between various models and types of Browning machine guns that would eventually spawn a whole host of sub-types and variants that remain the gun buffs' happy hunting ground, but are a quartermaster's nightmare.

From the M1919 came the M1919A1, intended for the US Army's Mark VIII tank, while the M1919A2 was mounted on a small tripod for use by cavalry. The M1919A3 was an interim model until the M1919A4 arrived on the scene in the 1930s.

The air-cooled M1919A4 became the most successful of the 0.30 Browning machine guns, so successful that it remains in service in large numbers to this day and there seems to be no technical reason for the model ever to pass from service.

Although it is an air-cooled design, the M1919A4 is a true multi-purpose weapon. It has been used for just about every type of application with which the machine gun has ever been involved, from armoured vehicle co-axial or defence weapon (on ball or pivot mountings) to tripod-mounted ground fire support weapon. There was also a special light tank version (the M1919A5), while the M2 and AN-M2 (not to be confused with the 0.50/12.7 mm M2) were early examples of a lighter-barrelled series of aircraft guns with ammunition feed possible from the left- or right-hand side and with provision for solenoid firing when used as wing or pod-carried weapons.

The M1919 series carried over the reliability and durability of the original M1917A1, and so great is the interchangeability of parts between models that numerous hybrids and sub-marks have been manufactured, even by the practice of assembling complete guns from spare parts.

The M1919A6 was an oddity, being an attempt to produce some sort of light machine gun for infantry use. Basically it was a M1919A4 with a light barrel, a bipod, a butt plate and a new trigger arrangement, but it made an unsatisfactory light machine gun, mainly because it was too heavy at

The air-cooled Browning 0.30 M1919A4 machine gun.

A Second World War picture of a Browning M1919A4 during training in the United States.

14.6 kg. In addition, it was an awkward and ill-balanced weapon and dangling ammunition feed belts are still not suited to the light machine gun role. It was not popular with the troops but it lasted until after the Korean War when it was phased out by the US Army. It was, hwoever, possible to modify the M1919A6 back to the M1919A4 standard. A total of 43,479 M1919A6s were manufactured but they are little seen now.

The last major variant of the M1919 series was the 0.30 M37, originally intended for co-axial or other uses on tanks but since employed as the fixed forward-firing armament on helicopters, typically as part of the Helicopter Armament System Subsystem XM1. The M37 was originally developed from the M1919A5 but differed in having feed capability from the left- or right-hand side and changes to the feed cover. M37s may still be encountered on the older models of M48 and M60 main battle tanks – the main model used on both was the M37C which has a hydraulic cocking (charging) system and an electrically operated trigger. At one stage M37 machine guns were trialled for installation in the

flying gun-ships such as the AC-47 'Puff the Magic Dragon' series used in Vietnam, but they were supplanted by 7.62 mm rotary Miniguns (see chapter 20).

The 1919A4 remains in service with many nations to this day, often as an armoured vehicle weapon for which it is still ideally suited. The one thing that signalled the eventual decline of the model was the adoption by many nations of the 7.62 mm × 51 NATO cartridge during the 1950s – the M1919A4 was produced to fire the 0.30-inch Model 1906 cartridge and the two are not compatible. Thus the M1919A4 may eventually fade from sight, but several nations have demonstrated that the basic design can be readily adapted to take the NATO round. The US Navy still retains one variant, the Mark 21 Model 0, which fires the 7.62 mm × 51 cartridge while South Africa makes use of the 7.62 mm MG-4 (converted in-country) as a combat vehicle weapon (see chapter 11). Both of these machine guns were originally M1919A4s converted to use the NATO ammunition. The 7.62 mm C1 is a similar weapon used by Canada.

A 0.30 L3A3 Browning machine gun, the 'British' model of the M1919A4, mounted on a Centurion AVRE 165 combat engineer vehicle.

There are still many Third World nations all around the globe that have yet to adopt or cannot afford the change to NATO standards, although they are getting fewer year by year. Many of those nations con-

A Canadian soldier firing a 7.62 mm C1 machine gun from a Snowmobile – the C1 is a Browning M1919A4 converted to fire 7.62 mm NATO ammunition.

tinue to use the 0.30-inch cartridge and thus retain the M1919A4 (or the M1917A1) to fire it. It will be many years before the last of them is retired. Between 1940 and 1945 729,423 0.30-inch air-cooled Brownings, including aircraft versions, were manufactured and more have been manufactured since.

The M2

By 1918 the coming of the tank indicated that armour was seen as one counter to the dreadful capabilities of the machine gun. Armour was also being increasingly used by aircraft, including a new type of aircraft, the ground attack fighter. American officers already in France issued a requirement for a new heavy-calibre machine gun firing a heavy bullet at a high enough muzzle velocity to penetrate the new armoured shields. It was suggested that something around a 0.50-inch/12.7 mm calibre would be about right.

The problem for the gun and ammunition designers was packing sufficient propellant and a heavy enough bullet into such a calibre to meet what was an exacting requirement. An experimental 11 mm cartridge sent over from France seemed to promise much, but the first attempts by Winchester to produce a 12.7 mm equivalent lacked power and were not very promising.

John Browning was involved with this programme because he designed the machine gun that was to fire the new cartridge, which was simply an M1917 scaled up to suit the larger calibre; the basic Browning mechanism remained unchanged except in detail. The first examples firing the new Winchester cartridge were ready on the day after the war ended but, as anticipated, the gun and cartridge combination did not meet the required specification.

In the aftermath of the Armistice, Winchester obtained a batch of German 13 mm *Tank und Flieger* (*Tuf*) cartridges; these were of considerable power since they were designed for firing from the Mauser *Tank-Gewehr* anti-tank rifle. By scaling this cartridge down to 0.50-inch/12.7 mm the performance specification could be met, but Browning had to incorporate an oil buffer into his design to prevent the resultant recoil forces from shaking the gun to pieces. Thus the 12.7 mm × 99 cartridge was created and it remains in large-scale service to this day, a NATO standard cartridge and one unlikely to be surpassed for some time to come. Browning's new machine gun was standardised in 1921 as the Model 1921, or M1921. It was a water-cooled weapon which was deemed to be perfectly satisfactory in every way but not many were purchased by the American military for the simple reason that funds during the post-war period were sparse. Attempts were made to market the weapon commercially. A Model 1924 was produced for sale by a consortium formed by Colt and the British Armstrong Whitworth company. Water-cooled ground and air-cooled aircraft versions were offered, but the project does not appear to have been a success in sales terms.

It was 1925 before the first M1921s were issued, and then mainly to the US Navy where they were primarily used as shipboard anti-aircraft defence weapons. They, and a modified version known as the M1921A1, were nearly all phased out from service by 1944 and replaced by other weapons.

Among those 'other weapons' were large numbers of the air-cooled version of the M1921 known as the M2. This had its origins in 1923 and was originally developed as an aircraft weapon – it was redesignated M2 in 1933. The M2 had provision to feed ammunition belts from either side, but apart from the air-cooled barrel the aircraft version differed little from the M1921 or the commercial Model 1924. It had a barrel 36 inches (914 mm) in length, later increased to 45 inches (1.143 metres) to improve the ballistic performance.

As it was intended for use on aircraft where short bursts are the norm, the original M2 proved to be something less than satisfactory when the first attempts were made to convert it for ground use, mainly on vehicle mounts, due to the weights involved (the M2 weighs over 39 kg) – anything other than very short bursts tended to make the barrel overheat. Thus a heavier barrel was introduced for ground use and the resultant gun was thereafter known as the M2 HB (Heavy Barrel); also introduced at the same time was a reduced rate of fire. With the new barrel the overheating problems were largely overcome other than under the most extreme firing conditions. Aircraft weapons continued to use various lengths of the lighter barrel; and even when heavier aircraft weapons were adopted, these light-barrelled aircraft weapons were still put to good use by the US Navy and many were employed as 'riverine craft' armament during the Vietnam campaigns.

The 'aircraft' M2s have a much higher cyclic rate of fire than the 'ground versions', the theory being that fleeting aircraft targets require more projectiles to ensure significant damage than the usual run of ground target. Aircraft M2s thus have a rate of fire of as much as 1,250 rounds per minute and incorporate special provisions, such as modified buffers and recoil springs, to cater with this rate. The ordinary ground

American soldiers on a firing range with a Browning 0.50/12.7 mm M2 HB heavy machine gun.

service M2 HB has a cyclic fire rate of 450 to 550 rounds per minute. M2s on anti-aircraft mountings could be modified to fire at rates as high as 650 rounds per minute.

Thus by 1941, when the United States entered the Second World War, the American armed forces had at their disposal a powerful heavy machine gun and cartridge combination that proved to be a world-beater. The problem then, as always, was that there were not enough of them. Calls came for more and more M2s to meet all manner of requirements, so that by 1945 a total of no fewer than 1,968,686 had poured from numerous production lines. Even America's enemies joined in by producing their own direct copies; the Japanese 12.7 mm Type 1 was an M2 clone.

They were used on all manner of vehicles and mountings, from Jeeps to trucks and from tanks to heavy tripods. Aircraft versions, both fixed and flexible, armed many Allied aircraft while others went to Allied navies; Over 82,000 examples of a naval version with a water-cooled barrel were manufactured to replace the old Browning M1921s. Multiple M2 mountings were introduced as anti-aircraft guns – the M45 Maxson mounting was but one of many and used four M2s on a trailer or vehicle carriage; these air defence versions were meant for use against low-flying aircraft. Many remain in service although some nations have converted the carriage to accommo-

date two 20 mm cannon in place of the original four M2s.

Throughout the Second World War American design teams did their best to produce an 'improved' M2. Most development attempts ended up as 'gilding the lily' exercises and although some detail modifications were introduced, such as replacing the original oil buffer by a simpler arrangement, at the end of it all the M2 HB was still basically the same weapon as produced back in the 1920s. Many of the wartime experiments, and many since, were directed towards not just 'improvement' but the provision of higher fire rates, revised ammunition feed systems or reduced weight for aircraft applications. Some programmes, such as that which led to the AN-M3, introduced so many modifications that the weapon became unrecognisable as an M2 other than the calibre used - even the ammunition was of a special type with a higher muzzle velocity plus a heavier projectile.

Production of the M2 HB Browning tailed off after 1945 and for a while it seemed as though the weapon was going out of fashion. The reasons were not hard to find. The M2 HB was a heavy brute to lug about so it was usually assigned to vehicle or other mobile mountings, or it had to be carried on some sort of conveyance. Once emplaced on an air defence tripod or something similar it was difficult to get in and out of action in a hurry, and other weapon

A Japanese armoured personnel carrier with a Browning 0.50/12.7 mm M2 HB.

types, such as automatic cannon, seemed to offer better firepower. Aircraft applications became fewer, even though the first F-86 Sabres in Korea still used six 0.50-inch Brownings as their main armament. These guns were the AN-M3, a souped-up version of the M2 with a rate of fire of 1,200 rounds a minute. (In truth the AN-M3 programme was something of a retrograde step, for combat experience during the Second World War demonstrated that cannon were far more efficient as fighter weapons. Later marks of Sabre, and other aircraft that came later, converted to 20 mm or heavier cannon.)

But the M2 HB still has considerable potential as an armoured vehicle weapon, either used co-axial to a tank's main armament or as a turret-mounted general-purpose weapon on light combat vehicles.

Four Browning 0.50/12.7 mm M2 HB heavy machine guns on an M45 multiple anti-aircraft mounting during the Second World War.

In a demonstration of the versatility of the Browning 0.50/12.7 mm M2 HB, this inflatable craft sports a special ring mounting for the weapon.

Even the latest US Army main battle tank, the M1A2 Abrams, sports an air defence M2 HB on the turret roof – many other models of tank and armoured vehicle have the same. Many NATO trucks have pro-vision to carry an M2 HB in a ring mount-ing on their cab roofs for air defence.

However, it is as a ground-mounted weapon that the M2 HB is making its definite come-back. There are several

A special version of the Browning 0.50/12.7 mm M2 adapted by FN to be mounted on an external pintle on helicopters.

A light inshore patrol boat with a formidable armament of two 0.50/12.7 mm Browning M2 HBs and a single 7.62 mm M60 machine gun.

reasons for this. One is that many armed forces now have a need for some form of anti-aircraft defence that is handier and more flexible than the expensive one-shot guided missile or equally expensive radar-controlled gun system. The M2 HB still has considerable air defence potential, especially when combined with the latest generation of 12.7 mm × 99 ammunition which, in addition to the usual jacketed ball round, encompasses such niceties as explosive, armour-piercing and incendiary projectiles, all of them highly effective against low-flying aircraft and that other battlefield innovation, the helicopter. Armour-piercing rounds, such as saboted light armour piercing, the so-called SLAP (more familiar as armour-piercing discarding sabot or APDS) with its muzzle velocity of 1,200 metres a second, also provide the infantryman with a destructive capability against light combat vehicles such as armoured personnel carriers and reconnaissance vehicles. There is even a 'multi-purpose' 12.7 mm × 99 round, the Norwegian NM140 produced by A/S Raufoss. This remarkable example of mod-

ern ammunition technology manages to pack into its small dimensions a capability for armour penetration (up to 11 mm of armour at 1,050 metres), an incendiary effect once the projectile is through the armour, and a fragmentation effect to add to the other on-target hazards.

All this weapon potential can be used by ground troops at a fraction of the procurement, training and manpower costs when compared to other more technologically advanced weapon systems.

There is also the distressing fact that the 12.7 mm × 99 projectile is a potent man-stopper. Most 7.62 and 5.56 mm bullet strikes will cause any recipient to lack any further interest in local proceedings, but under some circumstances, such as a peripheral wound or involving a hyped-up fanatic, a wounded enemy can still advance and cause injury or damage. Any hit from a 12.7 mm × 99 projectile will prevent such eventualities. Having said that, the M2 HB is usually employed to provide fire against material targets such as aircraft, soft-skinned vehicles, weapons and other equipment.

Examples of Olin-produced Saboted Light Armour Penetrating (SLAP) 0.50/12.7 mm ammunition with a sample of their penetration capabilities.

Another factor involves the introduction of the smaller-calibred light and general-purpose machine guns over the last few decades. This has often produced the result that effective automatic fire at long ranges can be lacking within infantry units; but the M2 HB can deliver its projectiles at ranges of up to 4,000 metres or more with no undue problems. Ammunition advances have also meant that the new rounds have a greater degree of inherent accuracy – at one time the 12.7 mm × 99 cartridge was notoriously inaccurate at long ranges, but that drawback has now been overcome by better propellant fillings and other ballistic technological refinements.

Then there is the introduction of modern technology to mountings. Using the M2 HB on a ground mounting such as the M3 tripod is something of an adventure, for the recoil forces are considerable and any mounting will jump and judder more than enough to make sustained accurate fire impossible. For some tactical applications this is no drawback, such as the provision of fire against an area rather than a specific target, but there are other instances where more accurate fire is required. Thus the last decade has seen the introduction of the 'softmount' buffered tripod or other type of mounting where hydraulic or spring-loaded cylinders absorb much of the firing shock and make steady and prolonged aim feasible. One of the proponents of the 'softmount' has been the Norwegian firm of Vinghøgs; their latest model is the NM152 and they also produce an adjustable-height anti-aircraft mounting to be used in conjunction with their 'softmount'.

The introduction of the 'softmount' has created the possibility for the latest generation of optical and night vision sights to be used in place of the rather rudimentary 'iron' sights provided on the standard M2 HB. Night vision sights can convert the M2 HB into an all-weather 24-hour anti-personnel and anti-material weapon, even at ranges of well over 2,000 metres, while optical sights can convert the gun into a long-range sniper-type weapon when firing in the single-shot mode.

Electronics have also introduced the possibility that each M2 HB could be converted into a highly accurate long-range fire support weapon. In the United States McDonnell-Douglas Astronautics have developed a miniature electronic fire control system known as the Multi-purpose Universal gunner's Sight, or MUGS. This small unit can be mounted on any M2 HB and employs a laser rangefinder, ballistic data stored in an electronic memory, environmental sensors such as thermometers and wind sensors, and sensors to determine the trunnion side angle (cant) and other factors. All these components permit a gunner to aim the weapon at a target then engage the MUGS unit and the laser rangefinder; the MUGS system computer will then instantaneously analyse all the available data and calculate the amount of barrel elevation and the necessary lead angle required to hit the target. The sight graticule in the MUGS will then be automatically off-set to the required amount to allow the gunner to have a high on-target hit probability. It is

even possible to provide MUGS with a night-vision capability. MUGS is still under development, but something very like it will be commonplace on heavy fire support weapons in the near future.

All these factors have made the M2 HB such a valued weapon that once again production is in progress at several locations around the globe. In the United States RAMO and SACO are both manufacturing M2 HBs while in the United Kingdom the Manroy concern is busy producing a wide range of Browning mountings, parts and accessories as well as complete weapons. In Belgium FN of Herstal (now known as Fabrique Nationale Nouvelle Herstal, or FNNH, due to corporate changes) continues its well-established connection with the Browning name by manufacturing several types of M2 HB, including a special remote-control M3P version in an underwing pod for light aircraft and helicopters. In the Far East Taiwan at one stage announced plans to manufacture its own M2 HBs, but how far those plans have progressed is not known.

One recent innovation regarding all Browning machine guns has been the elim-

A Browning 0.50/12.7 mm M2 HB heavy machine gun fitted with a night vision device.

A Belgian Army soldier with an FN-produced Browning 0.50/12.7 mm M2 HB heavy machine gun.

ination of the cartridge head space adjustment. When Browning machine guns were first manufactured it was not possible to make the distance, or head space, between the face of the breech block and the cartridge in the barrel chamber a constant dimension. But if this space was too short

Final assembly of Browning M2 HB heavy machine guns at the RAMO assembly line.

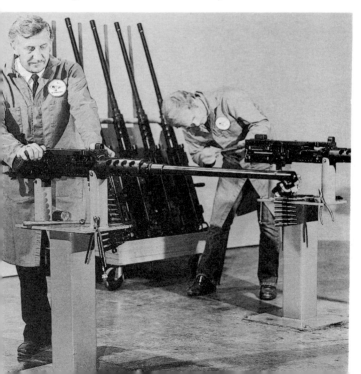

the breech block could not move forward sufficiently and the mechanism's inherent safeties would not let the gun fire – if it was too wide cartridges could be split apart to cause jams. John Browning overcame this problem by incorporating a method of using simple gauges and a ratchet system for the soldier in the field to carry out the necessary adjustment. Improved manufacturing methods and standards later did away with the need for this adjustment altogether, other than during workshop maintenance, but it arose again when the call came for some method of producing a quick-change barrel.

Changing any air-cooled Browning barrel is no major task, but the cartridge head space adjustment normally has to be checked every time it is carried out, which can be a time-consuming procedure when under field or combat conditions. Thus new systems of rapid barrel changing have been introduced involving bayonet-type lugs and grooves and no necessity to check the head space. RAMO, SACO and FN have all introduced their own particular systems to this end but, as far as is known, none has yet been adopted.

The same has applied to what was perceived as a requirement to produce a lighter version of the M2 HB, and these will be

Belgian paratroops undergoing training with a Browning 0.50/12.7 mm heavy machine gun — note that the gun is not loaded.

dealt with in more detail in chapter 19.

The M85, originally the T175E2, is a special variant of the M2 HB adapted for use as a co-axial or cupola-mounted gun on tanks; it is normally carried on M60 series battle tanks as a cupola gun for use by the tank commander. The M85 differs from the orthodox M2 HB in having a quick-change barrel and a dual rate of fire; this latter feature was introduced to provide the weapon with a higher rate of fire against aircraft targets. For normal ground targets

An FN-produced Browning 0.50/12.7 mm M2 HB fitted with a FN-developed quick-change barrel system — note the barrel-changing handle.

Above *A Browning 0.50/12.7 mm M2 HB with a quick-change barrel mounted on an assault landing craft belonging to the Swedish Coast Defence forces – note the buffered cradle and the foam pads on the shoulder rests.*

Below *A very rare bird observed in Chile – an air defence mounting with twin Browning M2 machine guns, probably taken from aircraft, modified to accommodate water-cooling jackets. Water is pumped through the jackets by a battery-powered motor.*

the M85 has a cyclic rate of fire of about 450 rounds a minute. When used against aircraft the rate of fire is increased to approximately 1,050 rounds a minute. If required, the M85 can be dismounted from its tank mountings and placed on a tripod for ground use, but this is seldom done. The American development system even managed to produce a ground-use version of the M85 known as the M85C, but it has long been withdrawn from service. Odd 'unlisted' variants of the M2 still crop up. One seen in recent years is a Chilean Air Force air defence mounting involving what appears to be two aircraft M2s. In order to fire long bursts from the light barrels, each barrel is enveloped in a thin water-cooling jacket with water circulated through each jacket by a battery-powered pump.

Another off-shoot of the M2 story involves an entirely different type of weapon, namely the 40 mm MK19 automatic grenade launcher. When a requirement arose for a weapon to fire 40 mm grenades in bursts, other than by the usual single-shot launchers, numerous small arms manufacturers put forward their own particular

AFUSTE DOBLE DE
AMETRALLADORA
BROWNING 50 PARA
TIRO ANTIAEREO

design solutions. The design selected after an intensive trials programme, the MK 19, was devised by SACO Defense Inc and employs a mechanism based on that used on the M2. Another odd comment on the M2 concerns a 30 mm automatic cannon known as the McDonnell-Douglas ASP-30. This potent weapon is intended to be a heavy fire support and vehicle defence weapon that might one day supplement or supplant the M2. Not surprisingly the ASP-30 was designed to be interchangeable with the M2 HB, employs the same overall dimensions and even uses the same ground and other mountings as the M2 HB – but there the resemblance ends, for the ASP-30 is a much heavier weapon all round.

The Browning M2 HB is still one of those weapons that is likely to be encountered just about anywhere in the world – other than in the former Soviet and Chinese areas of influence. Yet even there, many nations that have been provided with CIS or Chinese heavy machine guns of similar calibre still retain the M2 HB and field the two weapons together. The Browning M2 HB saga is far from over, for it seems extremely likely that the only replacement for the weapon is yet another M2 HB.

Twin Browning 0.50/12.7 mm M2 HB machine guns in an air defence mounting produced in Turkey – note the balancing counterweight hanging below the barrels.

DATA

Model	Model 1919	M2 HB
Calibre	0.30 or 7.62 mm	12.7 mm
Weight (gun only)	14.06 kg	39.1 kg
Length	1.044 m	1.653 m
Length of barrel	610 mm	1.143 m
Rate of fire	400-500 rpm	450-600 rpm
Feed	250-round belt	belt
Muzzle velocity	860 m/s	810 m/s

CHAPTER 3

THE GERMAN CONTRIBUTION

THE section relating to the output of Hiram Maxim has related how the German Army created such an impact with their employment of machine guns during the Great War. The German armed forces also made a considerable impression on the development of the modern machine gun to the extent that another historical backwards look is needed to appreciate how considerable that impression has been.

Germany entered the Great War with their version of the Maxim gun, the MG08, but ended the war with far greater numbers of the lightened version of that weapon, the MG08/15. This was developed to answer the need for a handy and portable automatic fire weapon to meet the tactical requirements of the man in the front-line trenches; the heavy MG08s and their like were usually organised under battalion or higher command in selected locations and were not always where the men in the trenches wanted them to be when they wanted them. They needed some light and handy machine gun operating at platoon or even section level.

The impression made by lightened forms of machine gun such as the American/British Lewis gun and the French Chauchat on the German front-line troops was immediate and they requested their own equivalents. The MG08/15 was the result, but it was a hastily devised design that was produced using as many existing MG08 parts and production facilities as possible – by 1916 the German industrial war machine was so stretched that it was either use the MG08/15 or recourse to making use of as many captured Lewis guns as they could. In the end the German Army ended up using both alternatives; indeed, one of the German machine gunner's standard handbooks contained details of how to operate and maintain Allied machine guns.

A careful and thorough post-war analysis of Great War operations carried out under the auspices of the German General Staff noted that the number of machine gun designs in service with the German Army during the Great War was too many for logistic and training comfort (apart from the DWM MG08 and MG08/15, the Germans used Bergmann, Dreyse, Madsen, and other types, plus captured examples). It also noted that the war had given rise to a requirement for two different types of machine gun, the heavy machine gun more or less permanently emplaced on a heavy tripod, and the light machine gun, a one-man portable weapon using a bipod. It was also noted that the main German attempt at a light machine gun, the MG08/15, was not exactly what the troops required. The lighter air-cooled lMG08/18 seemed to offer more, but too few were in the front lines by the time the war ended to make any impression.

It was decided therefore to combine the concerns regarding logistic and numbers of types into one long-term development programme, the initial stages of which were already under way before the Great War ended. The result of that programme was what we now term the General Purpose Machine Gun, or GPMG. The idea was that one 'universal' weapon would combine the attributes of the heavy machine gun, firing sustained bursts of automatic fire from a tripod or other heavy mounting, with the portability and low weight of a light machine gun. It was decided to fund a development programme, but at that time, the early 1920s, the terms of the Versailles Treaty forbade any machine gun development in Germany, so the immediate solution was to move the development programme elsewhere.

The Path to the MG34

Switzerland was the location of much of the early 'universal' machine gun development work and it was carried out by Rheinmetall-Borsig AG in association with the Swiss firm of Waffenfabrik Solothurn AG. The association formed the breeding ground for many weapon developments but few had so far-reaching an impact as the series of machine guns that commenced with the Solothurn S2-200, or Modell 29.

This was a long way from the final form of the modern GPMG but it indicated the way ahead. It was a light weapon with a bipod and all its components arranged 'in line', ie in a straight line from the butt to the muzzle. It used an air-cooled barrel with a novel quick-change device, and the rate of fire was quite high at around 800 rounds per minute. Ammunition was fed into the gun from a side-mounted 25-round box magazine.

The Modell 29 was developed into the Solothurn MG30 which was submitted for trials by the German Army during 1930, and they requested yet more development

The starting point for what we now know as the General Purpose Machine Gun, or GPMG – the Solothurn 7.92 mm MG30 machine gun.

work and the introduction of extra design features. The MG30 design was adopted by the Luftwaffe and eventually became their MG15, one of the German standard aircraft defence weapons and later adapted for ground use. Numbers of MG30s were sold to Austria and Hungary.

The Rheinmetall/Solothurn MG30 eventually became an all-German project as the need for the association with the Swiss became less and less necessary as time went on. The MG30 development work (by the early 1930s it had been transferred to Mausers in Germany) progressed rapidly and many features from existing weapons were gradually amalgamated into one design that was to become the 7.92 mm *Maschinengewehr 34*, or MG34.

The MG34 was the first answer to the German Army's request for a 'universal' machine gun. It was light and portable enough to be carried and fired by one man from a light bipod, yet it could also be mounted on a tripod as a crew-served weapon to deliver the sustained fire needed by fire support units – at one time it was even considered by the Luftwaffe for use as an aircraft gun, but that project lapsed. The gun's design followed the same general lines as the MG30 but many changes were introduced compared to that much-simpler weapon.

An MG34 in action somewhere on the Eastern Front.

The MG34 was not just a weapon, but was what would eventually be termed a weapon system, being itself but one item in a whole range of components and accessories that would enable it to be used for just about any machine gun role that could be devised. On a simple front- or centrally-located bipod and using a saddle-type belt drum holding 75 rounds, it was a light machine gun. On a heavy tripod and fed by 50- or 250-round metal belts, it became a heavy fire support weapon – a barrel quick-change device became involved when the barrel over-heated. Installed in a steel ball mounting, it was used for armoured vehicle secondary armament. On a tall tripod or on a special twin mounting it became an air defence weapon. These were only a few of the many forms of the MG34.

The mechanism of the MG34 was innovative. As a round was fed into the chamber, two inner rollers on the bolt head struck two cams on a cam sleeve and turned the bolt head to engage on threads on the cam sleeve. This locked the bolt at the instant that the trigger mechanism released the firing pin to strike the cartridge and fire the weapon. Part of the gas pressure produced on firing then expanded in a muzzle attachment to thrust the barrel backwards, whereupon the barrel and bolt, still locked together, started to move to the rear. After a short travel two outer rollers on the bolt head turned the head and unlocked the barrel and bolt. The barrel travel then ceased while the bolt travelled to the rear, carrying out the cartridge case extraction process and compressing a recoil spring. The bolt then impacted on a buffer and the compressed recoil spring returned it forward, loading a fresh round as it travelled. This mechanism could operate at a cyclic firing rate of 900 rounds per minute which was considerably higher than that of the old Great War Maxim guns it replaced.

The MG34 proved to be an excellent weapon, but the German armed forces soon discovered that it was too good: the cost of the weapon and the resources required for its manufacture were quite simply too ex-

May 1942 – South African troops manning a captured German 7.92 mm MG34 machine gun as an anti-aircraft weapon.

pensive for the German military authorities to consider for prolonged mass production under war circumstances. An attempt was made to develop a simpler version known as the MG34/41, but it was not adopted; something much better had by then been introduced on to the scene.

The MG42

That something was the *Maschinengewehr 42*, or MG42. It was a weapon devised under the supervision of one Dr Grunow, from a concern known as the Grossfuss-Werke of Doblen, Saxony. By examining the features of many development and production machine gun designs, Dr Grunow was able to utilise the ideas of many organisations and individuals and combine them all together into one single design that was to emerge as one of the best machine guns of all time.

Dr Grunow was not a gun-maker but an industrial engineer whose speciality was mass production. He was therefore not constrained by the usual gun-making skills of metal machining and attention to fine toler-

ances. Instead he specialised in the use of metal stampings and other processes that would cut down the time required to manufacture weapons while at the same time rendering them much cheaper and easier to produce. By the early 1940s there was already a precedent for such industrial procedures in the shape of the 9 mm MP40 sub-machine gun, a weapon that had revolutionised gun-making by its use of low-cost metal pressings, plastics and rivets in place of the normally highly engineered gun components. The result was still a very practical sub-machine gun that soon attracted the accolade of being copied (in principle) by the Allies – the British Sten gun was but one result. Dr Grunow applied the same approach to the machine gun.

The result emerged as the MG42 in which time-consuming machining processes were applied only to the barrel and the internal mechanisms where they were strictly necessary. The rest of the weapon employed steel pressings, rivets, plastics and castings which at first sight appeared to be crude, yet in operation the design proved to be superlative. It also proved to be simple and cheap to manufacture, requiring the minimum of machine tools and other processes. (Each MG42 cost the German Treasury RM 250 as opposed to RM 312 for each MG34). The overall finish was given little attention other than preventative coatings against rust and corrosion. The end result may have made many of the older generations of gun-makers weep, but German soldiers soon learned to appreciate the MG42 as one of the finest weapons of its type in the world. Allied soldiers grew to dread the distinctive tearing sound of the MG42's high firing rate.

The MG42 fired the standard German 7.92 mm × 57 rifle cartridge (as did the MG34) and it had many novel features, not the least of which was the barrel-change device which was both simple and quick to operate. The cyclic rate of fire was up to 1,500 rounds per minute, which meant that users normally had to restrict automatic fire to short bursts to prevent the barrel from over-heating too rapidly, but those short bursts could still put a considerable number of rounds on a target.

The operating mechanism used on the MG42 was the fruit of many minds but was based on a system devised in Poland before 1939. The man in overall charge of this aspect of the MG42 was one Dr Gruner who had no previous experience of gun-making and could thus approach his design task with an open mind.

On the MG42 there were no turning bolts. Instead, the chamber end of the barrel had an extension, or locking head, with cammed slots. As the bolt went forward during the loading process a moving locking stud struck a cam in the barrel extension to force locking rollers outwards and into slots in the barrel extension and thus produce a positive locking action. The weapon was then fired and gases expanding in a muzzle attachment forced back the barrel and bolt, still locked together. The barrel travel was arrested after a short movement, and at that same instant the rollers in the barrel extension were forced out of their slots by cams and the bolt was then free to continue its rearward travel, compressing a recoil spring and carrying out the spent cartridge case extraction as it moved. The recoil spring

A captured 7.92 mm MG42 on display in Paris in late 1945.

then forced the bolt forward again, loading a fresh round as it did so, and the sequence was repeated all over again as long as the trigger remained pressed.

Just as simple and innovative was the ammunition feed system which relied on a stud moving in grooves on the receiver top interior. The entire top of the receiver could be hinged forwards and upwards for loading and easy access to the moving parts.

The above account is again over-simplified but the locking roller and slot arrangement worked very well, so well in fact that there has never been cause to alter it in any way and it has been used in many other automatic weapon designs originating since 1945.

The MG42 itself underwent few changes during its Second World War career other than modifications to the muzzle attachment to prevent too much muzzle jump when using the weapon from a heavy tripod. But if the weapon itself underwent few changes, the rest of its 'system' certainly did.

The basic bipod and tripod con-figurations were carried over from the MG34, but the MG42 relied upon belt feed only for its feed system; 50- and 250-round metal belts were used. Armoured vehicle adaptations were produced, as were single and twin anti-aircraft mountings. There were also 'winter triggers', devices for firing the weapon from the cover of a trench, special remote control mountings for use on armoured fighting vehicles, optical sights (some carried over from the MG34), and clamping devices that enabled the weapon to be fired from tree stumps. More mundane accessories such as spare barrel carriers and ammunition belt fillers were introduced in profusion. Although many of these extras and accessories were carried over from the MG34, few of them were completely interchangeable with the earlier weapon system, adding to the German logistic load.

By 1945 five production lines were attempting to satisfy ever-growing demands for the MG42, aided by a whole host of sub-contractors and small workshops. By 1945 well over 750,000 MG42s had been manufactured.

However, one aspect of that 1920s staff analysis project was never realised, and that was the need to reduce the number of machine gun types in service. In 1945 the supplanted MG34 was still around in large numbers and the German armed forces were lumbered with an array of machine gun types (and differing types of ammunition for them) captured from all the corners of Europe. German industrial capacity, together with the efforts of the German designers, was never able to reduce the number of machine gun types in service. Instead, combat losses and the growing need to equip Germany's ever-expanding forces led to a quartermaster's nightmare out of all proportion to anything experienced by any armed force before or since.

MG42s are still likely to be encountered even now. The Germans themselves converted many old stock-piled MG42s to take 7.62 mm × 51 ammunition during the late 1950s and early 1960s, of which more anon. What was once Yugoslavia continues to manufacture the weapon as the SARAC M53 (see below) and nations still using numbers of the original MG42 include Albania, Algeria, Angola, Ethiopia and Somalia. Some were observed in militia hands during the internal strife in Lebanon.

Post-war MG42s

The MG42 was not the only Second World War machine gun design to influence other designers in the post-war period. There was an experimental MG45, with a revised roller lock mechanism and based on the MG42, which received a great deal of technical attention, and a Mauser aircraft gun, the MG 81, seemed to offer much. However, most of these post-war investigations were not to be converted into anywhere near hardware form for many years, for the post-war period saw just about every armed force throughout the world well provided with machine guns and with no particular

Italian troops manning a 7.62 mm MG42/59, licence-produced in Italy – note the blank firing attachment on the muzzle.

need for anything more for the foreseeable future.

That changed when West Germany became a part of NATO during the late 1950s. The new German armed forces had to be equipped from the ground upwards and, ever heedful of the lessons of 1939-45, decided from the outset to adopt the best equipment they could obtain. When it came to machine guns, there was no question as to what they would choose. It was the MG42.

The MG42 had been out of production since 1945 other than in Yugoslavia where production had re-started back in the early 1950s. The Serbs, Croats and Bosnians had maintained a precarious political and economic independence ever since they ejected their German occupiers in 1945 and a domestic arms industry was regarded as but one way to maintain that independence from others. By the early 1950s they were already manufacturing a wide range of small arms and ammunition and in 1953 commenced production of their SARAC M53 which was virtually a direct copy of the MG42, still in the German 7.92 mm × 57 calibre. Serbs, Croats and Bosnians continue to use the M53 to this day and others were sold to Ecuador.

But during the late 1950s there was no way that the (then) West Germans were going to procure a Yugoslav-manufactured weapon. The main reasons were that the newly-formed NATO nations had standardised on the 7.62 mm × 51 cartridge, and a political decision had been made that a re-armed West Germany should have its own armaments production infrastructure. The firm of Rheinmetall once more entered the picture and commenced production of new MG42s in 7.62 mm calibre. The result was the MG42/59.

The MG42/59 (Rheinmetall's commercial designation for the 'new' MG42) was virtually identical to the wartime MG42 apart from dimensional alterations to accommodate the new cartridge. Once the weapon was in service the *Bundeswehr* began to apply its own service designations. The first model was the MG1, firing the 7.92 mm × 57 cartridge, but it was a stop-gap measure until the 7.62 mm × 51 NATO version came into full production – that was the MG1A1. This latter model introduced some new features such as a chrome-plated bore which increased barrel life considerably and cut down the need to change overheated barrels quite so often as before. The MG1A2 had some changes to the ammunition feed to allow interchangeability of ammunition belts. However, none of these models were adopted by the West German armed forces other than as training and familiarisation weapons for the expanding

An Austrian Army 7.62 mm MG42/59 machine gun team in action.

Bundeswehr, but licence production of the MG1A2 was undertaken in Italy for the Italian Army.

The MG1A3 introduced modifications to speed production and became the first mass production and service model, using many of the design features of the earlier MG1 models, including the chromed barrel. The MG1A4 and MG1A5 are versions for fixed applications such as armoured vehicles and lack the usual bipod and other mounting attachments.

To add to the in-service inventories, numbers of old MG42s were taken from stockpiles and converted to the NATO stan-dard – they became the MG2.

The latest production variant produced by Rheinmetall is the MG3. This is based on the MG1A3 and utilises the various modifications introduced on earlier variants, but with some extra changes to the ammunition feed system that allow the weapon to accept ammunition belts of both German and American origin – some earlier variants were limited in what they could accept. The MG3 can accommodate a 100-round belt drum which removes the risk of dangling ammunition belts snagging or dragging in dirt or water. The MG3A1 is used in fixed installations.

A factory-fresh 7.62 mm MG3.

One aspect of the post-war MG42 variants is that they can use buffer arrangements and bolts of two weights, with a heavy bolt providing a reduced rate of fire (most German versions use the lighter bolt which produces a rate of fire of up to 1,300 rounds per minute). Licence-produced examples of the MG1A2 manufactured in Austria and Italy have the heavier bolt which limits the rate to about 900 rounds per minute. The Austrian MG42/59 is known locally as the MG74.

The Rheinmetall MG42/59 or MG3 is, or has been, licence-produced by several nations apart from Austria and Italy, including Pakistan, Greece, Spain, and Turkey. User nations are many and include

Above *German conscripts manning a 7.62 mm MG3 at some date during the mid-1970s. Note the blank firing attachment at the muzzle and the way the belt of blank ammunition is being allowed to get clogged up with earth .*

Austria, Australia (on their Leopard 1 tanks), Burma, Cape Verde, Chile, Denmark, Guinea-Bissau, Iran, Italy, Libya, Mauritania, Mozambique, Nigeria, Norway, Portugal, Saudi Arabia, Sudan, Togo and Tunisia. Some of these users may have obtained their weapons from sources other than Germany.

Heckler & Koch

One result of the re-growth of the post-war German defence industry has been the re-vival of the manufacture of small arms, complete with that country's reputation for innovation, sound design and high manu-facturing standards. Nearly all the old pre-

Right *A German soldier carrying his MG3 using the sling as a makeshift carrying handle.*

1945 German names associated with small arms design and development have been revived in one guise or another, but there has been one name that has become established since the 1950s and subsequently regarded as a world leader; that name is Heckler & Koch GmbH. To discover how that reputation was gained we have once again to make a short historical foray.

Heckler & Koch GmbH was formed by three former employees of the old Mauser concern during the late 1940s. As Mausers had virtually ceased to exist in 1945 there was a considerable pool of skilled labour available in the Obendorf-Neckar region. Heckler & Koch utilised those skilled workers to form a light engineering concern.

Among the industrial assets available to Heckler & Koch was the knowledge that just prior to the end of the war in 1945 some of the ex-Mauser employees had been involved in the development of an assault rifle known as the *Sturmgewehr 45(M)*, or Stug 45(M). This rifle used what was regarded as a highly promising roller-locking system, but the end of the war ended its prospects of progressing any further – or so it seemed at the time.

Many of the victorious Allied nations undertook technical investigations into the Stug 45(M) and its roller-locking action but during the years immediately after 1945 rifle development had a fairly low priority. However, during the early 1950s the Spanish armed forces expressed a desire to develop a modern rifle to replace all their bolt-action Mausers, and the Stug 45(M) design was revived under the auspices of CETME, a government-owned armaments organisation. Several experimental rifles were produced before the long-term implications of the imposition of a standard NATO 7.62 mm × 51 rifle cartridge were appreciated. CETME therefore concentrated on the NATO calibre; the CETME rifles went into production during the mid-1950s and they are still in production in Spain in both 7.62 and 5.56 mm calibres.

By the mid 1950s the newly-formed German *Bundeswehr* was also in need of a modern service rifle and decided that the CETME design offered considerable potential. Via a rather devious route the CETME rifle made its way back to Germany and the Heckler & Koch concern where further development work resulted in the 7.62 mm G3, adopted in 1959 as the standard *Bundeswehr* service rifle.

The G3 was to blossom in many forms, all of which carried over the use of steel stampings and other simplified production methods developed during the Second World War – but there has never been anything crude or unrefined regarding any of the Heckler & Koch products. They have always been well finished, sturdy and capable of absorbing hard wear under the most adverse conditions.

Much of the reliability of the Heckler & Koch line has been due to the fully-developed roller-locking system employed on just about every Heckler & Koch product and which had its origins in the Stug 45(M). The system employs a two-part bolt assembly, the bolt head being light and the bolt body relatively heavy. A driving spring is used to push forward the bolt body and firing pin as they move towards the chamber for firing and into a barrel extension piece. Between the bolt head and body are two rollers (the locking rollers) which are free to move outwards into recesses in the barrel extension. Further forward motion of the bolt body then causes the bolt head and body to move closer together and the firing pin can travel forward under control of the trigger mechanism to fire the cartridge.

At the instant of firing, pressure rapidly builds up on the face of the bolt head but at that instant the locking rollers are locked in their recesses and no rearward motion can commence. However, the recesses are shaped to act as cam faces and gradually drive the rollers inwards to force back the bolt body to a point where the rollers are in a position to allow the bolt head and body to be propelled to the rear under residual gas pressure. The locking rollers thus introduce a delay, after which the residual gas pressure is reduced to a level where it is safe for the spent cartridge case to be extracted from the chamber but with enough residual energy remaining to propel the bolt assembly to the rear and compress the recoil spring until the bolt assembly strikes a buffer. As the bolt assembly travels, the usual cartridge extraction and loading stages are accomplished.

Again, this process has been outlined in an over-simplified manner but it will be noted that there is no rotary action on the Heckler & Koch locking system and neither are there any complex lever mechanisms. This renders the system a sturdy and reliable method of locking just about any automatic fire weapon. Heckler & Koch have adapted it for employment not just on all their rifle products but also on the highly-successful MP5 sub-machine gun family and on their machine guns. The Heckler & Koch G3 rifle has been one of the most widely used of all European service rifles and has been licence-produced in many countries. So widespread and numerous have its sales become that it must now be the Number 3 rifle in the world, being beaten in numbers only by the Soviet AK-47 series and the American M16s. With such widespread use it follows that Heckler & Koch machine guns should have an equally large market. They have.

At first sight all the Heckler & Koch machine guns have the same general appearance as the G3 rifle. The base model of the machine gun family is the HK21 which was developed to act as a squad automatic weapon. In common with all modern machine guns, it is an air-cooled weapon with a quick-change barrel system and a belt feed. Standard NATO 7.62 mm × 51 ammunition is fired, although by changing the barrel, the bolt and the feed system it can be adapted to fire CIS 7.62 mm × 39 or NATO 5.56 mm × 45 ammunition.

The HK21 can be altered to use a 20-round box magazine or an 80-round double drum magazine instead of disintegrating link belts. By removing the butt it can be adapted for various vehicle mountings. But perhaps the best indication of the versatility of the Heckler & Koch machine guns is that by using various tripods and other mountings, the HK21 can be employed as a GPMG, although the barrel will have to be changed at rather frequent intervals.

The original HK21 is no longer in production, but was replaced by the HK21A1 which did away with the magazine feed option and uses only a belt feed, being able to accommodate just about any type of disintegrating link belt it is likely to encounter. The latest production model is produced in two versions, the HK21E and the HK23E, the latter being for 5.56 mm × 45 ammunition. Both versions involve a longer

The Heckler & Koch 7.62 mm HK21 general-purpose machine gun.

The Heckler & Koch 7.62 mm HK21A1 which differs from the HK21 in being belt-fed only.

barrel and receiver housing, revised sights and a trigger mechanism arranged so that three-round bursts can be fired in addition to the usual single-shot and fully automatic (plus safe). Other changes involve the belt feed mechanism, and are directed at reducing the stresses and strains caused by having to lift the weight of an ammunition belt and dragging it into the weapon. To make the weapon easier to handle in the 'assault' mode, a foregrip has been added under the forestock and a 'winter trigger' is provided to make firing easier when wearing mittens or NBC gloves.

The lighter HK11A1 is the latest version of the earlier HK11 which is no longer in production. Intended to be employed as a section light support weapon, it is virtually the same as the HK21 base model except that it uses a 20-round box magazine feed only – there is no provision for belt feed. The HK11A1 is virtually a heavy-barrelled G3 rifle with provision for rapid barrel-changing and is normally fired from a light bipod only. As with the HK21, the 7.62 mm HK11A1 can be adapted to fire CIS 7.62 mm × 39 and NATO 5.56 mm × 45 ammunition.

There were two other models following on from the old HK11. The HK12 was a 7.62 mm light weapon that could use 30-round magazines and a 100-round double drum, while the HK13 was calibered for the 5.56 mm × 45 round and used 20- or 40-round box magazines or a 100-round double drum. Neither remains in production.

Licence production of Heckler & Koch machine guns has been undertaken by several nations, and other countries have manufactured components to be assembled in other locations. One of the latter has been the United Kingdom, for the Royal Small Arms Factory at Enfield was at one time during the 1980s making all manner of Heckler & Koch weapons and components, even though the UK has never adopted any Heckler & Koch weapon for general service. (However, the Special Air Service does use the MP5 sub-machine gun, as do several British police forces.) At one time a production line for Heckler & Koch HK21A1 machine guns was established at Enfield to supply them to Kenya, Nigeria (6,000), the Sudan and Sri Lanka. The 5.56 mm HK23E was also licence-produced at Enfield for the United Arab Emirates. Other licence-producing nations have been Greece (the EHK11A1) and Portugal (the HK21). The Italian Franchi LF/23E light machine gun is basically a revised HK23E with polygonal rifling, and has also been trialled by the Italian Army.

All this licence production prompts the mention that, as the Heckler & Koch rifles and machine guns all share the same action, it is possible to exchange many parts between models and even types of weapon – for example, some components from the G3 rifle can be readily exchanged with parts on the HK21A1 machine gun. Not all Heckler & Koch components boast this interchangeability, but it is interesting that some parts can even be interchanged with those on their MP5 sub-machine gun.

Heckler & Koch machine gun users include Bangladesh, Bolivia, Brunei, Cameroons, Colombia, Germany (small numbers only), Greece, Jordan, Kenya, Malaysia, Mexico, Morocco, Niger, Nigeria, Portugal, Qatar, Senegal, Sri Lanka, the Sudan, Sweden (small numbers only) and Uganda.

It will be noticed that this list of users encompasses just about every corner of the world, and the prospects were that it would continue to grow. Unfortunately Heckler & Koch hit hard times during late 1990. Following a protracted development period reaching back to the late 1960s, the company was hoping for great things for a revolutionary new form of rifle to fire the caseless 4.73 mm × 33 round produced by Dynamit Nobel; the rifle to fire this innovative ammunition is known as the G11. Heckler & Koch invested heavily in the rifle's development and preparation for the anticipated prolonged production run to replace all existing German service rifles, and there was even a proposal to develop a light support weapon firing the 4.7 mm caseless round (see chapter 21).

Unfortunately for Heckler & Koch, the reunification of East and West Germany left the new all-German government with a considerable economic bill, and in anticipation of the size of this bill the scheduled funding for the new rifles was delayed – only a few G11s were ordered for special forces. That left Heckler & Koch over-extended and short of ready funds, so in early 1991 the British armaments concern Royal Ordnance purchased the firm.

Ironically, at one time Royal Ordnance had under its corporate wing the Royal Small Arms Factory at Enfield, now closed but in the past, as mentioned above, a prolific licence-producer of Heckler & Koch products. However, it seems likely that Heckler & Koch products, including machine guns, will continue to be manufactured.

DATA

Model	MG3	HK21A1
Calibre	7.62 mm	7.62 mm
Weight (gun only)	11.05 kg	8.3 kg
Length	1.225 m	1.03 m
Length of barrel	565 mm	450 mm
Rate of fire	700-1300 rpm	900 rpm
Feed	belt	belt
Muzzle velocity	820 m/s	800 m/s

CHAPTER 4

THE SOVIET MASSES

THE capacity of the Soviet military machine to produce and deploy vast numbers of machine guns was remarked upon in chapter 1 when it was mentioned that Russia and then the Soviet Union managed to produce well over 600,000 M1910 Maxim machine guns during a production life span that lasted over 40 years. However, such totals and the longevity of the production run have never been unusual throughout the history of the old Russian Empire (now the Commonwealth of Independent States—CIS) and subsequently the Soviet Union for several reasons.

One reason is that the sheer numerical size of the Russian, Soviet and CIS armed forces has always been extremely large and is still measured in millions. To this figure has to be added all the various supporting reserve and militia forces, and the manpower total thus expands even further. Just to equip armed forces of that magnitude is a massive industrial and organisational undertaking, while to keep them equipped with up-dated weapons and other items is an equally daunting and on-going task of huge proportions. Therefore just to equip the Soviet Army alone, leaving aside the navy, air force, border guards and all the rest, was a challenge that many Western

industrial infrastructures would still find difficulty in meeting. Yet ever since the early 1920s successive Soviet administrations met the challenge with a remarkable degree of success, although often at enormous cost and to the detriment of other aspects of the Soviet economy. The numbers of machine guns turned out by the old Soviet defence industry makes even the largest production totals achieved in the West look small - the only possible exception being the 0.50/12.7 mm Browning M2 HB heavy machine gun, the final production totals of which have yet to be determined.

This success has been achieved by following a few general guidelines as far as weapons are concerned. One has been to select a weapon design that is as simple and straightforward as can be devised. Another is to make that weapon as reliable and durable as possible, for the weapon will be used in some of the harshest and most demanding military environments that are likely to be encountered, even though it has to be accepted from the beginning that maintenance will be minimal and infrequent. A third requirement is that the weapon must be capable of being manufactured in the hundreds of thousands using

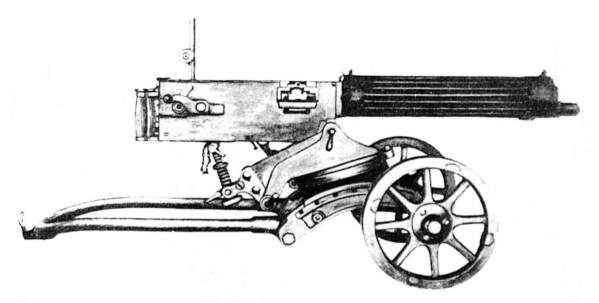

The veteran – the old 7.62 mm PM1910 Maxim, still likely to be encountered in odd corners of the world.

existing and often basic production facilities and with the added requirement of component interchangeability being possible between the first and the last examples off the lines. To all those requirements has to be added the ability of the weapon to be readily adaptable for many different roles and applications.

In the case of machine guns, most of these requirements were met by the introduction of the 7.62 mm PM1910 machine gun. It was as simple and well-tried in design terms as could be achieved, it was durable and reliable, and it was produced in huge numbers over a period spanning four decades. Throughout that period the weapon was altered but little. Training, supply and logistic problems were thus kept to a minimum.

These requirements have been carried over to the modern CIS machine guns, which are durable and reliable to a marked degree – they have to be, for they are used throughout the world in regions where the care and attention normally lavished on small arms is usually totally lacking. Yet these machine guns continue to work, often in extremes of heat and cold; any weapon which can continue to function normally throughout the extremes of a Russian winter has to be something to be remarked upon, but the same weapon will also function just as reliably in a Middle East desert.

CIS planners ensure, as did their Tsarist counterparts before them, that the standardisation enforced by the need for massive weapon totals is also carried over to the ammunition, thereby easing the supply and production situation considerably. Only a few small arms calibres are used by the CIS armed forces, a situation only recently matched by the enforcement of a rigid standardisation of NATO small arms calibres and ammunition – at one time NATO small arms calibres and ammunition types were as diverse as the nations involved, and it was the example of the CIS standardisation levels that to a great extent enforced the move to the NATO standards.

The Light Machine Guns

The lessons of the Great War that prompted other nations to develop light machine guns were also learned by the old Russian Army authorities, many of whom found themselves in much the same jobs when the Red Army was established. The one difference

5.45 mm RPK-74M3 light machine gun fitted with 45-round magazine and 1LH51 night sight: the RPK-74M3 weighs 4.6 kg and has a maximum effective range of 460 metres.

was that the newly formed Soviet armed forces were much more amenable to change than the old Tsarist military establishment, with the result that small arms development was provided with a considerable boost. However, the general upheaval following the Civil War and a general lack of funding kept any new weapons from the soldiers for some years.

On the light machine gun scene, the attempts made during the 1920s to modify the old M1910 Maxim machine gun to become some sort of light machine gun came to nothing. The results were too cumbersome and were in any event overtaken in 1926 by the introduction of a remarkable light machine gun design known as the *Degtyarev Pekhotnyy*, or DP, designed by a team led by Vasily Degtyarev.

The 7.62 mm DP, adopted by the Red Army in 1928, was a light gas-operated weapon with a distinctive flat pan-shaped magazine on top of the body and holding 47 rounds. The overall design was simple – so simple that most of its manufacturing processes could involve unskilled labour – yet it was extremely robust and was used throughout the Great Patriotic War of 1941-45. In 1944 the weapon was modified by the addition of an operating spring housing projecting over the top of the butt. A pistol grip was added and a stronger bipod was introduced – the designation then became DPM. Both the DP and DPM fired on fully automatic only, so the trigger mechanism was simpler to produce and maintain, having fewer parts to break.

The DP and DPM were both section fire support weapons and the amount of fire they could produce was limited to short bursts. On the DP some problems came from the operating spring inside the gas tube under the barrel. When this became hot, which was frequently the case when in action, it lost its tempering and caused malfunctions. It was therefore moved to a position over the butt on the DPM, hence the prominent housing there. The magazine continued to be a source of potential problems, proving to be easily damaged, but it could be easily replaced.

For all these faults, the DP and DPM were remarkable weapons. They were light, very simple and generally gave good ser-

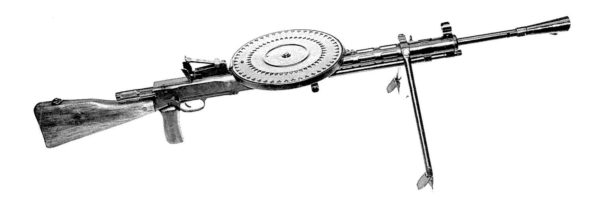

The 7.62 mm DPM with its distinctive 47-round flat pan magazine, still in service in some parts of Africa and produced in China as the Type 53.

vice. After 1945 they were gradually withdrawn from front-line use and were passed to the various Soviet militias or handed on to various 'freedom fighter' guerilla and other forces then sympathetic to the Soviet cause. Many continue to crop up in odd corners of the world to this day, but the DP and DPM are now regarded as obsolete.

The DT and DTM were DP variants used on armoured vehicles. At one time the Communist Chinese produced their own version of the DPM known as the Type 53, many of which remain in service with the People's Liberation Army and its various militia off-shoots.

The DPM was followed in service by the RP-46. This was a wartime attempt to develop a light machine gun capable of producing more sustained bursts than the DP and DPM. Wartime production and other priorities delayed the introduction of the RP-46 until 1946, when it emerged as a belt-fed weapon with a heavy barrel. Ammunition was fed in 50-round belts, but the 47-round pan magazine of the DP and DPM could still be employed in an emergency. The RP-46 proved to be capable of

providing the sustained bursts required and it was sometimes issued as a company as well as a squad fire support weapon.

The Soviet service life of the RP-46 was relatively short but it was overall a good weapon which seems to have had few drawbacks. It serves on with many nations throughout the world; the Chinese produced their own copy as the Type 58 and the North Koreans manufactured their own Type 64. Numbers of RP-46s still turn up in guerilla hands, especially in the Far East.

The short service life of the RP-46 – less than a decade – was mainly caused by the introduction of a new type of ammunition. The DP, DPM and RP-46 all fired the then standard Soviet rifle cartridge which dated back to Tsarist days, the rimmed 7.62 mm × 54. As early as 1943 a team of Soviet ammunition designers had commenced work on a less powerful 'intermediate' cartridge for use at the shorter combat ranges that careful operational analysis had demonstrated were the norm in modern warfare – the Germans had noted the same and worked along much the same lines to develop their 7.92 mm × 33 *kurz* cartridge.

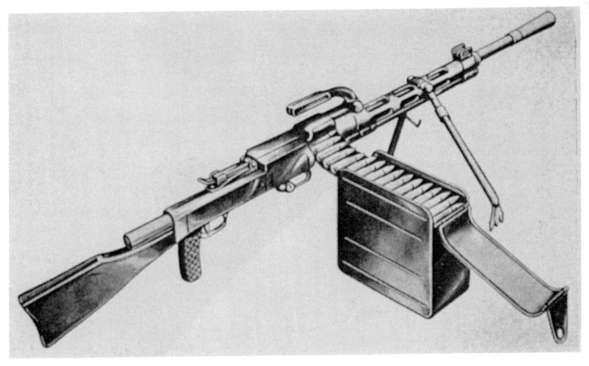

The belt-fed 7.62 mm RP-46 machine gun.

In both nations the intention was to use the less powerful cartridges to produce automatic fire from shoulder-fired weapons, and in both nations the result was what we now know as the assault rifle.

The new cartridge was the 7.62 mm × 39, and the first weapon designed to fire it was Simonov's SKS semi-automatic carbine. However, this weapon had a short service life in Soviet terms (even though it was produced in totals measuring hundreds of thousands) for it was soon overtaken by the superlative Kalashnikov AK-47 assault rifle. A new squad fire support light machine gun was also introduced to ensure ammunition commonality. This new weapon completed its development and became accepted for service as the RPD

The 7.62 mm RPD light machine gun.

during the early 1950s; the RP-46 was thereafter withdrawn from front line use.

The RPD was basically a much-improved DPM but with a 100-round disintegrating link belt held in a drum housing underneath the weapon at the centre of gravity. A bipod was located under the muzzle. The gas-operated mechanism was similar to that used on the DP and DPM but over the RPD's service life some modifications were introduced to overcome slight drawbacks discovered once the troops got their hands on them.

One aspect of the RPD that appeared to be a drawback was the absence of the barrel-change system which had been there on the earlier designs. It appears that the main reason for this was that although the DP and DPM did have barrel-changing systems, they were employed only infrequently in action. On the RPD this was acknowledged and the RPD barrel was fixed to make manufacturing that much simpler. Barrel overheating problems were overcome by the imposition of drills and training that ensured RPD users confined their activities to firing short bursts, the model firing on fully automatic only.

Few, if any, RPDs remain in front-line CIS service today, having been replaced by the later and lighter RPK machine rifles (see below). However, they are still likely to be encountered almost anywhere that the old Soviet sphere of influence reached, and

even beyond. Most of the old Warsaw Pact nations produced their own RPDs at one time or another and it was awarded the usual accolade of being manufactured in China for the People's Liberation Army (and for export) as the Type 56 and 56-1, the latter being an RPD with all the later modifications embodied. North Korea also produced the RPD as their Type 62, and it was also copied in Egypt as the 7.62 mm 'Suez' – the latter is apparently still in Egyptian Army service.

The RPD was produced as a section fire support weapon but being a Degtyarev design it came from a different design bureau than the Kalashnikov AK-47 and AK-47M assault rifles so widely used by the CIS armed forces until relatively recently. In logistic and manufacturing terms it made good sense to standardise a Kalashnikov-designed variant as a squad light machine gun, and by the early 1960s this had been achieved.

The new weapon is the RPK, or *Ruchnoi Pulemet Kalashnikov*, and is virtually a heavy-barrelled AK-47M assault rifle with the addition of a light bipod and the ability to accommodate larger magazines than was normal on the AK-47M rifle. The butt shape is also different from that of the rifle to make it easier to handle when firing.

The action of the RPK is exactly the same as that used on the AK-47M and details such as field stripping are the same

A 7.62 mm RPD light machine gun with the drum for the 100-round belt in position.

A 7.62 mm RPK light machine gun with its 40-round box magazine in position.

for both weapons. The **RPK** can use the 30-round box magazine of the AK-47M but is mainly intended for use with a curved 40-round box magazine and a 75-round drum magazine. The **RPKS** has a side-folding stock to reduce its overall length.

The **RPK** does not have a quick-change barrel system so, as with the RPD, bursts of fire have to be carefully controlled to prevent barrel overheating; the barrel is chrome-plated to reduce wear. This restricted fire burst drawback, combined with the light weight (weapon only, 5 kg) and limited capacity of the 40-round box magazine (the 75-round magazine is apparently only rarely used for offensive field operations) renders the **RPK** less of a light machine gun than a machine rifle. The arguments over this topic range and vary widely throughout the small arms industry,

The two outer troops of this tank-transported team are carrying 7.62 mm RPK light machine guns – the large machine gun visible in the background is a 12.7 mm DShK-38/46.

but the Russians do not seem to mind what the RPK is called as long as it works as and when required, and it has proved to be more than capable of that.

The RPK is widely used by nearly all the old Warsaw Pact nations. The seemingly inevitable Chinese variant is broadly based on the RPK and is known as the Type 81. In Yugoslavia a virtual copy of the RPK was produced as the M72 light machine gun. A later version, the M72B1, is fitted with a fixed wooden stock, while the M72AB1 uses a detachable folding metal stock for use by airborne or special units. To judge by examples produced for prospective exports by the Kragujevac Arsenal, the overall standard of finish on the M72 light machine guns is far higher than that provided on the CIS RPKs. One oddity regarding the Yugoslav M72 is that it was seen fit to produce an export-only version chambered for the NATO 7.62 mm × 51 cartridge; it is known as the M77B1 and is based on the M72B1 but using a straight box magazine holding 20 rounds. Two similar models chambered for the 5.56 mm × 45 NATO cartridge have also been aimed at the export market. They are the M82, with a fixed butt, and the M82A, with a folding steel butt. Both are generally similar in appearance to the RPK but, as with the 7.62 mm M77B1, they have a carrying handle incorporated.

There were reports that both the RPK and RPKS were manufactured within Iraq, where both weapons were known as the *Al-Quds*. At one time the RPK was manufactured in the former East Germany, whose army knew it as the LMGK.

The 7.62 mm × 39 cartridge used with the RPK is still a standard Eastern Bloc cartridge and it remains in large-scale production, but such is the speed of modern ballistic development that it has already been replaced in front-line service by a new cartridge, the 5.45 mm × 39. The Russians have thereby followed the general trend towards adopting a new high-velocity small-calibre cartridge for service rifles, and the acceptance of the 5.45 mm × 39

paralleled the adoption of the NATO 5.56 mm × 45. To produce a rifle to fire the new round the designers simply scaled down the internal dimensions of the AK-47M where necessary to produce the AK-74. To provide the matching squad fire support weapon, the RPK-74 was developed.

In virtually every way except weights and dimensions, the 5.45 mm RPK-74 is the same as the 7.62 mm RPK. Few details are available as yet but it seems safe to assume that the RPK-74 is employed in the same manner and uses similar capacity magazines to the larger weapon. A factory installed modification allows the weapon to use night vision sights. Few RPK-74s, if any, appear to have been issued to any force outside the CIS armed forces although some were no doubt captured by the Afghan Mujahadeen.

The only known RPK-74 variant, the RPKS-74, has a side-folding stock to reduce the overall length for airborne and other special force users. There is also an RPKN3 and RPKSN3.

The CIS Mediums

For four decades the standard Soviet medium machine gun was the PM1910 Maxim, but even during the Great Patriotic War it was appreciated that it was well past the time when it should have been replaced. Thus in the middle of the war a design team under Peter Goryunov developed an air-cooled medium machine gun that would eventually replace the old Maxim.

The new weapon first appeared in 1943. As it was produced under wartime conditions, one of the first design requirement priorities was ease of manufacture, so the original weapon, known as the *Stankovyi Goryunova 43*, or SG43, featured a smooth barrel exterior and an overall lack of finish. When time allowed, more refinements such as a fluted barrel to assist air cooling were added and the opportunity was taken to move the cocking handle from between the firing grips and locate it to the right of

Red Army troops dragging a 7.62 mm SG43 medium machine gun during the closing stages of the Great Patriotic War.

the receiver. Other late additions included the provision of dust covers to the ammunition feed, plus some other modifications. The SG-43 was a gas-operated weapon with the gas piston driving a breech block sideways for the locking action. The system was

strong and positive but the overall impression of the SG43 is that it carried over the weight characteristics of the PM1910 rather too excessively. This weight factor was also emphasised in the retention of a wheeled mounting not unlike that of the Sokolov carriage used on the PM1910. Later production models of the SG43 and its derivatives did away with the wheeled mount and used a more conventional tripod instead.

The ammunition feed used 250-round belts directed into the weapon from ammunition boxes. The round involved continued to be the 7.62 mm × 54 rifle cartridge dating back to Tsarist times, complete with its rimmed case. This meant that the feed mechanism was rather complex as the round had to be withdrawn from its metal belt before it could be directed forward into the mechanism. However, in practice this seemed to make little difference to the overall reliability of the SG43 and its variants, a reliability which can only be described as excellent. There were several variants of the basic SG43. One of the first was the SG43M, also known as the SGM, which incorporated many of the modifications such as dust covers, the repositioned cocking handle and the fluted barrel mentioned above. The SG43B was an early production

The 7.62 mm SG43 medium machine gun.

variant with a cartridge head space micrometer adjustment system used when changing the barrels. The SGMT was a version for use on tanks and had a solenoid firing system in place of the usual trigger group and grips, while the SGMB was used on other combat vehicles. The SGMB may be seen fitted with a retractable shoulder stock.

Nations other than the Soviet Union manufactured the SG43 and one of them, Hungary, introduced some local modifications such as a butt and pistol grip. The SG43 was also manufactured in Czechoslovakia and in China where it was known as the Type 53; the Chinese Type 57 was their version of the SGMB combat vehicle variant. In Egypt the Maadi Military & Civil Industries Company produced the SGM as their 7.62 mm 'Asswan'.

The SG43 and its variants are no longer used as front-line weapons by the CIS or any of the old Warsaw Pact nations (although they may still be held for reserve or militia use) but they still turn up in many corners of the world. They were encountered during the Vietnam campaigns and have been observed in action in Lebanon.

The SG43 was employed as a company level fire support weapon, and was eventually replaced by one of the more remarkable

of the modern CIS machine guns, the *Pulemyot Kalashnikova*, or PK. As its full designation implies, the PK is yet another product of the Kalashnikov design bureau and follows the usual practice of concentrating small arms development on one basic design. When the continued success of the Kalashnikov weapons such as the AK-47 rifle series and the RPK light machine gun are considered, it comes as no surprise to learn that the PK is a superb machine gun in its class and one that has attracted a great deal of attention from designers outside the Eastern bloc.

In common with most CIS small arms designs, the PK is a development of other weapons that have gone before. The overall mechanism owes much to that of the original AK-47 rifle and thus uses a gas-operated rotary bolt system. The ammunition feed system was adopted from a Czech design while the trigger arrangement was taken from that used on the RPD. There is one anomaly, which is the retention of the old 7.62 mm × 54 rimmed rifle cartridge, but as the PK is intended to be a fire support weapon the more powerful cartridge was obviously preferred over the reduced range and power of the 'intermediate' 7.62 mm × 39 round. The ammunition is fed in 100-, 200- and 250-round belts from

A bipod-mounted 7.62 mm PKM light machine gun.

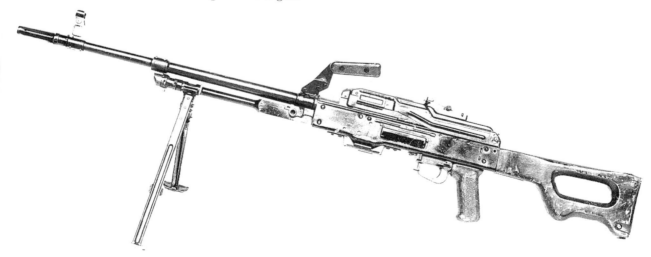

Infantry manning an armoured personnel carrier with (left) a 7.62 mm RPK and (right) a 7.62 mm PKM.

belt boxes. If required the 100-round box can be slung underneath the PK when it is carried in the 'assault' role.

The basic PK is a light machine gun using a bipod. When mounted on a tripod it becomes the PKS; the tripod is light and can be configured to become an anti-aircraft mounting. Both versions have a fluted quick-change barrel and a skeleton butt. The PKM is an improved version of the PK with a lighter, smooth barrel surface and making use of metal stampings where possible to reduce the weight of the weapon (the PK weighs 9 kg and the PKM 8.4 kg). When mounted on a tripod the PKM be-

comes the PKMS.

The PKT is a tank-mounted version of the PK and has a solenoid firing system in place of the usual pistol grip, butt and trigger arrangements. The PKB (or PKMB) uses twin spade grips and a thumb trigger so the usual trigger group is removed along with the butt; it is used as a pintle-mounted gun on light combat vehicles such as armoured personnel carriers.

The above list of PK versions indicates that the PK is a true 'universal' machine gun capable of fulfilling many applications. It is certainly reliable and capable of absorbing hard use, yet overall is remarkably

The 7.62 mm PKB, a PKM with the butt and trigger group removed and fitted with twin spade grips and a butterfly trigger.

light and simple. The PK seems set to remain in service for many years to come and many former Soviet bloc nations have it in service in one or more of its several forms.

As usual, the Chinese have chosen to produce their own close-copy version of the PKS known to them as the 7.62 mm Type 80, and described in their sales literature as a 'multi-purpose' machine gun. The Chinese PKB is the Type 59. They also produce their own version of the PKT and no doubt also the basic PK.

Yugoslavia licence-produced the PKT for some years for use on locally produced tanks such as the M-84, the Yugoslav licence-produced T-72. No doubt using experience gained from their production of the PKT, Kragujevac Arsenal technicians developed a machine gun known as the M84 and firing the 7.62 mm × 54 cartridge. To all intents and purposes the M84 is the same weapon as the PKM and may use either a bipod or a tripod mounting.

The Heavies

The first of the Soviet heavy machine guns was the DK, designed by Degtyarev in 1934. It was developed to fire the 12.7 mm × 108 cartridge but was produced in limited numbers only until 1938 when it was revised to accommodate a rotary type of ammunition feed developed by Georgio Shpagin. The resultant weapon became the DShK-38.

The DShK-38 was the standard Soviet heavy machine gun throughout the Great Patriotic War. As with so many other Soviet machine guns it was a weighty weapon and the ground mounting, which could be converted for anti-aircraft use, resembled a small artillery carriage, complete with the usual steel wheels and even a split trail arrangement with a rudimentary seat for the gunner. It was possible to fit a shield to this carriage and it could be towed by men, mules or light vehicles.

The DShK-38 was revised in 1946 to accommodate a scaled-up version of the

A 12.7 mm DShK-38 heavy machine gun on an anti-aircraft tripod.

ammunition feed of the 7.62 mm RP-46 machine gun. This made the feed much simpler and at the same time the fixed barrel of the DShK-38 was replaced by a quick-change system. The revised machine gun then became the DShK-38/46 (or DShKM) and it is this version that is most likely to be encountered today, although production of the series has ceased in the CIS. The DShK-38/46 was used by the Czechs in a special four-gun anti-aircraft mounting known as the M53, each gun having a 50-round belt feed drum, and although the Czech armed forces no longer use it, numbers were sold to Egypt where they were placed on BTR-152 wheeled armoured personnel carriers. A Czech twin-gun DShK-38/46 mounting was at one time used on light 4 × 4 vehicles. At least two of the towed four-gun M53 mountings were captured by the American armed forces following their 1983 invasion of Grenada; they probably came from Cuba, another M53 user.

The DShK-38 and DShK-38/46 have a performance not too dissimilar to that of the Browning M2 HB. The DShK-38 is now obsolete in CIS service but the DShK-38/46

What appears to be a 12.7 mm DShK-38/46 is actually a Chinese Type 54 heavy machine gun licence-produced in Pakistan by the Pakistan Ordnance Factories.

is still in widespread use as a vehicle-mounted weapon and as a light anti-aircraft weapon. Many CIS tanks carry a turret-mounted DShK-38/46, and light armoured vehicles such as the BRDM-1 amphibious scout car have the DShK-38/46 as their main armament.

Employment of the heavy ground mountings is now largely confined to the Middle and Far East nations to whom the DShK-38 and DShK-38/46 have been passed. Both models were encountered during the Vietnam campaigns and both models are in widespread service throughout Africa. Some of these may have come via China where the DShK-38/46 is still manufactured as the 12.7 mm Type 54. This weapon is used by nations such as Pakistan (by whom it is produced under Chinese guidance), Iran, Iraq (there were reports that at one time the DShK-38/46 was produced there) and Thailand, a nation which has procured

the Chinese Type 69 tank on which the Type 54 is mounted as a general-purpose defence weapon on the turret roof. The Type 54 is also used on the Chinese Type 77, Type 85, YW 531, YW 534 and WZ 523 armoured personnel carriers. The DShK-38/46 was at one time (the mid-1950s) produced in Czechoslovakia where it was known as the DSK vz 54.

The Chinese Type 59 is a modified Type 54, ie the DShK-38/46 with the muzzle attachment enlarged slightly to allow it to use sub-calibre armour-piercing projectiles fitted with sabots (known as armour-piercing discarding sabot or APDS) to increase their armour-piercing performance.

The DShK heavy machine guns are gas-operated weapons with finned barrels. The mechanism was based on that used for the old Degtyarev DP light machine gun, providing yet another example of the process of gradual evolution rather than drastic innovation employed by CIS machine gun designers.

The latest of the CIS 12.7 mm machine guns is named the NSV after its designers, Nikitin, Sokolov and Volkov. It has also been referred to as the UTES, and under either name it continues to use the 12.7 mm × 108 cartridge and may be encountered as a heavy infantry fire support weapon, as an anti-aircraft weapon or as a general defence weapon mounted over the commander's cupola on the tank turret (this version is the NSV-T).

Introduced into service during 1974, the NSV is yet another weapon based on the Kalashnikov gas-operated rotary bolt mechanism but scaled up to suit the calibre involved. As a tripod-mounted ground fire support weapon the ammunition is supplied in 50-round belts and the machine gun may be fitted with a pistol grip trigger group and an adjustable butt. Aiming is assisted by the provision of an optional optical (telescopic) sight.

As a tank-turret weapon the NSV is known as the NSV-T, the preferred heavy machine gun for the latest generation of CIS tanks. On the T-64 and the SMT-1989

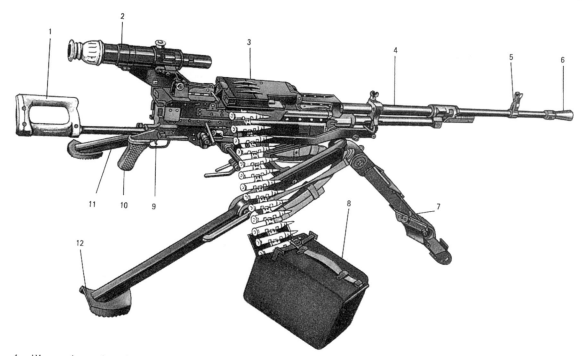

An illustration taken from an old East German military magazine showing the parts of a tripod-mounted 12.7 mm NSV heavy machine gun: 1 butt, 2 optical sight, 3 ammunition feed cover, 4 barrel, 5 foresight, 6 flash hider, 7 forward leg of tripod, 8 ammunition belt box, 9 trigger, 10 trigger grip, 11 tripod leg, 12 tripod foot.

the NVS-T can be aimed and fired remotely by the commander from within the turret with the hatch closed down. Aiming is accomplished using a periscopic sight located at the base of the cupola. On the T-72 and T-80 the NSV-T is aimed and fired from outside the vehicle using the gun's spade grips only. It has been noted during recent years that the NSV-T is being retrofitted to the earlier T-55M and T-62M tanks in place of the 12.7 mm DShK-38/46. The ordinary NVS can be mounted to fire out of the front ports of the BTR-D, the lengthened (six road wheels each side) armoured personnel carrier version of the BMD airborne combat vehicle. In all versions the practical rate of fire of the NVS machine guns is from 80 to 100 rounds a minute.

The NSV was licence-produced in the former Yugoslavia but has yet to appear on their list of locally made weapons available for export.

The largest of the CIS heavy machine guns is the 14.5 mm *Krupnokakalibernyi Pulemet Vladimironva*, or KPV. This heavy weapon was developed during the years following 1945 and was designed to fire the powerful 14.5 mm × 114 cartridge, available with armour-piercing or high explosive projectiles and originally intended for the anti-armour role with the 14.5 mm PTRD-41 anti-tank rifle.

Intended primarily for use as an anti-aircraft weapon, the KPV was designed for ease and simplicity of manufacture. The gun body is a steel cylinder to which other components are riveted or welded. Extensive use is made of steel stampings, but overall the construction is sound and strong while the life of the quick-change barrel is enhanced by the provision of chrome plating in the bore. The operating mechanism is gas-operated with the barrel and breech block being initially pushed back after firing by the propellant gases expand-

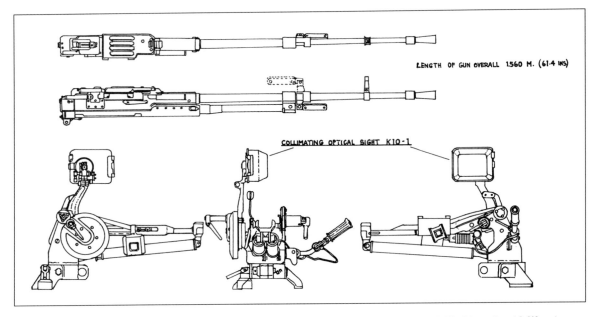

A drawing of a 12.7 mm NSV-T heavy machine gun as mounted on T-72 and T-80 tanks (Miltra).

ing in the muzzle attachment; however, due to the powerful 14.5 mm × 114 cartridge involved, the bolt has to employ a rotary locking action. The KPV is no longer in production in the CIS although at least one 'improved' variant is still manufactured in China.

The KPV has been widely deployed as a light anti-aircraft weapon from the early 1950s onwards, usually on vehicle-towed mountings known as the *Zenitnaya Pulemetanya Ustanovka*, or ZPU. The main versions of these are the ZPU-1, ZPU-2 and ZPU-4, the numeral denoting the number of guns involved. The ZPU-1 and ZPU-2 are both towed on single-axle carriages while the ZPU-4 demands two axles. As an anti-aircraft weapon, the KPV has an effec-

A side view drawing of the remote control mounting for the 12.7 mm NSV-T machine gun on T-64 and SMT-1989 tanks.

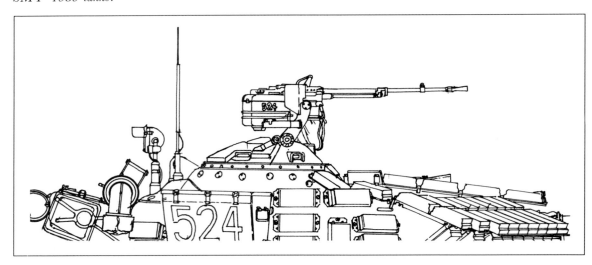

A 14.5 mm ZPU-4 anti-aircraft mounting with four KPV heavy machine guns belonging to the Maltese Task Force.

tive vertical range of 1,400 metres and a horizontal range of 8,000 metres, both of which make the ZPU mountings very effective air defence weapons. Despite this, however, they are no longer in service with the CIS (other than possible retention as reserve or militia weapons) or any of the old Warsaw Pact armed forces, but many nations throughout the world continue to value their air defence capabilities. These nations have been increased in number by KPVs and ZPUs produced in China and sold or passed as 'military aid' to many more nations. The Chinese ZPU-1 is the Type 75-1 and uses an 'improved' KPV; the ZPU-2 is the Type 58; and the ZPU-4 is the Type 56. ZPU-2s and ZPU-4s have also been manufactured in North Korea.

The KPV has also been widely employed as an armoured vehicle weapon for which its short inboard length makes it very suitable. (Some references make use of the designation KPVT for this variant.) This suitability is increased by the ability of the metal link ammunition belts to be broken into 10-round lengths for easy handling inside a vehicle turret, and belts can be fed into the gun from the left- or right-hand side (or even upside down for that matter). The armour piercing/incendiary (API) projectile fired by the KPV at a muzzle velocity of 1,000 metres per second can penetrate 32 mm of armour plate at 500 metres. Numerous former Warsaw Pact light armoured vehicles use the KPV as their main armament in turret mountings. Typical of these are the identical turret mountings used on both the Czech OT-64C and CIS BTR-80 armoured personnel carriers.

The cyclic rate of fire of the KPV is 600 rounds a minute, but for practical purposes this is decreased to about 150 rounds a minute. The gun itself weighs 49.1 kg.

Rotary Machine Guns

For some years there have been reports of a CIS four-barrel machine gun that operates using the rotary 'Gatling' principle. Little is known of it – not even the designation – but it is understood that it fires the 12.7 mm × 108 cartridge and does not rely on an external power source as do the American rotaries (see chapter 20). Instead, this rotary gun uses blank ammunition to commence a gas-driven operating cycle. This combination of blank-activated gas operation and a reported cyclic rate of fire of 4,000 rounds per minute would seem to indicate that the gun is intended for use on aircraft or helicopters rather than ground mountings.

DATA

Model	RPD	SG-43
Calibre	7.62 mm	7.62 mm
Weight (gun only)	7.1 kg	13.6 kg
Length	1.036 m	1.12 m
Length of barrel	521 mm	719 mm
Rate of fire	700 rpm	650 rpm
Feed	100-round belt	250-round belt
Muzzle velocity	700 m/s	800 m/s

Model	RPK	PK
Calibre	7.62 mm	7.62 mm
Weight (gun only)	5 kg	9 kg
Length	1.035 m	1.16 m
Length of barrel	591 mm	658 mm
Rate of fire	660 rpm	690-720 rpm
Feed	40-round box 75-round drum	belt
Muzzle velocity	732 m/s	825 m/s

Model	DShK-38/46	NSV
Calibre	12.7 mm	12.7 mm
Weight (gun only)	35.7 kg	25 kg
Length	1.588 m	1.56 m
Length of barrel	1.07 m	n/a
Rate of fire	575 rpm	700-800 rpm
Feed	belt	belt
Muzzle velocity	860 m/s	845 m/s

Model	KPV	RPK
Calibre	14.5 mm	5.45 mm
Weight (gun only)	49.1 kg	4.6 kg
Length	2.006 m	n/a
Length of barrel	1.346 m	n/a
Rate of fire	600 rpm	600 rpm
Feed	belt	45-round box
Muzzle velocity	1000 m/s	960 m/s

CHAPTER 5

THE SLEEPING GIANT – CHINA

THIS chapter is titled 'the sleeping giant' because China is a nation having immense industrial potential that has yet to be fully unleashed. That potential extends to China's armaments manufacturers, but it has to be stated right away that Chinese industry is already churning out small arms production totals that defy belief. It is difficult to apply precise statistics to these output quantities but a measure can be derived from the fact that over the past decade the Chinese have virtually re-equipped their entire armed forces (well over four million men, with reserves) with modern weapons, yet have still retained a capability to start export marketing drives as well as handing out or selling weapons to nations large and small all over the world. Despite all this, the true potential of the Chinese defence industries has still to emerge, for their production capacity to produce weapons of all types is as yet unrealised. To add to all this their inventive capacity to produce novel and advanced weapon designs has as yet been only hinted at.

The Chinese have always had their own home-based armaments industry – it must not be forgotten that the Chinese are credited with the discovery of gunpowder. Yet the present-day Chinese weapons industry has been established only since 1949, when the Communist Chinese armed forces took over the central government of the nation from the old Kuomintang forces led by Chiang Kai-shek.

The Communists inherited a shattered economy and a war-torn country which had been virtually destroyed by decades of internal dissension, invasion and civil war. By sheer hard work, ruthless discipline and a fair measure of outside assistance, the People's Republic of China has been able to organise and build its current industrial base virtually from nothing. It is a base that is still expanding in size and scope, for China's full manpower and raw material resources have yet to be fully exploited.

The Chinese defence industrial infrastructure did, however, inherit a few capabilities from previous regimes. From about the 1920s onwards fragmented efforts had been made to create some form of capacity to manufacture modern weapons, but these efforts were rarely co-ordinated or on any large scale. We have seen in chapter 1 how attempts were made to produce Maxim guns during the 1930s, attempts which were typically thwarted by Japanese invasion. Among such attempts were ammunition production plants (usually small arms ammunition) and pyrotechnics and explosives production – the latter both well-established Chinese industries. But these in-house production projects could usually supply only local needs. Any shortfalls were met by sporadic purchases from abroad or, after 1942, by American and other military aid.

Military aid from another source was already being directed towards the Communist Chinese for a period well before 1949. The old Soviet Union supported the Chinese efforts to create a Marxist-inspired state at that stage so military and other support was provided by them right across the board; during the early 1950s the coming rift between the Soviet Union and the new China had still to emerge. Soviet aid of all kinds poured into China, including weapons and the means to make them.

The Communist Chinese were anxious to establish their own defence industries and so were more than happy to accept Soviet guidance in the building and equipping of factories of all kinds. They were also happy to produce what would emerge as virtual clones of Soviet-designed weapons, for several reasons. The most obvious at that time was that the Chinese had virtually no design base of their own on which to draw and had to accept outside guidance. Another reason was that they could not afford to argue as to what they might manufacture. The Soviets were offering to supply machinery, guidance and training, and what they were offering in the way of weapon end products was as good as anything on the market elsewhere. Moreover, these products had all passed through the stage of being 'combat proven' on a massive scale and were tried and tested to a degree where no user or manufacturing problems could be expected. Added to that quality asset was the fact that Soviet weapons had to a large extent been designed for production using basic facilities and unskilled or semi-skilled labour. So why argue? Thus the newly established Chinese small arms industry (and much of their other defence industrial establishment) was founded on Soviet know-how and weapon

designs. That included machine guns.

Facilities to manufacture machine guns and other small arms were already in being during the early 1950s, and all the output went direct to the People's Liberation Army and other branches of the armed forces, which at that time were ill-equipped with a rag-bag of old Second World War weapons that were usually in dire need of replacement.

The machine gun designs of Soviet origin manufactured in China included (and still include in some cases) the weapons already covered in the previous chapter. There is therefore no need to cover the same ground again, so to keep things tidy all that is necessary is a tabulation of the Chinese models of Soviet origin together with the Soviet designations. (The Chinese Type number is the year in which the Chinese armed forces accepted that model for service, while a dash (-) denotes a sub-mark or variant.)

Type 53	7.62 mm DPM
Type 54	12.7 mm DShK-38/46
Type 56	7.62 mm RPD
Type 56-1	fully modified 7.62 mm RPD
Type 56	14.5 mm ZPU-4
Type 57	7.62 mm SG43
Type 57	7.62 mm SGMB
Type 58	7.62 mm RP-46
Type 58	14.5 mm ZPU-2
Type 59	7.62 mm PKB
Type 59	modified 12.7 mm Type 54
Type 63	7.62 mm SGM
Type 75	14.5 mm ZPU-1
Type 80	7.62 mm PKM
Type 81	7.62 mm RPK derivative

In addition to the above a 7.92 mm copy of the British/Canadian Bren gun was for some years manufactured in China as the Type 41.

How many of the above weapons are still in production in China is not known for certain, but one noticeable aspect of the Chinese armed forces is that they never seem to be able to throw anything away. Once a weapon has been withdrawn from

The NORINCO 7.62 mm Type 54, described as a tank anti-aircraft machine gun but actually a Chinese copy of the CIS 12.7 mm DShK-38/46.

front-line use it is given to one or other of the various Chinese armed forces' reserve organisations or People's militias. Failing that, they are passed to foreign 'freedom fighters' or other armed bands deemed sympathetic to the Communist Chinese way of political thought and thus end up in some rather strange hands. Much of the Viet

The NORINCO 7.62 mm Type 80, described as a multi-purpose machine gun but actually a Chinese-produced version of the CIS PKM.

The twin-barrelled 14.5 mm Type 58 light anti-aircraft weapon.

Cong and North Vietnamese weaponry deployed during the Vietnam campaigns had Communist Chinese origins.

Something Borrowed . . .

The above listing of copies of Soviet machine guns manufactured by the Chinese should not conceal the fact that they are now designing and manufacturing their own 'in-house' machine guns. The rift with the Soviet Union that developed into virtual hostility during the late 1950s and afterwards led to contacts with Soviet technicians being gradually reduced to virtually nil. While the skills of the Chinese gun-makers had reached the stage where they could copy weapons such as the 7.62 mm PK series without Soviet guidance, there was still the urge to demonstrate that national talents and self-reliance could develop machine gun and other weapon designs that would be as good as anything produced elsewhere.

One of the first known attempts to produce an indigenous Chinese machine gun resulted in the 7.62 mm Type 67. Although it might appear at first sight to be a new weapon it may be regarded as a product of the 'Meccano set' approach to machine gun development. The Type 67 is a general-purpose machine gun which uses features taken from a number of other extant machine gun designs which have been re-jigged.

For a start, the belt feed mechanism was taken direct from the old Type 24 Maxim gun produced during the late 1930s; as ammunition feed mechanisms can be quite complex this was a quick short-cut to avoid introducing possible difficulties with an entirely new system. The Type 67 is gas-operated, using the piston and bolt assembly taken from the pre-war Czech ZB26 light machine gun, the precursor of the British Bren gun and a weapon used throughout China during the Second World War. However, not all the gas operating system was ex-Czech since the gas regulator was taken direct from the Type 56/Soviet RPD. The trigger mechanism, another area of potential mechanical problems, was taken from the Type 53/Soviet DPM. Even design details are taken from other models; the sights, for instance, closely resemble those used on the Czech 7.62 mm Model 59. To round things off, the changing system for the air-cooled barrel was copied from that of the Type 57/Soviet SG43, along with the micrometer cartridge head space adjustment system. Finally, the round fired is still the old Tsarist/Soviet 7.62 mm × 54 full-power rifle cartridge.

This array of bits and pieces sounds like a mishmash but the end result is a sound and serviceable weapon that is widely used throughout the Communist Chinese armed forces and by others, including the People's Republic of Congo, Vietnam and Zambia. It is still in production and throughout its life has been gradually modified to make it more attractive to prospective export purchasers. There are Types 67-1, 67-2 and 67-2C, which appear to vary only in detail, although it is noticeable that the − 2 and − 2C versions have a handle that doubles as a barrel-changing aid and a carrying handle. All versions can be fired from either

A tripod-mounted 7.62 mm Type 67-1 machine gun.

a bipod or a light pressed steel tripod.

Ammunition feed is usually via 100- or 250-round belts or from a 50-round belt drum. The latter can be employed when the Type 67 is used in the anti-aircraft role, for which the weapon is also provided with a simple bead and optical cartwheel sight. When used in the air defence role, the Type 67 tripod can be re-arranged to act as an anti-aircraft mounting.

The 7.62 mm Type 67 was the first 'all-Chinese' machine gun to enter large-scale service, and has since been joined by others.

Something New . . .

The first indication that the Chinese design teams were breaking away from the Soviet mould came with the appearance of a squad-level light machine gun design known as the 7.62 mm Type 74. At first sight this appears to be yet another spin-off from the Kalashnikov AK-47 rifle design line; the Type 56 rifle, an AK-47 clone, had by the 1970s been rolling off the Chinese production lines in quantities measured in millions, so many soldiers and technicians were very familiar with all aspects of the Kalashnikov design.

On the Type 74 machine gun the overall gas operation system has been much revised and re-arranged, but the basic and well-tried Kalashnikov rotary bolt and piston mechanism appears to remain virtually unchanged, even if there is a prominent spring housing jutting forward over the barrel. This latter indicates that the Type 74 may have an entirely new operating system and provides a pointer to how Chinese weapon designers are beginning to make their mark on machine gun development. Unfortunately it has not proved possible to examine the interior of a Type 74, although they have been shown at defence exhibitions, so some mysteries still remain regarding this weapon. It appears to be in service with the Chinese armed forces and has been offered for export.

The Type 74 fires the 7.62 mm × 39 cartridge fed from a spring-loaded drum holding a substantial 101 rounds; if required, the 30-round box magazine from the Type 56 rifle can be fitted. Handling the weapon is very simple. The barrel is fixed so firing has to be limited to short bursts — there does not appear to be a single-shot facility. A handy and well-shaped wooden

The 7.62 mm Type 74 light machine gun.

foregrip makes the weapon easy to carry and aim in the 'assault' mode, and the simple bipod features no height adjustment method.

Another squad light machine gun design appears to have been developed and manufactured purely for export. This is the 7.62 mm Type 81, one of a 'family' of two weapons, the other being the Type 81 rifle (the latter having a fixed wooden butt, the Type 81-1 a metal folding butt), with much commonality of parts between them. Ex-

actly why the Type 81 light machine gun was developed is not clear for it appears to be a virtual copy of the CIS RPK, but with enough dimensional and other changes to render it a 'Chinese' design.

The Type 81 machine gun is slightly shorter than the RPK but weighs much the same and uses the same 30- or 75-round magazines; it has a carrying handle and the forestock appears to be longer than that of the RPK. There are also other small detail differences, but the Type 81 'family' seems

The 7.62 mm Type 81 light machine gun, one component of the NORINCO Type 81 gun family.

to offer few advantages over other weapons already available on the open market. Perhaps they were produced to take advantage of what has been one of the Chinese small-arms industry's main marketing advantages, namely a low unit cost which always seems to undercut the sum marked on competitors' price lists. This low unit price is made possible by the sheer scale of the manufacturing totals produced in the Chinese arms plants.

The Chinese have also produced two entirely new heavy machine gun models. The first of these is the Type 77 firing the 12.7 mm × 108 cartridge known to the Chinese as the Type 54 from its use on the earlier Type 54/Soviet DShK-38/46 heavy machine gun. From the long tube-like appearance of the receiver on the Type 77 and what seems to be a gas port and tube running under the barrel from a point half-way along its length, it appears to be a gas-operated weapon but exactly which operating principle is involved is not known for certain. Few Western technicians appear to have seen this weapon and available literature is restricted to a few sales brochures. Overall, the gun's construction

seems to be light for a weapon with a calibre of 12.7 mm, and the quoted weight of 56 kg, complete with the tripod, also appears to be on the light side when compared to other similar weapons.

The Type 77 may be used as a battalion-level fire support weapon or as a light air defence weapon; for the latter role it may be fitted with an optical sight. The same variable-height tripod is used for both ground and air defence employment and in both roles the weapon is fired using twin grips and a thumb trigger. Ammunition is fed into the weapon from a side-mounted metal box holding a 60-round belt. Judging from photographs it appears that there is some form of quick-change system for the fluted barrel. There is also a generally similar weapon known as the 12.7 mm Type W-85, but the weight of this weapon is even lighter than that of the Type 77. On the Type W-85 the weight of the gun in a 'combat state' and complete with tripod is quoted as 39 kg, which seems to be a remarkably low weight for what is supposed to be a battalion-level heavy fire support weapon. The Type W-85 is intended to be broken down for pack transport by man or animal with

The 12.7 mm Type 77 heavy machine gun mounted in a ground role.

A tripod-mounted 12.7 mm Type 77 as used in the light air defence role.

accurate aiming at long ranges – this sight is also claimed to have night-firing features but no infra-red or other night vision system appears to be incorporated. Field stripping is possible without the aid of tools and a malfunction rate of less than 0.2 per cent is claimed.

The ammunition fired from the Type W-85 is the same as that fired from the Type 77, the Type 54/CIS 12.7 mm × 108, and it is fed from the same 60-round metal box. Type 54 rounds are all armour-piercing but the Type W-85 literature makes mention of a 'tungsten-alloy cored bullet'. This is probably the same saboted 12.7 mm round (of an ammunition nature usually known in the West as armour-piercing discarding sabot, or APDS) as that used on the Type 59 heavy machine gun, a modified Type 54/CIS DShK-38/46 with an enlarged muzzle attachment to permit the use of such ammunition. It is very probable that this round is also fired from the Type 77. When fired from the Type W-85 the APDS sub-calibre projectile has a muzzle velocity of 1,150 metres per second compared to the 800 metres per second of conventional Type 54 armour-piercing projectiles, providing the APDS projectile with an improved performance against armoured targets.

The designation of the Type W-85 is somewhat confusing but it may be a manufacturer's code employed prior to service acceptance, after which a year code will be applied. As far as can be determined the

the heaviest part, the gun itself, weighing only 18.5 kg.

As with the Type 77, the Type W-85 is gas-operated and the two weapons appear to share the same tripod and general layout although there are many obvious differences, the smooth exterior of the Type W-85 barrel being but one. The Type W-85 definitely does have a quick-change barrel system and it does have a telescopic sight for

The 12.7 mm Type W-85 heavy machine gun, described in NORINCO literature as an anti-aircraft machine gun.

Type W-85 is not yet in service with the Chinese armed forces but it has been promoted for export.

The Chinese heavy machine guns are rounded off by their version of the 14.5 mm KPV, referred to in some references as the Type 56. The Chinese first produced the KPV in its original Soviet-inspired form but have since developed their own 'improved' version with a finned barrel to improve cooling and some alterations to the ammunition feed. This is the 14.5 mm Type 75 which is normally mounted on a light wheeled carriage that can be folded up to convert it to a towing trailer. It is also possible to break down the weapon and its carriage for pack transport. Laying is accomplished using mechanical elevation and traversing gears. For both air and ground target roles the sighting system can be mounted on a parallelogram arm with an adjustable height. Among the sighting systems available is an image-intensifying sight for use in low visibility or at night; with this sight the weapon and carriage combination is known as the Type 75-1. The 14.5 mm Type 80 is a further variation of the Type 75 with a capability to reduce the height of the carriage almost to ground level for firing at ground targets. The Type 80 carriage is heavier and more robust than that used on the Type 75 and is not so amenable for pack transport as it is intended to be towed behind light 4 × 4 vehicles.

NORINCO

All the above-mentioned Chinese machine guns, including those of Soviet design, are produced by a large State industrial conglomerate known as the China North Industries Corporation, usually referred to simply as NORINCO. This corporate monster, of which the defence industrial effort is but a section, is headquartered in Beijing and has centres in Guangzhou, Shenzhen, Dalian, Tianjin and Shanghai. It produces everything from optical equipment to explosives and from tanks to sporting guns. It also makes ammunition, explosives, rockets and bombs, to say nothing of small arms, artillery and even flame-throwers.

The growing self-confidence of the Chinese defence industries in machine gun production was further demonstrated by the establishment during 1985 of a production line to manufacture the 12.7 mm Type 54/DShK-38/46 heavy machine gun under Chinese technical guidance in Pakistan. An industry only recently reliant on outsiders for assistance is now in a position to offer help to others.

The 7.62 mm Type 56-1 light machine gun, a typical example of the Chinese producing CIS designs – this is actually a copy of the RPD.

Above *The Type 56 four-barrelled light air defence weapon involving four of the Chinese versions of the CIS 14.5 mm KPV heavy machine gun.*

Below *A 14.5 mm Type 75-1 emplaced ready for firing.*

The main point of this corporate message is that the Chinese are gearing themselves up to produce weapons on a scale that will soon outstrip anything seen hitherto, apart possibly from the CIS efforts. Already nations all around the world are availing themselves of the savings made possible by the Chinese economies of scale, and are re-equipping their armed forces with excellent weapons at a financial cost far lower than would be possible by using Western markets. The vast bulk of the NORINCO weapons on offer may be well-tried ex-CIS designs from a previous generation but they are extremely robust and reliable and their overall standard of manufacturing and finish leaves nothing to be desired.

These points cover all types of NORINCO weapons, including machine guns. We are certain to be hearing more of NORINCO-produced weapons in the future.

DATA

Model	Type 67	Type 74
Calibre	7.62 mm	7.62 mm
Weight (gun only)	9.9 kg	6.2 kg
Length	1.143 m	1.07 m
Length of barrel	597 mm	n/a
Rate of fire	650 rpm	approx 600 rpm
Feed	belt	101-round drum
Muzzle velocity	835 m/s	735 m/s

Model	Type 81	Type 77
Calibre	7.62 mm	12.7 mm
Weight (gun only)	5.3 kg	56.1 kg*
Length	1.024 m	2.15 m
Length of barrel	n/a	n/a
Rate of fire	approx 600 rpm	650-750 rpm
Feed	75-round drum	60-round belt
Muzzle velocity	735 m/s	800 m/s
		*with tripod

Model	W-85
Calibre	12.7 mm
Weight (gun only)	18.5 kg
Length	1.995 m
Length of barrel	n/a
Rate of fire (practical)	80-100 rpm
Feed	60-round belt
Muzzle velocity	up to 1150 m/s

CHAPTER 6

THE BELGIAN LEADERS – FN

FABRIQUE Nationale, known universally as FN, was formed in 1889 to manufacture Mauser rifles for the Belgian government. At the time of its formation it was able to draw upon a tradition of gun-making that had centred on the industrial city of Liege since the 15th century; Liege guns were known throughout the world for their quality and workmanship. Since 1889 FN has become a much-respected world leader in its field and has been the source of many novel and influential small arms designs that have produced an impact far outside the borders of Belgium.

FN's first significant industrial contact with machine guns began in the aftermath of the Great War when war booty in the shape of ex-German MG08 and MG08/15 Maxim machine guns were converted in Liege to accommodate the then standard Belgian 7.65 mm × 53 rifle cartridge. These 'Belgian' Maxims then went on to serve with the Belgian Army until 1940, and thereafter the Germans, but after 1945 few remained. Prior to 1914 FN had produced some spare parts for German-produced Maxims but no complete guns.

The next FN machine gun involvement was a result of the association between FN and the American weapon designer John Moses Browning (see chapter 2). FN manufactured the Browning Automatic Rifle, or BAR, from 1928 onwards and production did not cease (apart from the years 1940-45 and just after) until 1967.

The BAR was a great American armed forces favourite but it did not really catch on too well in Europe, where the only 'local' customers were the Belgian and Polish armies. The Belgians adopted the BAR during 1930 and, from 1932 onwards, took delivery of a number complete with light bipods and a barrel change system which converted them from being heavy automatic rifles into something close to light machine guns. Post-war production was mainly for export to countries such as Egypt and various South American states where some are rumoured to be still surviving in police and para-military hands. The BAR does not need to be considered here any further, other than to note that it was one of the first heavy-barrelled machine rifles of a type that now proliferates, and that its gas-operated mechanism was later adopted for use on the MAG (of which more later).

FN has long been involved in the manufacture of the other 'fully fledged' Browning machine guns, the first being produced in 1932. Numerous FN/Browning machine

An FN Heavy Machine Gun pod enclosing a 0.50/12.7 mm Browning machine gun being carried on the starboard side of a Sea Lynx helicopter.

gun models were produced with calibres ranging from 7.5 to 13.2 mm and, depending on the calibres, they were originally based on either the 0.30 Browning M1919 or the 0.50/12.7 mm M1921/M2. Both air- and water-cooled models were produced in many forms, mainly for export to all corners of the world.

Production of these export models had ceased by 1958 but in 1975 production of the 0.50/12.7 mm M2 HB re-started at Herstal and it has remained in production by FN ever since. (Herstal is a district of Liege and the location of FN's headquarters and main production plant.) FN technical staff have introduced their own refinements to the original Browning design and one available model is the M2 HB/QCB, a quick-change barrel (hence QCB) variant that does away with the need to adjust the cartridge head space when changing barrels. If required, the QCB option can be supplied in kit form for retro-fitting to existing M2 HBs.

FN also produce M2 HB tripods and other mountings and have also introduced several new natures of 12.7 mm ammunition such as armour-piercing explosive incendiary (APEI). They have also developed a streamlined pod which can be carried under the wings of light aircraft or helicopters. Known as the Heavy Machine Gun Pod (or HMP), it carries a special M2 HB variant known as the M3P, remote firing devices and a 250-round magazine. For more details of the M2 HB refer to Section 2.

FALO

One of the modern equivalents of the old Browning Automatic Rifle (BAR) is the FN *Fusil Automatique Lourd*, or FALO, also known as the FAL HB. This is a 7.62 mm squad fire support version of the famous *Fusil Automatique Legere* fitted with a heavy barrel (hence the sometimes encountered alternative name of FAL HB). The 7.62 mm FAL rifle has been one of the major European all-round leaders in the post-war military rifle field, being adopted and/or licence-produced by many nations all

A typical example of a 7.62 mm FALO, in this case an Australian L2A1 automatic rifle with the usual foregrip removed.

around the world, including the United Kingdom and many of the old British Commonwealth nations, after its commercial launch during 1953. It is still in production and is available from FN and many licensed manufacturers.

The FAL was designed to fire the NATO 7.62 mm × 51 cartridge, and such was its widespread adoption (by over 90 countries according to one source) that many nations requested a burst fire heavy-barrelled ver-

sion to act as a squad light support weapon. Thus the FALO was devised. It is really no more than a standard FAL rifle equipped with a revised trigger mechanism, a heavy barrel and a light bipod – a small carrying handle is usually added.

The end result is really too light to be accurately termed a light machine gun. It is limited in its ammunition capacity (no more than a 30-round box magazine and often just the standard FAL 20-round box),

Machine Gun 7.62 mm C2A1, a version of the FN FALO produced by Canadian Arsenals Ltd for the Canadian Armed Forces, seen here without a magazine fitted.

and, when being fired on automatic, it jumps around excessively due to its overall light weight. But since many FAL users have their rifles' trigger mechanisms limited to single-shot only, the FALO may be used to deliver the automatic burst fire support that can be so valuable at times, even if the bursts have to be limited in duration and somewhat erratic in aim.

The FALO has been licence-produced in nations such as Canada and Australia, but many users came to recognise its drawbacks and have since switched to more capable squad support weapons. However, it will be many years before the last FALO is withdrawn from service.

MAG

One of the most successful of all the post-1945 machine guns, in commercial, production and operational terms, has been the FN *Mitrailleuse d'Appui Generale*, better known to most of its many customers simply as the MAG. This remarkable weapon went into mass production in 1958 and it is still being manufactured, often far from Liege, for production licences have been acquired by many nations. (Some references mention the derivation of MAG to be *Mitrailleur a Gaz* – either way the initials MAG suffice. The term MAG-58 has also been used, from the year of introduction.)

The MAG was designed by a team led by one Ernest Vervier, a design engineer whose name deserves to be better known. M Vervier was one of the many small arms specialists who had been greatly impressed by the numerous small arms innovations to emerge during the Second World War, including the detail design features introduced on many of the pre-1945 general-purpose machine guns (GPMGs). He decided to employ FN's considerable engineering capabilities to design and develop a fully updated GPMG which would prove attractive to the armed forces of the then newly formed NATO nations and others.

The result was the MAG. In design terms it involves the simple and efficient belt feed

system of the German MG42 combined with the gas-operated mechanism employed by the Browning Automatic Rifle. As has been mentioned, the latter had been produced by FN for many years before the MAG was designed during the mid-1950s, so it was well understood by them. The BAR mechanism was accordingly modified and up-dated to bear the stresses of continued sustained firing and the loads imposed by a belt feed system. The barrel is air-cooled and involves the obligatory rapid-change feature with which the barrel-change handle doubles as a carrying handle. Other design features include a chrome-plated bore and the use of more chrome plating on parts of the gun that have to endure hard wear, such as the ammunition feed tray. Another feature is a novel gas regulation feature that permits variations in the cyclic rate of fire of between 650 and 1,000 rounds per minute.

However, there was one Second World War innovation that M Vervier decided not to adopt, and that was the mass production measures employed by many of the war-economy weapon designs. In place of the cheap steel pressings, welds and rivets introduced on weapons such as the MG42, the MAG continues to employ high-quality machined components carved from solid

The classic 7.62 mm FN MAG seen here mounted as a heavy machine gun on a tripod.

The 7.62 mm MAG light machine gun in use.

metal, involving an overall standard of engineering which makes few concessions to the rapid production approach. Such were the design procedures used for the MAG that it manages to involve all the refinements employed by previous generations of gun-makers yet remains highly amenable to the demands of mass production. The end result is a tough and reliable GPMG that is still repeatedly demonstrating just how good a weapon it really is.

In true GPMG style the MAG can be fired as a light machine gun from a bipod or mounted on a heavy tripod for sustained automatic fire. During its varied military career it has been mounted as an air or ground defence weapon on pintles, on ring and other types of vehicle mounting, on all manner of naval mountings (including simple lashings to guard rails during the 1982 Falkland Islands campaign), as a co-axial weapon on armoured vehicles, and has even been carried in light attack aircraft or helicopter pods – mention will be made of the latter two applications later. The MAG has also been produced as a ranging machine gun for the main armament of tanks.

Throughout its life the MAG has been produced with many variations to suit particular applications. Most of the variations apply to the weapons intended for use on tank and aircraft mountings, although there is a basic distinction between the weapons intended to use disintegrating (M13) or non-disintegrating ammunition belts; the feed systems are not interchangeable.

Three main MAG categories are known within FN. The Model 60-20 category includes the infantry bipod/tripod versions – 15 variants are listed with the basic model being the T1. The Model 60-30 category includes the aircraft/helicopter versions, while the Model 60-40 category includes the co-axial versions for fixed use alongside armoured vehicle main armaments or as a ranging machine gun. Thus the Models 60-30 and 60-40 do not have bipods, butts or sights, among other things. In each category there are models intended to suit particular mountings, but there is a considerable degree of component interchangeability between all the MAG categories.

One typical use of the Model 60-30 category of MAGs is inside a gun pod intended to be slung under the wings of light aircraft or from helicopters. The FN Twin MAG

Twin 7.62 mm MAG machine guns with their butts removed for use on a twin mounting carried on a Belgian Army Minerva Land Rover light vehicle.

Pod, or TMP, mounts two Model 60-30 category MAGs in buffered cradles inside a streamlined pod in such a way that most of the firing recoil forces are not transmitted to the carrier aircraft airframe. The TMP also has provisions for cooling ventilation. Firing is by remote control using electrical solenoids in place of the usual manual triggers. On the TMP the ammunition is belt-fed from 500-round boxes, one for each

A view taken from above and looking down into an armoured vehicle turret with two 7.62 mm MAGs mounted as co-axial weapons.

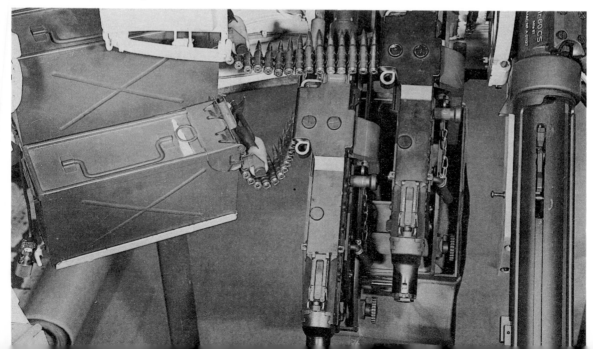

An FN MAG on a special post/pintle mounting on a M151 'Mutt'.

MAG, and provision is made in the design to ensure that the feed is not affected by sudden or violent aircraft movements. Apart from the TMP, other airborne MAG applications include fixed wing or fuselage mounted installations and column supports for firing from helicopter hatches.

The most numerous of the co-axial category 60-40 MAGs must be the one originally known to FN as the Model T3. This was adopted by the US Army as the M240 to serve as its main co-axial machine gun on

A 7.62 mm MAG mounted on an Israeli Army M60 tank.

battle tanks such as the M1 Abrams and the M60 series. The M240 is also used on other American armoured vehicles such as the US Army's M2/M3 Bradley infantry fighting vehicle (IFV) and the US Marine Corps's Light Armored Vehicle (LAV). The M240 employs an M13 disintegrating link belt that can be fed into the gun from the left; on the M240C the feed is from the right. Firing is from a solenoid trigger control, and cocking the weapon (or charging, to use the American term) can also be carried out remotely – many of the other category 60-40 MAGs can use a hand-operated trigger and have a cable-operated manual cocking system. If required, the M240 (and most of the other Model 60-40 guns) can be mounted on some form of ground mounting after fitting an adaptor kit.

The M240E1 is an American-derived anomaly in that it is a special variant provided with spade grips for operating from the flexible over-turret column mountings used on the wheeled Light Armored Vehicle (LAV) – thus the American supply system has managed to involve a fixed co-axial weapon design in the flexible vehicle mounting role. The original contract called for 739 M240E1s. M240s for the US armed forces are produced in the United States by an FN subsidiary located in Columbia, South Carolina. Production in the United States commenced during 1982.

Almost all MAGs fire the NATO 7.62 mm × 51 cartridge, the one major exception being the Swedish *Kulspruta 58* which originally fired the Swedish 6.5 mm × 55 round. Sweden was the first nation to adopt the MAG and originally their weapons were delivered direct from FN. In 1962 Sweden adopted the NATO ammunition standards, so the earlier weapons were converted to accommodate 7.62 mm × 51 rounds to comply. FFV Ordnance (now part of the Bofors AB conglomerate) licence-produces the MAG in Sweden (all production is now in 7.62 mm) and has devised many local accessories to cope with cold weather and other local environmental conditions, including a small sled to permit the bipod to

A special version of the FN MAG mounted on a light external pintle for helicopter use.

be used in deep snow conditions.

One of the most prolific of all MAG licence producers has been the United Kingdom. The UK's MAG production story is so involved and varied that the 'British' MAGs are dealt with in the next chapter.

Returning to the MAG variants, there has been a 'jungle' version (the Model 10-10) with a shortened butt and barrel, but as far as can be determined it has yet to be adopted by any customer.

Numerous accessories have been developed for the MAG, including a buffered tripod to absorb the recoil forces produced during sustained firing; this tripod even has a full 360-degree traverse head. There are also special anti-aircraft sights, cleaning and tool kits, blank firing devices to fit over the muzzle, and numerous other bits and pieces such as webbing bags to carry spare barrels or other parts.

The list of MAG user nations is a very long one, so an indication of the widespread employment of the MAG will have to be confined to the nations that have successfully negotiated licences to produce the weapon and/or its variants. The list includes Argentina, Egypt, India, Israel, Singapore (where it is manufactured and marketed *without* a licence), Sweden, the United Kingdom and the USA. Production continues in most of these countries and the MAG is, of course, still available direct from FN at Herstal.

In Taiwan the Combined Service Forces have developed a machine gun that closely resembles the FN MAG but has a finned barrel; it is known to the local armed forces as the Type 74.

The return to favour of the 'true' light machine gun as a squad fire support weapon in place of the GPMG or heavy-barrelled variety was in some cases made possible in part by the realisation that weapons such as the MAG are really too heavy for the light machine gun role. The MAG weighs 11 kg when being fired from its bipod (compared to the 6.83 kg of the FN Minimi) which means it is really something

of a load for the average soldier to carry and handle for prolonged periods. As a result the MAG is gradually being used more and more as a crew-served heavy fire support tripod-mounted weapon where its weight is not so much of a drawback. In the tripod-mounted role the MAG has few disadvantages other than, in common with all other air-cooled machine guns, the accepted fact that it cannot supply the prodigious amounts of fire once made possible by the old water-cooled designs.

Minimi

One very noticeable feature of FN small arms activity over the last few decades has been their far-sighted and innovative approach to the matter of small arms ammunition development. FN designers have always taken the viewpoint that the small arms projectile is the true weapon, not the rifle, machine gun or other delivery system, so projectile performance has to be given priority over other factors. This approach has led to FN introducing completely novel ammunition calibres and natures, recent examples being the introduction of the remarkable 5.7 mm × 28 round (together with its associated and equally remarkable P90 personal weapon) and the 15.5 mm × 106 round fired by the BRG-15 heavy machine gun (of which more later).

The introduction of novel calibres and ammunition natures has always entailed considerable commercial risks, but that has never prevented the FN management from undertaking potentially hazardous ventures. They have for years taken to placing their faith in accurately forecasting future trends and operational requirements such as when, back in the early 1960s, they started to develop a new weapon family to fire their then novel 5.56 mm SS 109 high-velocity cartridge.

Much of the early 5.56 mm ammunition development was carried out in the United States where the US Army's adoption of the M109 5.56 mm × 45 cartridge and the corresponding M16 rifle marked a distinct

A Browning 0.50/12.7 mm M2 HB heavy machine gun on an M63 air defence mounting.

A British Wessex Saker light strike vehicle armed with a Browning 0.50/12.7 mm M2 HB (top) and a 7.62 mm GPMG (next to driver).

MODERN MACHINE GUNS IN COLOUR

A tripod-mounted Browning M2 HB with a McDonnell-Douglas Astronautics Multi-purpose Universal Gunner's Sight (MUGS).

A Heckler & Koch 7.62 mm HK21 machine gun mounted on a RAMO RM-1 universal mount.

The dramatic Rattler multiple machine gun mounting intended for firing from the rear compartments of helicopters and seen here carrying four 7.62 mm MAGs.

A comparison between the Soviet 5.45 mm AKM-74 assault rifle (top), now the standard Soviet service rifle, and its squad fire support weapon partner, the 5.45 mm RPK-74 (bottom).

Top *One of the most successful machine gun designs produced since the Second World War – the Belgian 7.62 mm FN MAG general-purpose machine gun.*

Above *A pintle-mounted version of the 7.62 mm FN MAG intended for naval use.*

Below *The standard version of the FN 5.56 mm Minimi.*

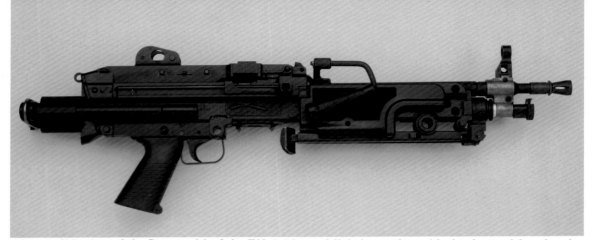

Above *Side view of the Para model of the FN 5.56 mm Minimi, complete with the shortened barrel and with the butt retracted.*

Top right *The British Royal Ordnance 5.56 mm L86A1 Light Support Weapon, the LSW.*

Middle right *A complete sustained-fire kit for a Royal Ordnance 7.62 mm L7A2 general-purpose machine gun.*

Bottom right *A tripod-mounted Spanish 5.56 mm Ameli.*

Below left *The FN Para Minimi, clearly showing its small overall dimensions.*

Below right *A hefty helicopter armament consisting of an FN Heavy Machine Gun Pod containing a 0.50/12.7 mm Browning machine gun (below) and an FN 7.62 mm MAG on a light external pintle.*

Above *US Army troops training in full chemical warfare protection equipment; the soldier in the fore-ground is operating a 7.62 mm M60 machine gun in the light machine gun role.*

Top left *Side view of the South African 7.62 mm SS-77 general-purpose machine gun.*

Middle left *The Swiss 7.62 mm MG51 in action as a light machine gun.*

Bottom left *The Italian AS 70/90 light machine gun with the bipod folded.*

Below *The 7.62 mm M60 machine gun in its bipod-mounted light machine gun form.*

GUN, MACHINE, 7.62 mm M60

A three-barrelled version of the American rotary 7.62 mm Minigun being fired from the rear of a long-range desert patrol version of the Land Rover Defender One Ten.

One of the three SUU-11/A pods used to house 7.62 mm Miniguns carried on 'Puff the Magic Dragon' AC-47s during the Vietnam campaigns. These pods were later replaced by more compact mountings.

In a dramatic demonstration of the power of modern machine gun ammunition a 0.50/12.7 mm HEPI (High Explosive Penetrating Incendiary) developed by FN has just penetrated a metal witness plate from the right-hand side.

milestone in small arms development and design trends. However, the Americans did not have the development field all to themselves. At FN Ernest Vervier and his successor Maurice Bourlet had also been investigating small-calibre high-velocity ammunition since the early 1960s, and their researches and forecasts led to an entirely new 5.56 mm cartridge which became known as the SS 109.

The SS 109 differed from the American M109 in many physical respects, not the least of which was a steel insert within the bullet and a more powerful propellant load. Externally the dimensions of the M109 and the SS 109 were identical, but their ballistic performances differed. For instance, the M109 cartridge was intended to give of its best at combat ranges of up to around 400 metres. By contrast the SS 109 produced a better range performance and also had better striking and armour-piercing parameters at those longer ranges.

The FN SS 109 appeared on the scene at around the time that the NATO nations were working towards the adoption of a new small-calibre standard cartridge, ie the mid-1970s. Inevitably the industrial situation and other factors virtually dictated that the NATO standard would have to be 5.56 mm, but the choice was seen to be between the American M109 and the Belgian FN SS 109. In reality this meant that the contest was between the industrial and political might of the United States and the technical faith and expertise of FN. It was a considerable challenge and an even more daunting commercial risk for FN to assume, for all the advantages seemed to be on the side of the Americans.

FN had by then already entered the 5.56 mm weapons market with their *Carabine Automatique Legere*, or CAL (later to become the FNC series). This scaled-down version of the famous FN 7.62 mm FAL rifle initially had only limited sales success, but it provided FN with a considerable degree of insight into the ballistics of the 5.56 mm calibre which convinced them that their SS 109 concept was correct. A decision was thus made to proceed with the design and development of a light machine gun to fire the SS 109 round and expand the marketing base of the FN 5.56 mm weapon family.

In the event the FN technicians and executives were vindicated when the SS 109 cartridge was adopted as the NATO standard following extensive trials which lasted from 1977 to 1980. The decision to develop the light machine gun was eventually seen to be equally far-sighted, for to date the numbers of marketable 5.56 mm light machine gun models have been few and far between, development having been almost universally directed towards rifles; machine guns have hardly been involved other than as heavy-barrelled equivalents of the rifles. Therefore a large potential market loomed for FN, of which their Minimi has been able to take advantage to a considerable degree, having rapidly become the most widely sold and used of any of the 5.56 mm light machine gun designs.

The first Minimi prototypes appeared during 1974, but full production did not commence until 1982. The years in between were directed towards crafting the Minimi to become a thoroughly reliable and robust weapon, and the FN technicians have once again proved that their innovative approach has produced the required results.

The Minimi bristles with features that demonstrate the attention to detail and craftsmanship that has always been a hallmark of FN weapons. The overall approach to the Minimi involves compactness and simplicity, but that has not prevented the introduction of features that have again shown FN to be design leaders.

Perhaps the most noticeable is a dual feed option by means of which the Minimi can, without modifications or rearrangements, use either a belt or magazine feed. In fact, FN claim that they have a three-mode ammunition feed system on the Minimi.

Two of the modes involve belts. On the first, belts of indeterminate length can be fed direct into the top-mounted feed tray, which has advantages when the weapon is tripod-mounted or on some other fixed

The standard version of the 5.56 mm Minimi.

mounting. However, foot soldiers who have to carry machine guns have long known that dangling ammunition belts have a

An FN demonstrator showing how the bipod of the 5.56 mm Minimi can be used as a foregrip when the weapon is fired from the hip.

habit of either snagging on anything in the vicinity or dragging themselves in dust and dirt to create malfunctions. FN have neatly overcome this old drawback by using a plastic box fastened underneath the receiver to keep a 200-round belt clean and out of the way. This box forms FN's second ammunition feed mode and is a most useful feature when the Minimi is fired from the hip during assault operations.

The third mode involves a standard rifle 30-round box magazine which can be fitted directly into the weapon from the left-hand side and at a slight angle, and which may be a standard American M16 type or FN's own (similar) FNC rifle magazine. In both cases the method is neat and easy and can make use of a rifle section's ammunition supply without the need for switching from magazines to belts.

Other Minimi features include a rotary two-position gas regulator with positions for normal conditions and what are termed 'adverse' conditions. The gas-operated mechanism uses a rotating bolt and is so arranged that the bolt always ceases its firing movements in the open position. This prevents live rounds being left in a hot chamber so that a potentially dangerous cartridge 'cook-off' may occur. To assist cooling, the barrel has a rapid-change

The 'Para' version of the 5.56 mm Minimi with the shortened barrel, seen here with the butt extended.

mechanism and the bore is once again chrome plated. Spent cartridge case extraction is considerably assisted by a smooth and progressive action which avoids the malfunctions sometimes caused by swollen or split cases after firing.

Detail design niceties can be encountered all over the Minimi. The trigger guard can be easily removed to permit operation when using cold weather or NBC protection gloves. The hand guard under the barrel houses a cleaning kit while the trigger pistol grip contains an oil bottle. In addition, a small button over the ammunition feed tray rises to indicate to anyone concerned that a cartridge is inside the feed.

The standard Minimi butt is a fixed steel skeletal component but to reduce the overall length of the weapon from the usual 1.04 metres to a possible 736 mm, a 'Para' model with a telescopic sliding butt is available; the 'Para' also has a shorter barrel. Another variant is a co-axial/vehicle version without a butt or handguard but with provision for an electrical firing solenoid; on this model the short barrel is an option.

As a squad fire support weapon the Minimi is provided with a bipod that can be adjusted in height as required. However, the Minimi can also be mounted on standard tripods, such as a MAG buffered tripod, to provide heavy support fire, although the 5.56 mm ammunition limits the effective range somewhat when compared to larger-calibre machine guns. However, the SS 109 round can be accurately delivered by a tripod-mounted Minimi to over 800 metres, at which ranges the ability of the Minimi to accommodate optical or night vision sights becomes yet another asset.

Throughout this description of the Minimi the accent has been on the use of the 5.56 mm SS 109 cartridge, and this combination does indeed provide an excellent combat performance potential. However, some nations have yet to adopt the SS 109 and still retain the M109. These can be fired by the Minimi but for optimum results the barrel rifling has to be altered. This simply involves fitting a suitable barrel – the M109 barrel demands rifling with one complete twist in 12 inches (305 mm), while the SS 109 requires a rifling twist of 7 inches (178 mm). Ball, armour piercing and tracer rounds are available for both the M109 and the SS 109.

A measure of the excellence of the Minimi can best be seen in the adoption during 1982 of the Minimi by the US Army and Marine Corps to become their M249 Squad Automatic Weapon, or SAW. The M249 differs from the standard FN Minimi only in details which are mainly confined to slight 'American standard' alterations to permit production in the United States at FN's South Carolina subsidiary. Nearly 60,000 M249s were originally ordered, but once the type had been in service for a while some problems were reported.

The main snag appears to have originated in the dual ammunition feed system. American M109 ammunition could not always provide the energy necessary to drag heavy ammunition belts through the feed system at certain angles, while the cyclic fire rates produced when using the box magazine, with its much reduced feed loadings, were deemed to be too high. A switch to SS 109 standard cartridges eliminated those problems. It was at the same time noticeable that all the complaints came from the US Army – the Marines had no complaints at all and still enthuse over their M249s. The significance of these early 'problems' can be seen in the fact that at the beginning of the 1991 Gulf campaign the US Army issued an urgent request direct to FN for a further 1,000 M249 SAWs. More such requests will no doubt follow.

No other Minimi users appear to have had any significant problems and the weapon has generally gained a reputation for outstanding reliability. Apart from the

A Canadian soldier (note the helmet camouflage) with a 5.56 mm Minimi, known to the Canadian Armed Forces as the C9.

United States other Minimi-using nations include Australia (licence production and known as the F89), Canada (known as the C9), Indonesia, Italy, Sri Lanka, the United Arab Emirates and Zaire. Numbers of Minimis are rumoured to be used by the British Army's Special Air Service (SAS) and it has also been adopted by the Swedish Navy to equip the Ranger companies within their unique *Amfibiebataljon 90* amphibious coastal defence battalions.

Although few illustrations have yet to be published it would appear that the K3 squad automatic weapon produced for the Korean armed forces by Daewoo Precision Industries of South Korea owes much in design terms to the FN Minimi. Taiwan also produces a 5.56 mm squad automatic weapon that closely resembles the Minimi; it is known as the Type 75.

Surprisingly the Minimi has yet to be adopted by the Belgian armed forces themselves who have, to date, procured only a few for their special force units. A dearth of defence funds is quoted as the main reason.

BRG-15

As has already been mentioned, FN have never been reluctant to promote novel ammunition and other concepts and are willing to develop completely new ammunition calibres and types if they can be convinced that future tactical requirements will demand such innovations. They have therefore carried out investigations into the demands that the coming years will create and have discovered a 'slot' between the 0.50/12.7 mm heavy machine gun and the 20 mm cannon. Here they feel that there will be an operational requirement for an intermediate calibre automatic weapon to penetrate the denser layers of protection carried by future light armoured vehicles, such as armoured personnel carriers, and at long ranges.

The first investigative forays made into this area by FN technicians resulted in a cartridge with dimensions of 15 mm × 115. However, attempts to fire a conventional

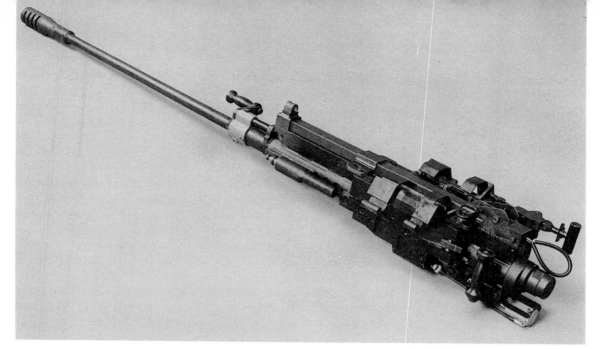

One of the 15 mm prototypes of the FN BRG-15.

jacketed bullet at the required high muzzle velocity in this calibre simply wore test barrels out at an unacceptable rate. A drastic alteration of approach resulted in a slightly wider but shorter 15.5 mm × 106 cartridge with the projectile being a steel slug with a plastic driving band, the overall impression being not unlike that of a miniature artillery projectile.

FN have already developed several types of ammunition in this new calibre. The intended basic projectile is known as PB-AP for Plastic Banded – Armour Piercing. This can apparently penetrate 19.5 mm of vehicle armour at 800 metres, which is far better than the performance put up by the Soviet 14.5 mm × 114, the only cartridge that can be rated as anything approaching an equivalent. Other more involved armour-piercing cartridges with high-performance sub-calibre penetrators are under development, and there will be a PB-HEPI (Plastic Banded – High Explosive Penetrating Incendiary), all of which bodes ill for future light armoured vehicles.

The automatic weapon developed to fire this new ammunition is the FN BRG-15. It is a heavy weapon at 60 kg, but its recoil forces are reduced by an internal buffer system to a level such that the gun can be mounted on ground mountings suitable for the 0.50/12.7 mm M2 heavy machine gun or similar vehicle and naval pintle mountings. The BRG-15 is a gas-operated weapon with a rotating bolt plus all the usual features such as a quick-change barrel that is fluted to assist cooling.

The BRG-15 has an ammunition feed system that is now common on large-calibre automatic weapons but unusual below the usual run of cannon calibres. This is a dual ammunition feed on which two belts, each containing a different ammunition nature, can be fed into the weapon, one from each side. At a flick of a selector switch the gun operator can select the type of ammunition most suitable for the target involved, eg armour-piercing or high explosive. The cyclic rate of fire is a hefty 600 rounds a minute and the muzzle velocity is stated to be 1,055 metres per second. The maximum effective range is quoted as 2,000 metres.

The BRG-15 and its ammunition were still under development as these words were written, but even then the future of this promising project was in some doubt, although not for technical reasons.

By late 1990 FN was in corporate trouble, for in spite of all the considerable direct and licence sales successes, together with promises for the future, FN found itself in considerable financial difficulties. Despite some attempts to realise suitable levels of funding, FN were taken over during late 1990 by the French defence industrial giant known as Giat Industries. In the process the old *Fabrique Nationale Herstal* became part of *Fabrique Nationale Nouvelle Herstal*, or FNNH.

The new FNNH title will no doubt become common currency one day, but the change of ownership will probably bring in its train the usual corporate round of seemingly unavoidable internal rationalisations and reorganisations. In the process, projects such as the BRG-15 and its ammunition might well founder for, despite all their considerable promise, development is still at an early stage and many years might pass before any return on invested finances or resources could be realised. It will be a great pity but the BRG-15 project might suffer in the cause of keeping the rest of the expertise and capabilities of the old FN concern in being in order to maintain their position of respected leaders in their field.

DATA

Model	MAG	Minimi
Calibre	7.62 mm	5.56 mm
Weight (gun only)	10.85 kg	6.83 kg
Length	1.26 m	1.03 m
Length of barrel	545 mm	466 mm
Rate of fire	600-1000 rpm	700-1000 rpm
Feed	belt	belt or 30-round box
Muzzle velocity	840 m/s	925 m/s
Model	BRG-15	
Calibre	15.5 mm	
Weight (gun only)	60 kg	
Length	2.15 m	
Length of barrel	n/a	
Rate of fire	600 rpm	
Feed	belt	
Muzzle velocity	1055 m/s	

CHAPTER 7

MADE IN BRITAIN

BETWEEN the years 1914 and 1918 the status of the machine gun within the British military establishment changed from being a barely tolerated ancillary weapon to that of prime infantry firepower producer. A mixture of combat experience and the influx of new minds completely converted the British approach to war after the grim experiences of the opening year of the Great War. During the years that followed the British Army introduced the concept of the man-portable light machine gun by their active promotion of the Lewis gun, completely re-organised the way in which fire support machine guns were organised, and deployed and made massive efforts to increase the numbers of machine guns available to a nation at war.

After 1918 it all fell apart. The British Army was reduced once again to a relatively small cadre of professional soldiers while most of the new weapons that came into prominence during the Great War were either shelved or allowed to deteriorate. In the machine gun field not all the skills and experience that had been gained so expensively were forgotten, but as 'the War to end all Wars' had just been fought, there was thought to be little need for new equipment or the investigation of new tactics.

Thus the British Army returned to its former role of colonial policing and the machine guns were returned to the armouries. The old Great War Hotchkiss and Lewis guns were retained throughout the 1920s and early 1930s and the bulk of the military establishment took the opinion that there was no need to even contemplate any replacement for the hallowed Vickers machine guns.

However, a few forward-looking soldiers did anticipate the need to replace the old Hotchkiss and Lewis guns. Both were complicated and generally unhandy weapons, so even by the early 1920s, when extremely limited funds were becoming available once again for new equipment, a long-term decision was made to adopt a new light machine gun to act as a platoon and squad support weapon. The original intention was that a 0.303 version of the American Browning Automatic Rifle, the BAR, would be selected, but trials dragged on, and although other promising designs were tested, the end results were inconclusive.

By 1930 it seemed highly likely that a Franco-British design known as the Vickers-Berthier would be selected, but this overlooked the fact that a military attache based in Czechoslovakia had already, by 1930, sent to the United Kingdom reports of a Czech light machine gun that seemed to offer considerable promise.

Indeed, the reports from Czechoslovakia were so glowing that an example of the Czech weapon was procured by the British authorities for examination. Throughout the subsequent trials the gun, known as the ZB26, performed well. But there was a snag.

The ZB26 had originally been designed to satisfy the requirements of the Czechoslovak defence ministry. Born out of the old Austro-Hungarian Empire during the aftermath of the Great War, Czechoslovakia and her armed forces had inherited stocks of ageing weapons of all types and calibres to the extent that some form of ammunition and weapon standardisation was urgently needed. The strong sense of national pride that soon became evident in the new Czechoslovakia virtually dictated that as many of the new standard weapons as possible should be Czech designed and produced, and one of several weapon study and production concerns set up to meet the standardisation demands was the *Praga Zbrojovka*, the Prague Armoury.

On the design team of this concern was one Vaclav Holek, a gun-designer possessing a considerable talent that was about to emerge. He was mainly responsible for a series of light machine gun designs that eventually reached the form known as the ZB26 that had attracted the attentions of the British military attache. It was an excellent weapon, and is still thought by many to be worthy of consideration as one of the best light machine guns ever designed. It was light (only 9.6 kg), gas-operated, simple, durable, and years ahead of its time in design terms. The Czechs had developed a winner and the ZB26 went into production for the Czech Army and for export.

However, for the British Army there was that one major snag with the ZB26. The Czechs had understandably chosen to standardise on the well-tried 7.92 mm × 57 (Mauser) cartridge, then commonly used throughout Central Europe. This used a rimless cartridge case while the long estab-

lished British round was the rimmed 0.303 (actually 7.7 mm × 56). The Czech design would thus require some modifications for British use, but the overall design was so promising that the British authorities concerned decided to go ahead and develop it further, in association with Vaclav Holek and his team. Further consideration of the Vickers-Berthier contender was subsequently abandoned by the British Army (in fact, that gun was adopted by the Indian Army, a body that often went its own way as far as equipment and other matters were concerned).

Development work commenced using a refinement of the original ZB26 known as the ZB27, which had revised components in its gas-operated system but was basically the same as the earlier gun. Further changes were made to permit the gas system to accommodate the cordite-propellant British rounds, and alterations were made to the receiver construction that allowed the gun to be manufactured more easily and at the same time allowed it to be stripped down in a simpler fashion. The Czech ZB26 thus made the transition to the British Bren gun.

The Bren

The revised Czech design was selected to become the British Army's new light machine gun in 1933. An agreement was drawn up between the *Brno Zbrojovka* (whence Czech production had been transferred from Prague) and the British Government whereby the fully modified design would be produced at the Royal Small Arms Factory at Enfield, just north of London.

The new machine gun was soon named the Bren, from Brno and Enfield, and production was established and well under way when the Second World War commenced. Throughout that war the Bren gun repeatedly demonstrated that it was an excellent weapon, so excellent that it is still in widespread service to this day.

It gave sterling service throughout the Second World War and was produced in large numbers, 220,000 at Enfield alone and over 416,000 elsewhere. War production necessities inflicted simplifications and economies to parts and accessories and production centres were established elsewhere, but the basic Bren gun was changed but little. Some produced in Canada even reverted to the 7.92 mm calibre and were sent to China to join numbers of ZB26 guns exported there prior to 1938. The Chinese did the 7.92 mm Bren gun the compliment of copying it to become their Type 41, apparently to the extent of retaining it in production after the Communist take-over of 1949.

The Bren gun is a gas-operated weapon with some of the bullet propellant gases tapped off via a point under the barrel to drive a piston assembly on which is supported a tilting breech block. This simple piston and block arrangement provides a positive lock at the instant of firing but is released by a system of cammed surfaces to drive back and compress the usual return spring. The overall system is so simple that the entire gun can be stripped down for cleaning and maintenance within seconds. Each component unit, or group, rarely requires further attention beyond the usual

cleaning. A quick-change barrel system allows the Bren to be mounted on a tripod for heavy support fire but its main combat asset was, and still is, as a bipod- or vehicle-mounted light machine gun.

Drum magazines were developed to augment the usual 29- to 30-round curved box magazine and a range of mountings was also produced to give the Bren an anti-aircraft capability, some of which (such as the Motley) mounted two Brens. In addition, versions of the small tracked Universal Carrier were developed to carry the Bren gun and its crew (two men at most) in mechanised infantry formations; in fact, the name Bren Gun Carrier was often incorrectly applied to all Universal Carrier models.

Numerous trial programmes were carried out using the Bren as a basis but they need not concern us here as none of them led to any in-service results. What does concern us is what happened during that post-war period when the British Army adopted the 7.62 mm × 51 NATO standard cartridge.

Once again the Bren gun design proved amenable to a change of ammunition and calibre, leading to a production line conversion programme which was initiated back at

The starting point, a 0.303 Bren gun.

Enfield during the late 1950s. Conversions are still available today, for the Bren gun is with the British Army still and with many other armies as well, especially those who were once part of the old British Empire. However, few 0.303 Brens remain available for conversion since most potential customers seem to have been catered for already. This is mainly due to simple logistics, for the old 0.303 ammunition is now produced in significant military quantities only in India, a nation that at one time also produced the Bren gun; in any event most of India's Bren guns have also been converted to 7.62 mm NATO standard by now. South Africa, Greece and Portugal are possible sources of 0.303 ammunition, but even there the output is dwindling as the local markets diminish.

The 7.62 mm Bren gun has some visual differences compared to the old 0.303 versions and some of the components have been changed. One of the two most noticeable changes involves the barrel, which now has a flash eliminator in place of the old cone-shaped flash hider. The second change is that the curved 0.303 magazine, which had to accommodate the rimmed 0.303 rounds, has been replaced by a much straighter magazine – the capacity of 29 or 30 rounds remains the same. Otherwise the two ver-

sions look very much alike. Internally some items have been modified to suit the NATO cartridge, but the main internal difference that would be spotted by an old Second World War soldier is that the interior of the 7.62 mm barrel is now chromium-plated.

The introduction of this plating has made one significant difference to the Bren gun team. The 0.303 Bren guns were issued complete with two barrels, for in action they had to be swapped over at fairly frequent intervals to assist cooling – hence a Bren gun team was usually two men with one carrying the spare barrel and most of the ammunition ready-loaded in magazines. By chromium-plating the barrel the internal wear is much reduced and so is any build-up of heat; thus only one barrel is needed for all but the most demanding of tactical situations, and the second man of the old team may now carry out other combat duties. The present-day Bren gunner still has to carry the weapon but relies on the rest of his section to carry extra magazines or else take recourse to the sections' standard L1A1 rifle 20-round magazines if the need arises – the new 30-round Bren and 20-round L1A1 rifle magazines are interchangeable.

The term Bren gun has now been officially dropped within the British Army, the modern designation being 7.62 mm

Side view of the 7.62 mm L4A4 machine gun.

An Australian Army soldier firing a 7.62 mm L4A4 machine gun.

Machine Gun L4A4, but the name still lives on. The L4A4 is but one of a series of 7.62 mm Bren gun conversions, most of which were not adopted in quantity or were never made. For instance, the L4A9 features a dovetail mounting into which the sight from a GPMG can be fitted; it is seldom encountered. The L55A1 is an inert demonstration and training version of the L4A4 which cannot be fired.

The L4A4 is still widely used throughout the British armed forces even though it was more than partially replaced by the L7A2 GPMG (see below). Units such as the Royal Artillery and Royal Engineers continue to be issued with the L4A4 in place of the

A 7.62 mm L4A4 machine gun mounted on the commander's cupola of a Royal Engineers FV432 armoured personnel carrier; the tubes in the background belong to a Ranger land-mine projector.

A 7.62 mm L4A4 fitted with special sights for the air defence role. At one time the Royal Artillery used these weapons as their turret-mounted vehicle defence weapons.

GPMG, usually as a demountable vehicle defence weapon. It is also issued to Home Defence Territorial Army units and others not expected to be in the immediate front line, as well as being used by many overseas armed forces, especially those with historical ties to the United Kingdom.

The L4A4/Bren is still an excellent weapon. Generations of soldiers have trained with it and used it in action all around the world, and it would appear that future generations will require to know it as well, for there is still no sign of it fading from the scene.

Signallers defending their position with a 7.62 mm L4A4 in the foreground.

GPMG

The Vickers machine gun served the British Army well during two World Wars and gradually accumulated a respect and aura all of its own – it appears on the cap badge of the Small Arms School Corps to this day. Despite this reverence, by the 1950s even some old soldiers were beginning to admit that their beloved Vickers guns might be getting a bit long in the tooth in some respects, so when the change-over from the old 0.303 ammunition to the new 7.62 mm NATO standard was imposed during the late 1950s it was decided that the time had come to make a change. After 50-odd years of service the old water-cooled but capable Vickers had to be replaced by something more modern.

The British Army accordingly made a belated switch to the general-purpose machine gun (GPMG) concept and the weapon selected was the Belgian FN *Mitrailleuse d'Appui Generale*, the MAG mentioned in the previous chapter. However, although the overall MAG design and operating principles remained unchanged, by the time the weapon had been modified to allow it to comply with the British methods of production used at the Royal Small Arms Factory at Enfield, there were few parts that could be interchanged with their counterparts on Belgian-made MAGs. The Belgian MAG had become a 'British' machine gun.

The official designation of the British-made MAG is General Purpose Machine-gun, 7.62 mm L7 Series; to all and sundry it is the GPMG or 'Jimpy'. Until relatively recently (of which more anon) the British Army did indeed employ the L7 series of guns as a true GPMG; each section had its own bipod-mounted L7A2 and more were retained at company and battalion levels for tripod-mounted heavy fire support duties. However, the L7 series was gradually expanded to assume other roles so that a whole series of British MAG types gradually evolved, most of which owed little to any Belgian equivalent other than in general outline.

The best way of describing all the various GPMG models is to describe them under a listing, starting with the L7A1. (Throughout the listing the 'L' denotes Land Service, the first number the model, and the 'A' and number the modification state of the equipment.)

L7A1. The first British production model, equivalent to the Belgian FN Model T1. This version uses a 200-round disintegrating metal link belt feed.

L7A2. The main British GPMG version with provision for mounting a 50-round belt box under the receiver and with a revised feed mechanism.

L8A1. The tank version of the L7A2 with the butt removed, the trigger group replaced by a firing solenoid and modifications to the feed system. Some parts such as the cocking handle are reduced in size to save space. It is possible to use a kit to convert the L8A1 for the ground role but it is seldom, if ever, used. The L8A1 is used as the co-axial weapon for the Chieftain tank series.

L8A2. An improved version of the L8A1 that can also be used on the Challenger 1 tank.

L19A1. An L7 series model with a heavier barrel to remove the need for frequent barrel changing when carrying out sustained firing. Seldom issued.

L20A1. Intended for use in pods or other external mountings on helicopters and light aircraft. This version can be fed from the left- or right-hand side and, as would be expected, it is controlled electrically. No sights are fitted and the pronged flash-hider at the muzzle is unique to this version.

L20A2. Only slight differences from the L20A1.

L37A1. This is an armoured combat vehicle version and is basically a combination of L7 and L8 components. A special barrel is used to permit a greater proportion of tracer

An early publicity photograph of the L7A1 general-purpose machine gun soon after it entered British Army service in the 1950s.

rounds than normal to be fired for aiming purposes and the weapon can be dismounted and fitted with a bipod and butt to enable it to be employed in the ground role for local defence. This version is used in turreted FV432 armoured personnel carriers and as the commander's cupola weapon on the Chieftain tank.

A twin L7A2 mounting on the rear of a British Army SAS long-range patrol Land Rover Defender One Ten.

A 7.62 mm L37A2 machine gun on the commander's cupola of a Challenger 1 tank.

L37A2. A generally improved L37A1 that can also be used on the Challenger 1 tank.

L41A1. A drill and training version of the L8A1 which cannot be fired.

L43A1. This version was specifically to be used as the ranging machine gun for the 76 mm main gun on the Scorpion tracked reconnaissance vehicle. It also doubles as a co-axial weapon and is generally similar to the L8A1, although it lacks the latter's muzzle attachment. Now being withdrawn.

L44A1. A helicopter-mounted version of the L20 used by the Royal Navy.

L45A1. A drill and training version of the L37A1 that cannot be fired.

L46A1. A skeletonised training version of the L7A1/A2 that cannot be fired.

The above listing should not shroud the fact that the vast output of the British MAGs are ground-mounted L7s, and mainly L7A2s at that. The use of the GPMG at both squad and battalion level within the British infantry battalion provided a high degree of logistic commonality within the battalion but that advantage had to be purchased at a price.

The price was that as a light machine gun the L7A2 is on the heavy side. It can indeed deliver the bursts of fire required and is portable enough to be lugged from one position to another at the normal infantry

The L43A1 version of the 7.62 mm GPMG.

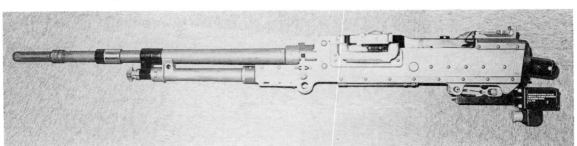

Above *A 7.62 mm L7A2 on the mounting employed on the British Army's Saxon wheeled armoured personnel carrier.*

Below *A 7.62 mm L7A2 being fired from a ring mounting normally carried on the roof of a truck for local air and other defence but seen here mounted as a ground mount for training.*

pace, but it was noticeable that the biggest and strongest man in each section was the one who usually ended up with the Jimpy – for the average soldier it was quite simply too much of a load to be carried far.

This drawback was acknowledged and lived with for many years until the advent of the 5.56 mm Individual Weapon (IW), of which more anon. The introduction of the IW and its associated Light Support Weapon (LSW – also see below) removed the L7A2 from the infantry platoon, but the GPMG is still used as a company and battalion level heavy fire support weapon mounted on a tripod. At this higher level the weight of the L7A2 and its associated bits and pieces can be more readily accommodated – and the bits and pieces are indeed something of a load. However, many battalions, especially those earmarked for Home Defence or those who have yet to be issued with the new 5.56 mm weapons, still retain the L7 series as both a light machine gun and for the heavy support role.

For the heavy fire support role the L7A2 is provided with a sustained fire kit developed at the old Royal Small Arms Factory. In essence the kit comprises a few extra parts for the gun itself, a buffered tripod complete with a 360-degree traverse head, and an optical sight assembly.

The buffered tripod (the L4A1) is able to absorb the bulk of the recoil forces produced during prolonged periods of automatic fire in such a way that reciprocating movements of the gun itself are kept to a minimum; elevation and traverse angles are normally locked. Firing stresses are further reduced by the replacement of the usual recoil buffer at the rear of the receiver by a stronger component; the butt is removed when this buffer is in use. The gun is also provided with at least two barrels for regular changing to avoid overheating.

The optical sight assembly supplied with the kit permits indirect laying for use at long ranges (up to about 1,800 metres) when the target, usually an area target rather than a defined point target, may not be visible from the firing position. Happily for the British infantry battalion, the sight unit involved with the sustained fire kit is the C2 Trilux, the same sight unit used with the 81 mm L16A2 mortar, the battalion's main fire support weapon, so in theory everyone has at least a basic idea of how the sight unit should be operated. In the sustained fire role ammunition is normally fed in 200-round belts and two men serve the weapon.

For on-board air and local defence the Royal Navy uses the L7A2 on a pintle mount, another Royal Small Arms Factory product. This mount is adjustable in height and can carry an ammunition box bracket and spent case container. Two pistol grips assist the gunner to aim the weapon when in action and the cradle has buffers to reduce firing stresses. If required this pintle mount can accommodate the L37A1 variant.

Production of the L7A2 GPMG has now ceased although some of the variants are still available and there will be a turn-over in parts and accessories for years to come. But they will not be made at Enfield, for the old Royal Small Arms Factory is no more. The parent organisation, Royal Ordnance (itself now part of British Aerospace), sold the site and moved all its small arms pro-

duction activities to Nottingham. None the less the British GPMG lives on and will remain around for many years to come; many of the old British Commonwealth nations use the L7 GPMG series in one form or another.

LSW

The general reluctance of the British Army to adopt the machine gun back in pre-war days should not give the impression that it was loath to consider new weapons of all types. The Army has always been conservative and new equipments tend to upset well-known procedures and training methods, but as long as changes have been evolutionary rather than revolutionary, as was the initial situation with the machine gun, there has always been a sector within the British military establishment that is amenable to new ideas. Thus as far back as the pre-Great War period the officers involved in musketry matters were already considering a change from the 0.303 cartridge to a smaller and higher-velocity 0.276-inch equivalent.

The original intention was to provide the average foot soldier with a more accurate long-range rifle. Considerations such as the reduced bulk and weight of the cartridges involved were secondary and in any event the outbreak of the Great War put an end to the project. The period between the wars was hardly conducive to expensive changes in standard calibres either, so the enduring advocates of the smaller calibre had to wait until the early 1950s before they once again had a chance to suggest any change of policy involving a new type of round.

The British ammunition designers proposed a new cartridge with a calibre known as 0.280 (actually 7 mm × 43) which was arrived at using a combination of ballistic and combat experience analysis. A rifle that was designed primarily as a combat weapon and with no consideration for tradition or past experience was devised to fire the new cartridge and, known as the EM-2, it at one time seemed certain to replace the old Lee-

Enfield 0.303 bolt action rifle as the new British service weapon.

But that was not to be. The political might of the United States enforced the adoption by NATO of the 7.62 mm × 51 cartridge, and the 0.280/EM-2 combination was promptly removed from the scene as the Belgian FAL became the new British rifle.

Many at the time thought the wrong decisions had been made and plugged on with their researches; in time those doubters were to be proved correct. The 7.62 mm × 51 gradually emerged as a cartridge that is over-powerful for the combat ranges of modern warfare and too bulky in logistic terms. The United States were among the first to realise their error and, not without reservations in some high-ranking quarters, they made the significant decision to adopt the smaller high-velocity 5.56 mm × 45 round and the AR-15 (later the M16) rifle from which to fire it.

Actually British ammunition technicians were working along much the same lines as their American (and Belgian) counterparts. Over the years they conducted a series of exhaustive studies that revealed several promising calibre/propellant load/bullet shape and weight combinations that seemed to offer much. The Army followed these investigations in the hope they they would one day be able to adopt a small rifle calibre if one ever appeared. Thus when the 5.56 mm/AR-15 combination arrived on the scene they grabbed the chance to procure a batch of about 10,000 AR-15s plus their ammunition. That was in 1961 and it is interesting to note that the British Army procured the AR-15/M16 rifle before the US Army decided to adopt it.

The British Army used their new rifles for jungle warfare and other specialist roles and were favourably impressed to the extent that they requested their own home-grown ammunition and weapon equivalents. The result was an entirely new cartridge, the 4.85 mm × 49, and a new weapon to fire it from, but this time not just a rifle but a matching rifle and light machine gun duo. The combination became known as the Enfield Weapon System.

But once again it was not to be, at least not in its original form – the United Kingdom had to comply with the demands of NATO standardisation. Although the 4.85 mm cartridge came through the 1977-80 NATO small-calibre cartridge selection trials with credit, it was a virtual certainty from the start that a 5.56 mm would be the 'winner'. And so it emerged that the Belgian FN SS 109 cartridge became the new NATO standard (see chapter 6).

Thus the 4.85 mm cartridge died almost as soon as it was born, but the Enfield Weapon System did not. The rifle and light machine gun, together later re-named Small Arms 80 or SA80, were altered to accommodate the new 5.56 mm round and a protracted development period commenced.

The two components of SA80 are a combat rifle, the Individual Weapon or IW, and a Light Support Weapon or LSW. Both have basically the same layout known as a 'bullpup', with the trigger group located ahead of the magazine (as employed on the earlier and unfortunate 0.280 EM-2). This layout considerably reduces the weapon's overall length and makes it much easier to carry and stow in confined spaces. All the components are arranged in a straight line, ie 'in line' from the butt to the muzzle. The gas-operated mechanism relies on the now virtually universal rotating bolt head principle for locking.

The intention was always that the LSW would act as the squad support weapon for the IW. As it turned out there are two LSWs to six IWs in each infantry section, although this proportion can vary. In order to ease the training, spares and logistic situation within the infantry battalion, the IW and LSW have over 80 per cent of their components in common. Both share the same 30-round box magazine, and the LSW differs from the IW mainly in having a longer and heavier barrel and a bipod firing arrangement.

The old argument immediately arises as to whether the LSW is actually a light

The 5.56 mm L86A1 Light Support Weapon (LSW).

machine gun or a form of machine rifle – the odds seem to favour the latter. It uses the same 30-round box magazine as the IW so lengths of burst have to be limited to conserve ammunition and to take cognisance of the fact that the barrel is fixed. Even so, it was some time before the LSW was deemed acceptable for service, even for firing short bursts.

The original 4.85 mm LSW was known as the XL65E4 (the 'X' denotes experimental). When modified for the 5.56 mm cartridge it became the XL73E2.

At that stage the LSW bipod was located just forward of the foregrip and when firing bursts the weapon juddered to such an extent that controlled firing was very difficult. At around the same time the LSW's development stage had reached the point where changes were being introduced to the original design to make automated manufacturing on computer-controlled production lines possible, so a decision was taken to alter the bipod layout completely.

Loading a magazine into a L86A1 LSW.

A 5.56 mm L86A1 LSW mounted on the roll bar of a Royal Artillery Land Rover.

The opportunity was taken to create a bipod extension forward of the foregrip so that the bipod is now located under the muzzle. To enable the firer to exert increased control when firing, an extra grip was added just behind the magazine. This combination cleared the burst-firing problem.

The engineering and final development changes resulted in a new designation of

A Rifleman holding aloft a L86A1 LSW for inspection during a demonstration held at the School of Infantry, Warminster.

L86A1, and as such the LSW started to enter service in 1989. It retains the optical SUSAT sight of the IW and is now an accurate long-range weapon capable of providing section fire support out to a range of about 800 metres, although most combat ranges are less than that.

Production of the LSW is still under way to meet the requirements of the Army's front line infantry battalions, the Royal Air Force Regiment and the Royal Marines. When their needs have been met the LSW will no doubt be issued to other units.

One small footnote to the LSW – it is manufactured to suit right-hand users only. Any attempt by a left-handed person to fire the LSW from their natural side will prove to be a most uncomfortable experience as hot ejected cases will be directed straight into the user's face (if it is any help, the same thing happens on the IW as well). Many similar light and other automatic weapons overcome this potential difficulty by ejecting spent cases directly downwards.

DATA

Model	L4A4	L7A2
Calibre	7.62 mm	7.62 mm
Weight (gun only)	9.53 kg	10.9 kg
Length	1.133 m	1.232 m
Length of barrel	536 mm	679 mm
Rate of fire	500 rpm	750-1000 rpm
Feed	30-round box	belt
Muzzle velocity	823 m/s	838 m/s

Model	L86A1
Calibre	5.56 mm
Weight (gun only)	5.4 kg
Length	900 mm
Length of barrel	646 mm
Rate of fire	700-850 rpm
Feed	30-round box
Muzzle velocity	970 m/s

CHAPTER 8

THE FRENCH FURROW

THE French have always ploughed their own furrow when it comes to machine gun design and development. In the beginning they had no opportunity to do otherwise for when the French armaments industry first began to take an interest in automatic weapons, during the early 1890s, Maxim and Browning had between them managed to obtain patents on virtually every automatic weapon principle and design detail that seemed possible – at that time.

However, one French company, Hotchkiss et Compagnie, managed to get round the patent barrier by adopting a new principle, the one we now know as gas operation. An Austrian had designed a prototype using the notion that propellant gases tapped off from the barrel could power the automatic mechanism. Hotchkiss technicians took over and developed the idea to the stage where a viable automatic weapon could be offered to the French military authorities.

The resultant series of weapons became known as the Hotchkiss machine guns. There were several of them but all were air-cooled weapons as it was thought that water-cooling did not lend itself to the gas operation principle. To assist cooling, the Hotchkiss barrels were provided with what

came to be a virtual Hotchkiss trademark, namely a series of metal vanes, or 'doughnuts', around the chamber end of the barrel which acted as extra cooling radiators.

With time the mechanism of the Hotchkiss guns proved to be reliable enough and they served the French Army well throughout the Great War and after. Most were chambered for the 8 mm Lebel rifle cartridge, but there was also an 11 mm 'balloon model' that was intended to fire incendiary bullets at observation balloons. For all their widespread use, the early models did demonstrate some lack of thought on the part of the designers. One example was that they were heavy and awkward weapons to move, especially as early tripods had no provision for gun traverse or elevation which was another avoidable drawback. In time the latter was rectified, but another and more serious failing was carried over to later models and that was the type of ammunition feed adopted. All the Great War era Hotchkiss guns had their ammunition fed into the feed mechanism secured on thin steel clips resembling small trays, each holding 24 or 30 rounds. These clips were a constant source of potential feed troubles since they were prone to damage, twisting and the ingress of

dirt and debris. They also tended to limit the length of bursts and, although it was possible to join clips together to make longer bursts possible, it meant that one member in each Hotchkiss team, apart from the gunner, had to do little else other than guide the clips into the gun and constantly monitor their progress through the feed system. For some reason this problem was never entirely eliminated and although Hotchkiss machine guns were still in service during the Second World War, they were tolerated rather than treasured and were used only if nothing else was to hand. For all that, the Japanese used Hotchkiss copies throughout their various wars.

Attempts to overcome the shortfalls of the Hotchkiss mainly resulted in failures, such as the mle 1907 Puteaux which was withdrawn almost as soon as it was issued. However, there were several other examples of French weapon designers going their own way. One was the project which resulted in the infamous Chauchat of 1915, an early attempt at a light machine gun. The introduction of the 8 mm Chauchat into French (and later American) service was transformed into a series of major political and financial scandals by the involvement of dubious contracts, cheap materials, indifferent manufacture and an overall poor initial design. The Chauchats that were issued to troops in the trenches were of such poor quality as weapons that their users usually took to repairing the numerous malfunctions by simply throwing the weapons away.

Other and later French machine guns were more successful. Hotchkiss had a measure of sales success with various models of a new light machine gun produced during the 1920s, although few went to the French armed forces who had decided to adopt a new cartridge to replace their elderly 8 mm Lebel round. The first attempt, issued during the mid-1920s, was the 7.5 mm × 58 mle 1924, and a new light machine gun, loosely based on the Browning Automatic Rifle but with enough alterations (such as an overhead 25-round box magazine) to make it 'French', was produced to utilise the new round.

This new machine gun, the mle 1924, was produced at Chatellerault and St Etienne arsenals but it soon transpired that the new cartridge was not completely satisfactory – indeed, it was sometimes downright dangerous since it had a nasty tendency to cause unwanted explosions in the chamber. The situation was rectified by the issuing of a modified and shorter version, the 7.5 mm × 54 mle 1929, so the mle 1924 light machine gun was modified to take the new round, becoming the mle 1924/29 in the process.

This variation, along with drum-fed fortification and tank-mounted variants, served the French Army until 1940 and for several years after 1945. Numbers may still be found in service with some of the African and other nations where French colonial influence still holds sway, and some are reported to be still retained as reserve weapons by some of the various French gendarmerie units, but they can now be regarded as obsolete.

The mle 1924/29 was not the only example of French machine gun development between the wars. Another model, the gas-operated Darne, pioneered the mass production procedures adopted during the Second World War years by its extensive use of pre-fabricated pressed steel and other easily made components. First seen in 1918, it attracted a great deal of attention, at one time even being considered for possible adoption by the British armed forces, but it never achieved any major sales successes other than as an aircraft gun on some Czech and French Air Force inter-war aircraft.

AAT 52

After 1945 the 'new' French armed forces were mainly equipped with American weapons such as 0.30 and 0.50/12.7 mm Browning machine guns. However, a sense of national pride meant that there had to be at least some French-designed weapons in the national armoury and a machine gun

The 7.5 mm AAT 52 general-purpose machine gun mounted on a tripod.

seemed to be a priority. Accordingly one was devised to fire the French 7.5 mm mle 1929 cartridge, briefly resurrected in order to provide the new weapon with a full French flavour. The new machine gun was intended to be a general-purpose machine gun, so was named the *Arme Automatique Transformable mle 52*, usually known simply as the AAT 52 or AA 52.

The AAT 52 was yet another example of the French ploughing their own furrow, for at a time when other nations were adopting all manner of advanced and highly efficient locking systems, many tried and tested in the heat of wartime action, the French designers decided to adopt a modified form of the blow-back principle. This is widely used in low-power ammunition weapons such as sub-machine guns, the recoil forces produced on firing being used to push a breech block back to the rear. Only the mass of the breech block is available to overcome the forces involved at the instant of firing when internal pressures are at their highest, so blow-back weapons usually add some form of forward motion, initially derived from a recoil spring, to add forward

momentum and assist the locking mass of the breech block.

For low-powered cartridges the simple blow-back principle is adequate and efficient, but for more powerful cartridges, including rifle cartridges, the principle is not so sound, as chamber internal pressures are much higher.

However, it was the simplicity of the blow-back principle which probably attracted the French designers, who devised a simple two-piece bolt in which a lever is set. At the instant of firing the lever is located in a recess, but as the recoil forces are applied to the bolt face they tend to use the mechanical influence of the lever to push back the rear part of the bolt which then moves more quickly than the front under the influence of the lever, thereby delaying the front portion of the bolt long enough to allow chamber pressures to drop to a lower level. However, the pressure stresses within the cartridge case are such that to assist extraction (the internal pressures force the case outwards against the chamber walls as well as against the cartridge base, ie to the rear), part of the chamber around the neck of the case has to

Side view of a 7.5 mm AAT 52 machine gun clearly showing the butt monopod.

be fluted to reduce the area in contact with the case, thereby allowing the case to be eased from its seating. Even so, AAT 52 spent case extraction is sudden and violent to the extent that deformed and ruptured cases are not unknown, but somehow the principle seems to work – but it must operate on the lower limits of efficiency.

The AAT 52 was produced in two forms, one having the usual light bipod and quick-change barrel for the light machine gun role (plus the novelty of a short monopod under the retractable butt which is supposed to assist in producing steadier fire), and the other with a heavier barrel for firing from a tripod (usually a modified M2 tripod, normally used for the 0.30 Browning machine guns).

The AAT 52 was put into production for the French Army and for export to many of the nations that were once French colonies in North Africa and elsewhere. However, it was not long before production had to switch to a new model, this time known as the 7.62 mm mle NF-1. The 7.62 mm provides the clue to the need for the change, for the mle NF-1 fires the NATO standard

round, which does nothing to assist spent case extraction since the internal pressures produced are, if anything, higher than those of the older 7.5 mm cartridge.

Only the mle NF-1 is now produced, being still in production by Giat Industries in both light and tripod-mounted forms, but it cannot be said to have had many sales outside the usual French colonial markets. Few observers outside France would agree that the NF-1 is a very good design. By going their own way and insisting on an all-national product, the French designers managed to produce a weapon with some awkward features that more prolonged practical experience might have helped them to avoid.

Apart from the already mentioned doubtful efficiency of the modified blow-back mechanism employed, the barrel-change system involved when the mle NF-1 is used as a light machine gun may be used as an example of this lack of practicality: the barrel release mechanism can be operated easily enough, but as the barrel is removed it takes the bipod with it, leaving the gunner to struggle with a hot gun and no forward

support. Watching even an experienced gunner carrying out this operation is quite a sight for prospective machine gun designers. Another odd point is the use of a monopod under the butt. In theory this appears to be a sound idea, but in practice it can be a decided hindrance, especially when engaging multiple targets. In addition, even though the weapon is belt fed there is no provision for a belt box or any other form of ammunition feed support.

In favour of the AAT 52/mle NF-1, it must be stated that it is easy to manufacture at low cost and is relatively compact, light and simple to operate. Tank and aircraft/helicopter versions have been produced, and there are provisions for mounting optical sights and night vision devices.

Many nations have introduced these weapons to their armouries by purchasing French-produced armoured and other vehicles, for the AAT 52/mle NF-1 is often mounted as a local and air defence weapon for vehicles of all kinds. Consequently, current users outside the usual French sphere of influence include Argentina, Bolivia, the Congo, Iraq, Kenya, Spain and the Seychelles. AAT 52/mle NF-1 machine guns have also been observed in the hands of various militias during their squabbles in Lebanon.

Above *Smile please! A French soldier carrying a 7.62 mm NF-1 light machine gun.*

Below *A 7.62 mm NF-1 machine gun on a cupola pintle mounting.*

As far as can be determined there are no major French machine gun development programmes under way at the moment, although no doubt something is brewing in one or other of the various French defence research establishments. Perhaps the acquisition of the Belgian FN concern by Giat Industries might introduce some changes to that situation (see chapter 6).

For their heavy machine gun requirements the French armed forces continue to rely on the well-trusted Browning 0.50/12.7 mm M2 HB.

DATA

Model	NF-1
Calibre	7.62 mm
Weight (gun only)	10.6 kg
Length (butt retracted)	1.08 m
Length of barrel	500 mm
Rate of fire	900 rpm
Feed	100-round belt
Muzzle velocity	830 m/s

CHAPTER 9

A SPANISH FLAVOUR

SPAIN has for centuries had a respected armaments industry that has always embraced small arms of all kinds, but for some reason machine guns were never strongly featured among locally developed products. The Spanish Army initially adopted Hotchkiss machine gun models of many kinds, usually for their 7 mm × 57 Mauser cartridge, so there was no real incentive for Spanish weapon designers to turn their attention to machine guns.

It would appear that the first 'Spanish' machine guns were actually French Darne models produced in Spain at Guernica during the 1920s. It would also appear that Darne machine guns were produced in Spain mainly because they could be manufactured there at less cost than would be possible elsewhere, but the Darne machine gun had few sales successes and gradually dropped out of sight. The destinations of the Guernica output went largely unnoticed.

The machine gun scene in Spain altered out of all recognition during the Spanish Civil War of 1936-39. Machine guns poured into Spain in vast quantities by the then current market standards, although much of the material involved was, by any standard, of very dubious combat worth. Some of the weapons involved, such as the ma-chine guns provided by the Soviet Union, were of excellent quality but much of the rest was culled from old Great War stock-piles dragged out from all around Europe.

Out of all this quantity the post-Civil War administration managed to pick the best as examples from which to develop some locally produced designs. They understandably decided that the Czech machine guns originally imported for the Nationalist forces were among the best to hand, although during the chaos that followed the events of 1936-39, funds within Spain for new weapons were scarce. Only one of the selected Czech designs got anywhere near even limited production, and that was based on the well-known ZB26. The Spanish result, known as the FAO, was virtually a direct copy of the ZB26 and was used as the basis for a later weapon known as the FAO Model 59. The latter was again based on the ZB26 but converted to belt feed and chambered for the NATO 7.62 mm × 51 cartridge.

Another Spanish design was the ALFA Model 1944, a more original design but largely based on Italian weapons such as the Breda modello 37; it was a tripod-mounted machine gun with a belt feed and was produced in some numbers at Oviedo. It also underwent the conversion to fire the 7.62 mm NATO cartridge and then became the ALFA Model 55.

All the FAO and ALFA models have now faded from the Spanish scene, for the military authorities there decided to take up licence manufacture of the German Rheinmetall MG3, the post-war version of the wartime MG42. Production of the MG3 was undertaken by the concern of Empresa Nacional de 'Santa Barbara', headquartered in Madrid. Enough MG3s were manufactured by Santa Barbara to allow the old FAO and ALFA machine guns to be retired from the Spanish armed forces. Santa Barbara MG3s have also been exported to Saudi Arabia and Pakistan; the latter transactions mainly involved components for local manufacture.

Santa Barbara then decided to turn their attentions to producing a Spanish machine gun.

Ameli

The Santa Barbara design staff commenced their project with a thorough market survey that indicated that there seemed to be a definite market for a really light light machine gun firing the 5.56 mm × 45 cartridge; such a weapon seemed to have many attractions for special forces and airborne troops who would normally have to rely on larger-calibred weapons for fire support. The project was known at one time as the Special Purpose Assault Machine gun 5.56 × 45, or SPAM. Not surprisingly, that unflattering name was changed and the Ameli was born.

The 5.56 mm Ameli visually resembles a miniature MG42/MG3 machine gun but internally it has many points of its own. It uses the same roller-locking mechanism as the many assault rifles produced by the Spanish CETME concern and also by the German Heckler & Koch. This system is positive yet simple and has proved to be highly efficient on the Ameli.

The Ameli is small and light, being only 970 mm long and weighing 6.71 kg in its

Firing the standard version of the 5.56 mm Ameli light machine gun from the hip.

standard unloaded form. It is thus an easily operated assault weapon when fired from the standing position and suspended from a shoulder sling, or it can be fired from a two-position bipod. For both these roles the Ameli can use 100- or 200-round belts held inside a disposable plastic box magazine that clips on to the weapon on the left-hand side. If required the Ameli can also use free-hanging disintegrating link belts of any length, but this type of feed is usually employed only when the Ameli is mounted on a tripod.

Development of the Ameli has extended for well over a decade and during that time many useful features have been engineered into the design. The rear sight bracket is arranged to combine with the barrel-change handle, thus providing a carrying handle over the weapon. A really rapid barrel-change system is employed which

The lightweight version of the 5.56 mm Ameli light machine gun.

enables the user to swap barrels in only 5 seconds, according to Santa Barbara claims. Optical and night sights can be fitted. The cyclic rate of fire could at one stage be either 800 or 1,200 rounds per minute with alterations being made by the changing of only one part, but this feature has now been removed. An even lighter variant with a revised muzzle brake/flash suppressor is under development; this version weighs only 5.2 kg.

Handling and firing the Ameli present no problems and overall it is handy and a delight to use. It is a true one-man machine gun for not only can one man carry and fire it, but the overall size and weight are such that the same man can also simultaneously carry a canvas satchel containing a spare barrel, spare parts and a cleaning kit.

However, to date the Ameli has been ordered only for Spanish special operations units and export sales appear to have been made only to Mexico, although in what quantity is not known.

Santa Barbara is now part of the CETME organisation.

DATA

Model	Ameli
Calibre	5.56 mm
Weight (gun only)	6.71 kg
Length	970 mm
Length of barrel	400 mm
Rate of fire	900-1,250 rpm
Feed	100 or 200 round belt
Muzzle velocity	875 m/s

CHAPTER 10

CZECHOSLOVAKIA

IN chapter 7 we left the newly formed Czech small arms industry just as they produced their excellent ZB26 light machine gun, *en route* to its being converted into the British Bren gun. The Czech contribution to modern machine gun development did not end with the ZB26, and there have been other machine guns of Czech origin since then.

The ZB26 was closely followed by the ZB27 and ZB30 which were all basically the same weapon but with slight changes to introduce improvements of some nature or another. They were all used by the pre-1939 Czech armed forces, as was the ZB53 or *vzor 37*, an advanced air-cooled 7.92 mm general-purpose machine gun that could be mounted in armoured vehicles without modification. The ZB53 was yet another Czech design and a sales success that was once again deemed worthy of British Army acceptance, this time still in its original 7.92 mm calibre and destined to grace the mantlets of many wartime British armoured vehicles. There was also a heavy 15 mm ZB60, a large air-cooled weapon usually employed as a light air defence weapon by nations such as Greece, Iran and Yugoslavia prior to 1940.

The ZB26, 27, 30, 53 and 60 are rarely encountered now other than in guerilla or other para-military hands, for after 1938 the Czech nation was gradually merged into the Third Reich and all Czech weapon-manufacturing facilities were directed towards supplying the needs of the German armed forces. During the years after 1945 many of these old weapons were either sold or provided as 'military aid' to nations throughout the Middle East (at least 4,000 ZB53s were sold to Israel while more went to Libya) and Africa.

After 1945 Czechoslovakia was a nation once again but with a supervisory occupation force. Nevertheless, Czech originality and inventiveness once again won through to the extent that the reformed Czech armed forces were able to take advantage of home-grown weapon design and manufacturing talents. Virtually alone among the old Warsaw Pact states, Czechoslovakia was able to resist the usual large-scale incursions of Soviet designed and supplied weaponry and managed to equip its armed forces largely with locally produced weapons.

One of the first of the Czech post-war machine guns was an odd attempt to produce a general-purpose machine gun based on the pre-war ZB26 series but able to accommodate either a belt or box magazine

An example of what is generally considered to be one of the finest light machine guns ever developed, the 7.92 mm ZB26 (for the record this is actually a ZB27, but the differences between it and the ZB26 are slight).

ammunition feed system without modification. Known as the *Lekhy Kulomet vzor 52* (*vzor* or vz translates as 'model'), this weapon had many unusual features such as a two-portion trigger for firing either single-shot-only on one sector and fully automatic on the other. The need for mass production was acknowledged by the use of a stamped steel receiver body inside which were attached the various necessary machined portions.

However, the vz 52 had one very odd feature – the use of a Czech cartridge known as the 7.62 mm × 45. It would appear that the Czech armed forces were so intent on supporting their nation's individuality that this round was developed in defiance of the otherwise strict standardisation measures imposed within the old Soviet sphere of influence. Introduced in 1952, the new Czech cartridge was destined to have a short life, for by 1957 Soviet pressure had dictated the introduction of the 7.62 mm × 39 Soviet and Warsaw Pact cartridge. The Czech weapons already manufactured to fire the Czech cartridge had to be converted to accept the Soviet calibre and thus the vz 52 became the vz 52/57.

The 7.62 mm vz 52, an attempt to convert the pre-war ZB26 series to belt feed that has now largely been withdrawn from use.

It was all to no avail, however; the vz 52 and 52/57 failed to find acceptance outside Czechoslovakia and were disposed of in odd corners of the world, the type eventually fading from view. The vz 52/59 is, however, reported to be still in service with Algeria, Angola, Chad, Cuba, Egypt, Ethiopia, Guinea and Mozambique, although its exact status in all these countries is uncertain.

The design of the Finnish KK62 light machine gun was greatly influenced by the vz 52. Chambered for the Soviet 7.62 mm × 39 cartridge, it is still in service with the Finnish Army (see chapter 16).

vz 59

With the removal of the vz 52/59 from production, the authorities at the Brno Arsenal were requested to turn their attentions to a general-purpose machine gun firing a fully powered cartridge. As Czechoslovakia was part of the Warsaw Pact organisation, it had to adopt the old 7.62 mm × 54 cartridge which dated back to the days of the Russian Tsars but which is still a good performer at long ranges and is still used with the latest generation of CIS machine guns, including the PK series (see chapter 4).

However, the Brno designers adopted their own form of feed link belt in which the complete rimmed round can be pushed forward through the belt, producing a much simpler feed mechanism and a more positive feed. The link system was so thoroughly designed that the links can be re-used time and again, and such was the Czech approach to what many would regard as a minor logistical matter that they went so far as to design a small link re-filling machine that can be clamped on to an ammunition box.

However, the feed belt was a minor part of a design approach that resulted in a weapon known as the *Kulomet vzor 59*, or vz 59. This gun is really a revised version of the earlier vz 52 and 52/57 but chambered for the larger cartridge and with the capability to use a box magazine feed removed – only the belt feed is involved on the vz 59. It is also a true machine gun, being provided with two types of barrel, light and heavy, with the heavy barrel being slightly longer.

The light-barrel version uses a bipod, the heavy-barrelled version a tripod, but there are odd 'interim' variants such as a heavy barrel and bipod combination. In fact, whenever the vz 59 is used on a bipod it is known as the vz 59L. Whichever barrel is used with this model, the ammunition belt can be held in a 50-round metal box which is slung on the right-hand side of the receiver.

Thus only the tripod-mounted version can accurately be designated the vz 59. This

A bipod-mounted 7.62 mm vz 59N general-purpose machine gun.

A Czech Army vz 59N in action during manoeuvres.

version is used not only for the ground fire support role, but the tripod can also be revised and raised in such a fashion that the gun may be used for air defence. In both roles the vz 59 is commonly used in combination with a telescopic optical sight which is claimed to enhance accuracy at long ranges – the normal 'iron' sights are calibrated up to 2,000 metres.

To confuse matters somewhat, the ammunition employed with the vz 59 guns, although based on the CIS pattern, is produced in Czechoslovakia in two forms, one with a standard bullet and the other with a heavier bullet; the latter is mainly employed when the vz 59 is mounted on a tripod and provides a longer range.

There is also a vz 59T for use on armoured vehicles which has provision for remote firing, while another variant is the vz 59N which was produced as a prospective export model chambered for the 7.62 mm × 51 NATO cartridge – however, as far

as can be determined it has not met with any major sales success since the few vz 59-user nations outside Czechoslovakia itself all have the CIS-cartridge version. These users include Libya, Mozambique and Tanzania.

DATA

Model	vz 59
Calibre	7.62 mm
Weight (gun only)	8.67 kg
Length (heavy barrel)	1.215 m
(light barrel)	1.116 m
Length of barrel (heavy)	693 mm
(light)	593 mm
Rate of fire	700-800 rpm
Feed	50-round belt
Muzzle velocity (max)	830 m/s

CHAPTER 11

DOWN SOUTH – SOUTH AFRICA

SOUTH Africa is not a name that immediately springs to mind when machine gun developments are considered, and no doubt there are many residents of that country who would be happier if things had remained that way. However, the manner in which the white sector of the South African community chose to conduct their internal affairs from the early 1960s onwards engendered so much disquiet among other nations that South Africa became increasingly isolated from international commerce and other affairs. In time this disquiet eventually led to the total embargo on armaments sales and associated matters imposed by the United Nations in 1977.

By that time the South African Government had been provided with plenty of warning of the actions that were to be taken against them and had laid their long-term plans accordingly. It was obvious that a state of self-sufficiency regarding arms supplies would have to be adopted and the state-owned Armscor (Armaments Development and Production Corporation of South Africa) was established to supervise and control the indigenous design and development of weapons for the South African Defence Forces (SADF).

Armscor has more than managed to achieve the required state of armaments self-sufficiency to an extent that has surprised many observers of the defence scene. The process has been expensive but can only be rated as a remarkable example of the ability of the South African nation to look to its own resources and successfully reach a self-appointed objective. In the process South Africa has changed from being an arms importing nation to becoming one of the world's major arms exporters.

The array of weapons and other military equipment, including a wide range of ammunition, produced by the South Africans over the last two decades or so has been a remarkable achievement by any standards. Usually starting from scratch, and by using a multi-channel approach of careful requirement definitions, obtaining talent and technology, fostering and channelling local resources and by overall hard work, Armscor have overseen many major weapon projects. These have included the world-beating 155 mm G5 and G6 artillery systems, the 127 mm Valkiri multiple-launch artillery rocket system, the Ratel infantry fighting vehicle series, a whole range of naval vessels, and the Cheetah strike aircraft, to name but a few examples.

Set against such major projects, small

The 7.62 mm MG-4 machine gun, a South-African conversion of the Browning M1919A4.

arms feature on a much smaller scale but even there the South Africans have come up with some remarkable weapons which, along with all their other indigenous weapon projects, have been specifically developed to meet their own demanding operational conditions.

As far as machine guns were concerned, the SADF had a stock of weapons to hand when the United Nations embargo was imposed. A quantity of FN MAG machine guns had been obtained from Belgium during 1960 and these were used to augment the numbers of in-hand 0.30 Browning M1919A4s, 0.303 Brens and Vickers machine guns, and a stock of 0.50/12.7 mm Browning M2 HBs.

By dint of careful maintenance, the 0.50/12.7 mm M2 HBs are still in service today. The other weapons were either modernised in some way or retained for possible future use; for instance, the 0.303 Vickers machine guns were converted to fire the 7.62 mm × 51 NATO round. As far as is known, the South Africans were the only nation to adopt such a course, as the modifications required to accommodate the NATO cartridge must have been extensive. In the event the converted 7.62 mm Vickers were used only by various Citizens Force

units and were gradually withdrawn; most now adorn local museums.

It would appear that at least a few of the old 0.303 Bren guns underwent the conversion to 7.62 mm NATO standard, but they too appear to have been withdrawn from use.

MG-4

Perhaps the most important conversion programme was undertaken with the old 0.30 Browning M1919A4s, which underwent the re-barrelling procedure to convert them to 7.62 mm × 51 NATO. At the same time some other significant modifications were also introduced. For a start, the trigger mechanism was modified so that the firing cycle always ceases with the breech open, thereby avoiding the possibility of 'cooking-off' a cartridge left in a hot chamber. More modifications were made to the feed system so that the modified gun can now accommodate disintegrating metal link belts. Other detail changes were introduced to improve reliability and to ease maintenance. The resultant weapon was renamed the MG-4. In fact, it would appear that not only were old M1919A4s converted to 7.62 mm MG-4s but also completely new weapons were

A 7.62 mm MG-4 AA in action as the turret gun of a Rooikat wheeled reconnaissance vehicle; this vehicle also has a co-axial MG-4 CA.

produced, although this is not confirmed.

Two versions are in service: the MG-4 CA is a co-axial weapon without sights or a pistol grip, while the longer-barrelled MG-4 AA is used as a pintle-mounted weapon and may be seen mounted as the commander's weapon on armoured vehicles such as the SADF's Olifant (modernised Centurion) tanks and Rooikat wheeled reconnaissance vehicles – both vehicles also use the MG-4 CA as co-axial machine guns.

The MG-4 AA can be mounted on standard Browning tripods but is more often employed as a vehicle-mounted weapon,

A 7.62 mm MG-4 AA mounted on the rear cupola of a Ratel infantry combat vehicle.

sometimes on locally produced mountings carrying two MG-4s side-by-side.

SS 77 L9

The standard general-purpose machine gun for the SADF was the FN MAG but the South Africans realised that a lighter yet equally versatile weapon would eventually be required to keep their infantry units adequately armed to meet future threats. At the time that the new machine gun concept was first proposed, South Africa seemed to be beset by many threats, both internal and external, so the requirement was seen as urgent.

That was in 1977, when two Armscor engineers (Smith and Soregi – hence SS 77) assumed the task of examining as many current machine gun designs as they could obtain to select the best features of each for incorporation in their new design. The intention was mainly to hasten the development process, but the end result is not just the usual 'dog's dinner' visual impression of various other weapon features that such approaches usually assume. The resultant weapon, the SS 77, is in many ways a carefully designed machine gun.

One of the most noticeable features of the SS 77 is that it retains the full-power 7.62 mm × 51 NATO cartridge. This was adopted because over most of the SADF's operational areas the greater range and accuracy capabilities of 7.62 mm ammunition make it far more effective than the then fashionable 5.56 mm, especially as SADF operational doctrine emphasises aimed fire rather than the area suppressive fire approach adopted by many other nations. One result of this combination of requirements is that the SS 77 is, at 9.6 kg, somewhat heavier than many of its light machine gun contemporaries, but is proportionally that much more durable to match the weight.

The SS 77, also known as the L9, was designed from the outset with reliability, even under the most adverse conditions, and simplicity very much to the fore. Development actually commenced during 1977 but production did not commence until 1987, the interim being marked by periods when the perceived short-term threat diminished and development work had to be set aside to cater for other more pressing priorities.

The SS 77 uses the gas-operated sideways breech-locking mechanism of the CIS SG-43 machine gun. By adjusting the gas regulator at the tap-off point under the barrel, using the base of a spent cartridge case, the

The 7.62 mm SS 77 machine gun – this example has a pre-production type of butt which was modified for production.

The full production version of the 7.62 mm SS 77 machine gun.

cyclic rate of fire can be varied between 600 and 900 rounds per minute. (This feature was eliminated on late production models.) Ammunition feed is from the left using non-disintegrating or disintegrating belts with M13 or DM1 links. When the SS 77 is used as a light machine gun the usual dangling belt problem can be overcome by containing the belt within a 100-round pvc pouch that clips on to the receiver beneath the feed slot. At other times the SS 77 is fed by 200-round belts from a plastic or steel box.

One SS 77 feed novelty is the use of two milled slots in the feed table that engage the belt's leading empty link when loading. This allows the belt to be engaged securely as it is aligned and the feed cover closed, eliminating the usual 'three hands' fumbling required on many other weapons.

Synthetic materials are used throughout the construction of the SS 77 but this has not been to the detriment of the overall standard of finish. The SADF insist on high standards of finish on all the equipment and consumables they use, rightly taking the view that the weapons will probably have to be used under the worst possible conditions so quality has to be superlative to start with. Field stripping the SS 77 is simple and few

Right-hand view of the 7.62 mm SS 77.

A 7.62 mm SS 77 machine gun field stripped down to its main assemblies.

parts are involved. Each weapon is issued complete with two fabric rolls, one containing spares and the other a cleaning kit.

One unusual feature of the SS 77 is a side-folding butt, introduced to reduce stowage length; handling and the ammunition feed remain unimpaired when the stock is folded. Other features include a butterfly safety switch located just in front of the trigger guard and controlling a double-sear

A 7.62 mm SS 77 machine gun in action in the South African bush.

system that can withstand the shocks of dropping with complete safety. The feed and ejection ports are kept covered by spring-loaded flaps to prevent the ingress of dust and other debris.

Overall the SS 77 is an excellent combat weapon that can be mounted on a variety of mounts, including all the usual standard Browning and other tripods; the bipod is an integral component. When mounted on a tripod the SS 77 may be fitted with an indirect fire sight known as the H-019. Vehicle pintle and co-axial mountings have also been devised for the weapon and it can be fitted with a solenoid for remote firing.

An unusual twin mounting for the SS 77 has been devised with the two guns side-by-side behind a shield, and this can be used for either the vehicle or ground role. Another and more dramatic mounting is known as Rattler. This is intended for mounting in helicopters for firing through rear area hatches, and can be configured in several ways, one being the mounting of a single 20 mm GA1 cannon. However, the Rattler can also mount either four FN MAGs or SS 77s together with a ready-use total of 2,000 rounds. The gunner is seated behind the guns and aims them using a reflector sight.

DATA

Model	MG-4	SS 77
Calibre	7.62 mm	7.62 mm
Weight (gun only)	approx 15 kg	9.6 kg
Length (MG-4 AA)	1.015 m	1.16 m*
Length of barrel	595 mm	550 mm
Rate of fire	600-750 rpm	600-900 rpm
Feed	belt	belt
Muzzle velocity	840 m/s	840 m/s
		*943.5 mm with stock folded

CHAPTER 12

SINGAPORE SLING

AS with South Africa, the tiny island nation of Singapore is not a name that immediately springs to mind when machine guns are being considered. Yet Singapore has over the last two decades been able to make an impression on small arms and other weapon design and production that is out of all proportion to its geographical size.

All ground-based weapon design and development undertaken in Singapore is carried out by the state-owned Chartered Industries of Singapore, usually known as CIS, and not to be confused with the Commonwealth of Independent States. CIS was established in 1967 and its first major task was the licence production of a variant of the American 5.56 mm AR-15/M16 assault rifle. This was used to arm the local armed forces and yet more were produced for export. However, CIS considered that the M16 series were really too costly for them to produce and turned to Sterling Industries of the United Kingdom to design a new assault rifle for them. The initial result was eventually to emerge as the 5.56 mm SAR 80 which has been produced by CIS in some numbers. The CIS 5.56 mm SR 88 was to emerge later.

To complement the licence-produced M16 rifles, the Singapore armed forces imported a batch of 2,100 M16A1 heavy-barrelled rifles to act as light fire support weapons. They soon discovered the drawbacks of the machine rifle type of weapon and as a result the Singapore Ministry of Defence (known as Mindef and the owners of CIS) decided to commence the development of an indigenous light machine gun, with reliability and ease of handling being priorities. As with the programme that led to the SAR 80 assault rifle, it was decided to once again consult established weapon designers from overseas.

In 1978 development work was initiated by a team that included the American James Sullivan, who had at one time been involved with the design of the AR-15/M16 assault rifles. One of the earliest design parameters accepted was the use of the 5.56 mm × 45 cartridge, which was selected due to the lower recoil forces involved and the reduced weapon sizes and weights that could be made possible. These considerations were deemed important, for experience had taught the Singapore armed forces that the weights and recoil forces involved with most 7.62 mm weapons were too great to be comfortably handled by the small-statured local population.

The first firing test-beds for the new

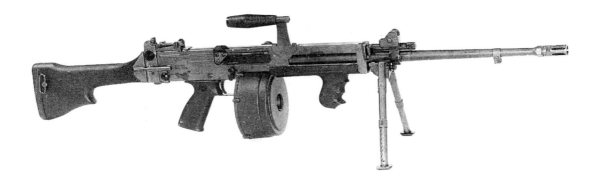

A 5.56 mm Ultimax 100 Mark 2 with fixed barrel.

weapon were ready during 1978 and the first full prototypes were ready during mid-1979.

Ultimax 100

The new light machine gun was named the Ultimax 100, the prototype being known as the Ultimax Mark 1. The first production version, which made its debut during 1982, was the Mark 2, with a fixed barrel. This was later followed by the Mark 3 which has a quick-change barrel.

In either of its two production forms one feature that has to be noted regarding the Ultimax 100 is its low weight. The Ultimax 100, even with bipod, sling and a fully-loaded 100-round magazine, weighs far less than any other comparable weapon when empty. With a full 100-round magazine it weighs 6.5 kg, which can be compared to the 6.83 kg of an unloaded FN Minimi or the 6.88 kg of the unloaded Spanish Ameli. For a further indication of the low weights involved, an empty Ultimax 100 weighs just 4.7 kg, even with its bipod. These weights alone are enough to mark this weapon as something special, but there is more to come.

To match the low handling weights, the

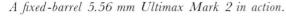

A fixed-barrel 5.56 mm Ultimax Mark 2 in action.

A 5.56 mm Ultimax 100 Mark 3 – note the different position of the carrying and barrel-change handle compared to the Mark 2.

Ultimax 100 seems to produce virtually no recoil, even when fired using sustained bursts. The weapon employs a gas-operated mechanism which is so arranged that it takes advantage of an early point along the barrel from whence the actuating gases are tapped. The resultant high pressures provide a rapid but definite piston action while at the same time acting as a self cleaning measure to provide increased reliability.

The locking system is the now widely used rotating bolt action, but the recoil spring involved is long, so long in fact that the bolt group, which extends over the chamber to the actuating piston, is arranged on a guide rod in such a manner that it never has to impinge on the normal internal buffer or receiver back-plate to generate the usual recoil forces. This long

The 5.56 mm Ultimax 100 Mark 3 light machine gun in use.

spring and the adoption of a relatively low cyclic rate of fire (500 to 540 rounds per minute) together produce very low recoil forces to be transmitted to the firer. In fact, the designers have produced a 'constant recoil' concept in which the impulses generated from the bolt action cancel one another during each operating cycle. The result is that the Ultimax 100 can be aimed and fired using one hand, should such an unlikely procedure ever have to be assumed in action. Using a more common combat practice, the Ultimax 100 can be easily fired from the 'assault' hip position with a high degree of user control. Even more control can be adopted when the weapon is fired from its integral bipod. It is even possible to produce aimed fire from the shoulder when standing, ie in much the same manner as one would fire an assault rifle.

The construction of the Ultimax 100 is simple and it is relatively inexpensive to manufacture. The receiver is made from two steel stampings welded together, with extra strength being derived by the internal guide bar for the bolt. The resultant loose fit of the bolt inside the receiver means that the weapon can continue to operate even when clogged with dust, sand or mud. In addition to the loose bolt fit, a six-position gas regulator is provided to ensure that the weapon can be kept firing under the most adverse conditions. In fact, the Ultimax 100 has been demonstrated undergoing numerous and repeated mud-bath and other similar tests, and is able to keep firing when other weapons would have ceased to function.

To reduce costs the barrel interiors are not chrome-plated but this does not reduce performance. The Ultimax 100 has again been repeatedly demonstrated firing 100-round bursts (an unlikely probability during almost any action) without problems, even with the fixed-barrel Mark 2 version.

Ammunition feed is from a 60- or 100-round pre-loaded drum, with the 100-round drum being the most commonly encountered. The employment of the drum feed removes the problems that can result when using ammunition belts, and loading a drum into the feed slot takes only a few seconds. The drums used are made of a sturdy plastic and have a clear rear face through which the rounds inside can be easily observed for visual quantity-remain-

Singapore Defence Forces troops advancing with 5.56 mm Ultimax 100 light machine guns.

A field-stripped 5.56 mm Ultimax 100 Mark 3.

ing checks. During peacetime training periods the drums can be re-loaded several times, although in action it is expected that spent drums will simply be discarded and replaced by others carried in a shoulder satchel holding four drums. When no more drums are available, standard 20- or 30-round box magazines of the widely-used M16 type can be slotted in to replace them.

The integral bipod is adjustable in height and its bracket allows a fair degree of barrel traverse and roll to each side. As with many other similar designs, the bipod can be folded back alongside the receiver, but is not then used as the usual foregrip; instead

the Ultimax 100 is provided with a proper sub-machine-gun-type foregrip. In confined spaces the butt can be detached to reduce the overall length to 800 mm.

The Ultimax 100 can be mounted on tripods, on vehicles and on aircraft or helicopters. One attractive and very simple vehicle mount involves placing two Ultimax 100s on their sides and side-by-side, with the pistol grips pointing outwards. This simple arrangement can be attached to points such as a truck tailgate or a wall to double the amount of potential fire available.

The Ultimax 100 can fire either the M193 or the SS 109 5.56 mm rounds, as all

A rare sight – a 5.56 mm Ultimax 100 Mark 3 fitted with a sound suppressor.

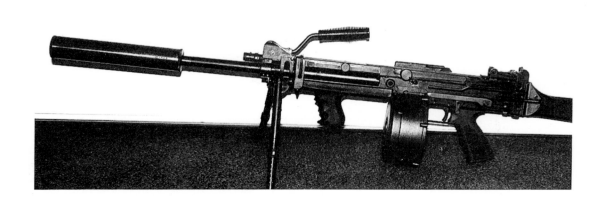

that is necessary is to change the barrel to one with the appropriate rifling twist. However, it is interesting to note that CIS data rates the maximum effective range of the M193 round fired from the Ultimax 100 as 460 metres; for the SS 109 round the figure is 1,300 metres.

The Ultimax 100 is probably the only light machine gun that can be fitted with a bayonet. One is listed as an Ultimax 100 accessory, along with the usual items such as a shoulder sling and a blank firing attachment for the muzzle. However, there is one accessory that is not listed but has been seen fitted, and that is a sound suppressor. Again, the Ultimax 100 is unusual in being able to accommodate such an accessory but there is no technical reason why other similar weapons could not be fitted with such an item. However, it is not easy to see exactly what tactical use a sound suppressor could have when fitted on an automatic weapon, and the Ultimax 100 fires on fully automatic only.

The Ultimax 100 is the standard light machine gun of the Singapore armed forces (they use the fixed-barrel Mark 2 version) and it has been actively promoted elsewhere. However, the only known overseas users announced to date are Honduras, the Philippines and Zimbabwe. Some have turned up in Croatia.

Above and below *Two views of the 12.7 mm 50MG heavy machine gun.*

50MG

In 1983 CIS began the design of a new 0.50/12.7 mm heavy machine gun which they determined should be lighter, simpler and easier to use and maintain that the

well-established Browning M2 HB. In addition, the new design was to be able to fire the effective armour-piercing saboted light armour penetrator (SLAP) ammunition.

The result is known as the 50MG, and in appearances at least it appears to owe much to the results of the now-defunct American General Purpose Heavy Machine Gun (GPHMG) and 'Dover Devil' programmes (see chapter 19). The weapon is gas-operated and fires from an open bolt, thereby eliminating the risk of 'cook-off' produced by leaving a round in a hot chamber. A modular design approach was adopted which results in five basic assemblies, or groups. The use of this approach makes maintenance much easier and the entire weapon can be readily field-stripped without recourse to tools.

The first group is formed by the receiver which is made of pressed steel. This includes two tubes which extend forward on either side of the barrel to enclose the bolt carrier group's gas system pistons and recoil spring guide rods.

The second group is the ammunition feed. On the 50MG this is a dual-feed single-sprocket-wheel system that enables the weapon to feed in ammunition from the left or right. The system also allows the firer

to switch from one side to the other rapidly so that two natures of ammunition may be held ready to suit whatever target might appear, eg ball ammunition on one side and armour-piercing on the other. There is usually no need to field strip this group.

The trigger group is self-explanatory and involves a twin spade grip, the safeties and the fire selector.

The barrel group involves one of the 50MG's main attributes, mainly a barrel quick-change system that does away with the need for the cartridge head space adjustment required on the Browning M2 HB. On the 50MG the head space is fixed so barrel-changing takes seconds. The barrel group also includes a three-position gas regulator and a muzzle attachment to reduce recoil.

Finally there is the bolt carrier group, complete with two pistons and recoil rods.

Using the modular approach, the overall weight of the 50MG is relatively low at 30 kg, of which 10 kg is the barrel. The 50MG can be fitted on to a standard M3 tripod by using an adaptor, and pintle mounts have been developed to allow the 50MG to be carried on armoured vehicles and light naval vessels.

The 50MG is understood to be in production although to date the only customers

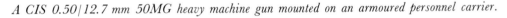

A CIS 0.50/12.7 mm 50MG heavy machine gun mounted on an armoured personnel carrier.

appear to be the Singapore armed forces.

Others

The Singapore armed forces have procured various versions of the FN MAG general-purpose and co-axial machine guns, both from the Royal Small Arms Factory at Enfield and direct from FN at Herstal. The Ordnance Development and Engineering Company of Singapore (Pte) Limited, a member of the Singapore Technology Corporation (as is CIS), market the FN MAG although it is understood that they have no licence to either manufacture or market this weapon. They produce the MAG in two forms, a standard infantry version and a co-axial version without a bipod or butt.

DATA		
Model	Ultimax 100	50MG
Calibre	5.56 mm	12.7 mm
Weight (gun only)	4.7 kg	30 kg
Length	1.03 m	1.778 m
Length of barrel	508 mm	1.143 m
Rate of fire	500-540 rpm	600 rpm
Feed	drum	belt
Muzzle velocity	945 m/s*	890 m/s
	*SS109	

CHAPTER 13

ISRAEL'S DESERT WIND

ISRAEL is a young nation that has spent its entire existence under a state of war with its neighbours, and this experience has made it a state for whom all matters relating to defence rate the highest of priorities. One of those priorities has always been that it must be as self-sufficient in defence material as possible. In the past this has not prevented the Israel Defence Forces (IDF) from obtaining weapons from any available source (including the use of captured material), but the emphasis has always been on self-reliance wherever possible.

Small arms have become one area where Israel has been self-reliant, although it is noticeable that as far as machine guns are concerned much of the Israeli arsenal is either the usual run of American weapons or the Belgian FN MAG. While Israel has been able to produce rifles such as the Galil and sub-machine guns such as the Uzi, Israeli machine guns have been noticeable by their absence.

Attempts have been made to produce machine guns in the past; back in the early 1950s an Israeli example known as the Dror was produced locally in small numbers but soon faded from the scene and does not appear to have been much of a success – hence the importing of the FN MAG

and the acceptance from the United States of approximately 23,000 Browning M1919A4s, most of which were converted to fire 7.62 mm NATO ammunition soon after they arrived.

However, for infantry squad fire support the M1919A4s were of limited value. The United States did supply just over 1,000 M1919A6 light machine guns in 1981 which provided at least some form of squad weapon, but for most of the Israeli infantry their only section weapon has been the heavy MAG or the Model ARM, a heavy-barrelled version of the Galil rifle with a bipod, which was produced in both 5.56 and 7.62 mm forms.

The problem with the Model ARM is that it is really only a machine rifle. Even if the largest magazine holding 50 rounds is used, the barrel is fixed and automatic fire has to be limited to short bursts. Something better was therefore required and the result was the Negev.

Negev

The Negev was first shown publicly during 1989 and is a product of the Weapons Division of Israel Military Industries (IMI – now TAAS – Israel Industries Limited).

A 5.56 mm Negev machine gun surrounded by some of its accessories - note the short assault rifle barrel in the foreground.

It is now in production for the IDF.

This light machine gun is based on the Galil assault rifle family and is consequently modelled on the CIS AK-47 series. However, the Negev is something more than just a 'breathed on' Galil, for it may be regarded as an original and unusual approach to weapon design.

It is a 5.56 mm weapon that can be belt fed or fed using standard rifle magazines. It has a quick-change barrel but the entire weapon is so designed that by removing the bipod and fitting a shorter barrel and a box magazine, it can be converted into an assault rifle. All barrels are fully interchangeable and any accidental release of the barrel catch is prevented by a cover on the receiver.

This combined machine gun and assault rifle approach is somewhat unusual to say the least, the usual approach being to convert assault rifles into something approaching a light machine gun. Yet the Negev is a light machine gun intended for squad fire support and it thus has a belt feed mechanism fitted over the front of the receiver. The gun was designed to be used within the tight confines of vehicles and so has an unusually short feed cover for operation in constricted areas such as a patrol vehicle cab, an ergonomic feature which is regarded as one of the finer points of the Negev design.

The Negev retains the basic Galil/AK-47 rotating bolt locking system, but arranged to fire from an open bolt to prevent 'cook-off' after firing bursts. As an alternative to the belt feed, and for use when the Negev is configured in the assault rifle mode, a feed slot under the receiver can accept the usual Galil 12-, 35- or 50-round box magazines (an 'export' version can accommodate the 30-round M16 box magazine, as can the standard version after fitting an adaptor), or one of the various commercial drum or other high-capacity magazines that have appeared on the market in recent years. When the belt feed is involved, the belt may be carried inside a protective pouch that clips into the magazine well on the left-hand side of the receiver.

The Negev gas regulator has three positions. The first position provides a cyclic rate of fire of 650 to 800 rounds per minute, while the second provides 800 to 950 rounds per minute. The third position is used only when rifle grenades are fired from the muzzle – this is normally carried out in conjunction with the 12-round Galil magazine containing ballistite propelling cartridges. Construction of the Negev is simple, and it can be field stripped down to only six sub-assemblies, including the sturdy bipod. The Galil rifle-type butt can be folded to reduce the overall length and the weapon can be

A 5.56 mm Negev machine gun mounted to fire from a front windscreen position on an Abir wheeled internal security vehicle - note that the stock is folded to save space.

fitted on to standard vehicle and other mountings. Throughout the construction of the Negev considerable use is made of machining, either from the solid metal or from castings; this makes the Negev heavier than some other similar weapons but it will be extremely durable and have a long service life. The barrel is chrome plated.

An integral adaptor on top of the receiver can be used to mount various types of optical and night vision sights, and a fabric shoulder sling is a standard accessory.

It is anticipated that the Negev will eventually replace the FN MAG in IDF service. It was adopted for service by the IDF in February 1990 although the assault rifle option does not appear to have been favoured. Production was expected to commence during early 1991. In the meantime

TAAS are actively marketing the Negev and it will be surprising if it does not end up in service with armed forces far from Israel.

DATA	
Model	Negev
Calibre	5.56 mm
Weight (gun only)	7.2 kg
Length (long barrel)	1.02 m
(short barrel)	890 mm
Length of barrel (long)	460 mm
(short)	330 mm
Rate of fire	650-800 or
	800-950 rpm
Feed	belt or box
Muzzle velocity	850 m/s

CHAPTER 14

BRAZILIAN BIRD

DESIGNING and developing a new machine gun is not a straightforward or simple process. Readers may have noted from accounts provided in this book that machine guns designs are usually the products of evolution rather than dramatic innovation – the innovations were made by famous names such as Maxim, Browning and Holek, who introduced the original designs and concepts with which others have worked, and it is very noticeable how many so-called modern machine gun ventures utilise features or mechanisms lifted directly from earlier models.

This formalised plagiarism is not all dishonest or even blameworthy. Once a concept has been perfected there is no need to 'reinvent the wheel' just for the sake of the exercise. It is far more sensible to copy the AK-47, the rotary bolt locking system, or some other similar well-established mechanism.

However, some novel machine gun designs have appeared during recent years, and from areas that had until then been devoid of any reason for machine gun design even to be contemplated. That was the situation in Brazil in 1969 when a three-man engineering team working in a military research institute in Rio de Janeiro was given the task of designing a machine gun. With few ideas of how to actually go about the task, the team managed to produce three prototypes that actually worked, but their lack of experience in the field led to no end of troubles with their progeny. They had quickly learned that machine gun design is not a paper exercise but a very practical hands-on business.

The Brazilian Army became involved in the project with the prospect of an indigenous Brazilian machine gun appearing to be a very attractive proposition. They took the design from the research institute and handed it over to to an industrial concern that had even less idea of the complexities of machine guns than the original researchers. Not surprisingly that move proved to be a non-starter and the project was handed back to one of the original three-man team that had initiated the whole operation. Working in isolation he gradually progressed until the prototypes came to look more and more like a viable proposition. The results were accordingly passed to a further state-run research institute for yet more work.

During 1977 a commercial engineering firm was given the task of producing two test and evaluation prototypes for the

Brazilian Army; these were extensively tested and the whole project was finally approved for production.

The resultant machine gun is known as the Uirapuru (after a well-known Brazilian jungle bird) and is produced by Mekanika Industria e Comercio Limitada of Rio de Janeiro. Chambered for the 7.62 mm × 51 cartridge, the Uirapuru is a general-purpose machine gun with a distinctly odd, elongated and ungainly appearance bestowed mainly by the construction method involved. Its receiver is basically a tube containing the bolt body and return spring. Everything else is somehow connected with that tube, including the box-like structure that houses the ammunition feed system. Gas operation is employed along with a belt feed, and the weapon can be either bipod or tripod-mounted, with the butt removed

The 7.62 mm Uirapuru general-purpose machine guns shown both bipod- and tripod-mounted.

when the latter role is assumed. There are few frills and everything is very basic and easy to manufacture.

Apparently the Uirapuru operates well and is now in service with the Brazilian Army, where it is used both as a light and medium machine gun. Co-axial and pintle versions are understood to be in production for armoured vehicles, and a solenoid-operated version is available for use on aircraft and helicopters.

DATA

Model	Uirapuru
Calibre	7.62 mm
Weight (gun only)	13 kg
Length	1.3 m
Length of barrel	600 mm
Rate of fire	650-700 rpm
Feed	belt
Muzzle velocity	850 m/s

CHAPTER 15

RISING SUN

IN 1945 Japan was a shattered nation. Years of war, the effects of Allied bombing and the final humiliation imposed by the Americans' use of the nuclear device had brought the Japanese to their knees. Yet within a few years the nation was largely rebuilt and was even in the early stages of re-arming.

The rise of Japan after 1945 has been one of the social and economic phenomena of the century. Not only was the nation's social infrastructure re-established and re-modelled, but industry was also able to rise from the ruins to become a world leader in many aspects of engineering and electronics. Defence was among the many new industrial ventures established, and it included new manufacturers eager to assist in the arming of the new Japanese Self-Defence Force.

This force was established in 1954, at a time when the occupying Americans were anxious for the emerging Japan to reassume at least part of its national defence stance. In their turn the new Self-Defence Forces were anxious to ensure that as many of their requirements as possible would be met by local resources. Among the many requirements was a new machine gun.

The pre-1945 Japanese machine gun ar-senal was a motley collection, much of it based on old French Hotchkiss designs that were retained in service well past the time when they had been discarded by other nations. This was simply because Japan at that time had few industrial or other resources to replace them with anything better; the few local examples they produced were often noteworthy for their unusual design approaches (such as the hopper-fed Type 11 light machine gun) or were copies of Czech designs. After 1945, the few machine guns that the Japanese were initially allowed to use were nearly all the usual American hand-outs – indeed, the Japanese Self-Defence Force still uses the Browning 0.50/12.7 mm M2 HB.

When the time came during the mid-1950s to design a new Japanese machine gun, all the relics of the past were swept away. The designers, led by one Dr Kawamura, commenced with a completely clean sheet and took advantage of the many innovations introduced during and after the Second World War. They eventually produced two designs, one of which was approved for service in 1962 and entered production soon after.

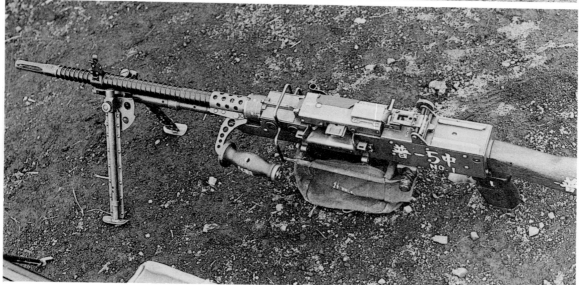

Rear and top views of a 7.62 mm Type 62 general-purpose machine gun.

Type 62

The new machine gun was given the design bureau designation of 9M but in service it became the 7.62 mm Model 62 (*62 Shiki Kikanju*). It is a gas-operated disintegrating-link belt-fed general-purpose machine gun with few design items of note other than it uses a cam-operated tilting block combined with lugs that move into recesses at the instant of firing to ensure a very positive lock. This system is unique to the Type 62, but otherwise there is little to note on the weapon other than that it is very solidly built and the standard of finish is very high. That high standard of finish combined with the fact that only about 3,500 Type 62s were actually made (by the Nittoku Metal Industry Company of Tokyo) means that, in unit costs, the Type 62 must be one of the most expensive machine guns produced since 1945.

In the foreground is a 7.62 mm Type 62 general-purpose machine gun on a bipod mounting; the weapon to the rear is a 7.62 mm Type 64 assault rifle, the standard Japanese service rifle.

The Type 62 may be encountered mounted either on a tripod or a bipod. For the portable light machine gun role, belts are often carried in a fabric pouch connected under the receiver. When on a tripod the wooden butt is usually removed and a periscopic optical sight may be employed.

For co-axial use on their armoured vehicles (Japan is one of the few nations that actually designs and manufactures its own armoured vehicles), the Type 62 was modified to become the Type 74. In most mechanical respects both types are identical, but the Type 74 uses trigger grips or a solenoid for firing and is manufactured from heavier materials to further improve dura-

bility, weighing 20.4 kg compared to the Type 62's 10.7 kg. If required, the Type 74 can be mounted on a tripod for ground use.

DATA

Model	Type 62
Calibre	7.62 mm
Weight (gun only)	10.7 kg
Length	1.2 m
Length of barrel	524 mm
Rate of fire	600 rpm
Feed	belt
Muzzle velocity	855 m/s

CHAPTER 16

NORTHERN ENDEAVOURS – FINLAND

FINLAND is a nation that has throughout its history been dominated either by Russia or Germany. In 1918 it gained independence from Russia after a struggle from which the new state emerged victorious and in possession of about 500 Maxim guns of Russian origin. These guns formed the main machine gun equipment of the new Finnish armed forces for some time to come, although during the pre-war years the Finns introduced their own Maxim-based developments and produced new guns. The last model being adopted as late as 1932, and it featured the 'snow cap' on top of the barrel cooling jacket into which snow could be packed for barrel cooling. This feature was later adopted by the Soviets for their late production PM1910 Maxims.

During the 1920s the Lathi Model 26 appeared, to become one of the first really light light machine guns that, despite all the attentions paid to it in many machine gun accounts, was not used outside Finland and is now regarded as obsolete.

After the Winter War of 1939-40 Finland once again came under Soviet influence and is still bound to the CIS by treaty agreements to a state of armed neutrality, although Finland remains an independent state. The CIS influence can be seen among much of the equipment of the Finnish armed forces although a fair proportion of their defence material is still purchased from the Western bloc nations. However, many small arms of local design are produced within Finland. Finnish rifles and associated products (including sound suppressors) are highly regarded for their quality, as is their target-shooting quality ammunition. However, this aspect has not been marked by any substantial weapon export sales during recent years.

As far as machine guns are concerned the Finnish armed forces use several models of CIS origin such as the RPD, the PK series and the DShK-38/46. However, one in-service model of machine gun is of Finnish origin and is known as the KK-62.

KK-62

The 7.62 *Konekivaari Malli 62* (KK-62) was produced by Sako Valmet and, as its designation suggests, it entered service in 1962, the prototype having appeared in 1960. It is still in service and is a gas-operated light machine gun firing a derivation of the CIS-designed 7.62 mm × 39 cartridge produced in Finland with a slightly altered ballistic performance compared to the Soviet original. Firing this cartridge the KK-62 has a relatively high cyclic rate of fire of from 1,000 to 1,100 rounds per minute, and on automatic only – there is no provision for it to fire single shots. In practical terms the rate of fire is reduced to around 300 rounds a minute. Ammunition is fed into the gun in 100-round non-disintegrating metal link belts which can be held in a pouch secured to the right-hand side of the receiver.

The gas-operated mechanism of the KK-62 is based on that of the Czech ZB26, or to be more exact the post-war vz 52, and uses a tilting breech block that locks into the roof of the receiver. There is a quick-change barrel mechanism and the barrel has a distinctive pronged flash suppressor at the muzzle. Another odd feature of the KK-62

7.62 mm KK-62s in action under typical wintry Finnish conditions and during a training exercise.

The Finnish 7.62 mm KK-62 light machine gun.

is that, in deference to Finnish conditions, there is no trigger guard, which permits thick mittens to be worn when operating it. To provide some measure of trigger safety the usual trigger guard is replaced by a rudimentary open trigger bar positioned vertically in front of the trigger itself.

By all accounts the KK-62 is a thoroughly serviceable and well-made light machine gun, but only a few were sold outside Finland, to Qatar, whose armed forces at the same time purchased a quantity of Valmet Model 62 and Model 76 assault rifles. Production of the KK-62 was completed some years ago.

Valmet also produced a light machine gun design known as the Model 78 and based on the receiver of their Model 62 and Model 76 assault rifle, but only a few were made for trials, after which the project did not proceed further.

DATA	
Model	KK-62
Calibre	7.62 mm
Weight (gun only)	8.3 kg
Length	1.085 m
Length of barrel	470 mm
Rate of fire	1,000-1,100 rpm
Feed	100-round belt
Muzzle velocity	730 m/s

CHAPTER 17

THE SWISS ARSENAL

IT is often forgotten that Switzerland has the largest army in Europe, well over 560,000 men, plus almost as many assigned to civil defence. It is also often forgotten that the vast bulk of that total is formed from reservists who carry out a complex system of on-going training and who can also move out to defend their country direct from their homes.

Even today Switzerland organises and maintains a system of national defence upon a network of fortifications plus natural and other obstacles that combine to hinder and delay any possible invader. The fixed fortifications are backed up by conventional armoured and infantry formations operating in the areas between the natural and fortified barriers.

For the large numbers of fully trained soldiers involved, provision has to be continuously made to supply them with weapons and all other material requirements. As far as can possibly be arranged, Switzerland supplies all national defence requirements from within. All too often in the past any reliance on outside sources has led to problems when links with those sources have been broken either by external conflicts or by the imposition of export embargoes.

Thus in the field of small arms Switzerland tends to rely almost entirely upon national resources – and they are many. Despite Swiss neutrality and the well-known and respected national stance of peace and conciliation, the Swiss defence industrial base is wide and experienced. Everything that a modern armed force requires, from aircraft to tanks and artillery, and from ammunition to trucks, can be made within Switzerland and using Swiss industry. This includes machine guns.

One Swiss machine gun has already been mentioned in chapter 1. That was the series of Maxim guns manufactured at the Waffenfabrik Bern, all marked by their superb standards of finish and overall quality, and which continued to be used until the 1950s, especially in the mountain fortifications and strongpoints. Their many forms can be seen in museums throughout Switzerland, still looking as though they had just been turned out from the factory.

But Swiss machine guns were not all Maxim guns. An attempt was made during the 1920s to produce a locally designed light machine gun. Known as the MG25, or Furrer, this emerged as a functional but rather complex gas-operated weapon with a side-mounted box magazine containing 30 rounds. It is now rated as obsolete but apparently some are still retained for possible use as reserve weapons.

The associations with Swiss engineering concerns by treaty-breaking German defence companies during the 1920s led to many innovative machine gun designs, but few of those concerns retained any machine gun production facilities after the German design teams returned to Germany during the early 1930s. The most obvious example of this Swiss-German association was Waffenfabrik Solothurn AG, the producer of the MG30 that eventually led to the MG34 and everything that followed (see chapter 3). After the 1930s Solothurn concentrated on other weapon products such as anti-tank rifles and automatic cannon, leaving other concerns such as the Schweizerische Industrie-Gesellschaft, better known as SIG, to produce light machine guns such as the KE7. These were sold in small numbers to China and elsewhere, but were not adopted by the Swiss forces and are almost unknown today.

The MG25 and the Maxims were the main types of machine gun used in Switzerland during their defensive period which lasted throughout the Second World War. Despite their neutrality the Swiss military authorities closely observed the many innovations that arose between 1939 and 1945, among them the many and various changes in the approaches to small arms manufacture and the new types of mechanism that were introduced.

Among the innovations selected for further study within Switzerland was the German MG42; the designers at the Waffenfabrik Bern decided to produce a local version of this weapon which they eventually designated the MG51.

MG51

The Swiss MG51, also known in multilingual Switzerland as the M51 (from the French *Mitrailleuse*), was not a direct copy of the German MG42. One of the most obvious differences was that the Swiss, with their long tradition of high-class engineering, could not accommodate the concept of using the steel stampings, rivets and welds of the MG42 and opted instead to produce the MG51 using all the usual stages of machining from solid metal and other high-quality manufacturing procedures. The result is that although the Swiss MG51 resembles the MG42 it is really a different and much more expensive weapon. It is also far more durable and heavier.

The MG51 fires the Swiss 7.5 mm × 55 rifle cartridge which is also known as the M1911 or M11. This is a fairly powerful

The Swiss 7.5 mm MG51 general-purpose machine gun.

cartridge, so to accommodate the chamber pressures involved the Swiss designers at Bern rather over-compensated and decided to adopt a more positive system of locking flaps in place of the rollers used on the MG42 – otherwise the Swiss and German mechanisms function much the same.

Being a general-purpose machine gun the MG51 may be fired from a bipod, but its more usual ground mounting is a sturdy and rather heavy steel tripod which can be arranged to be carried as a back pack by mountain troops. When on the tripod the MG51 is often used in association with optical sights of superlative quality.

Such sights are also used on the various fortification mountings with which the MG51 is associated and which are complex and expensive, using steel mantlets and ball mountings. For many of these mountings the butt is removed, a practice also followed when the MG51 is used as a co-axial weapon on armoured vehicles such as the Swiss-produced Pz 61 and Pz 68 tanks. A similar arrangement is also produced for the Pz 87, the Swiss version of the German Leopard 2 tank, but here more changes proved necessary, resulting in a new machine gun designation of MG87.

The MG87 fires the 7.62 mm × 51 cartridge (some versions were produced for the 7.5 mm × 63) and has a revised mounting sleeve, a butt cap with no provision for a butt, an electrical firing mechanism, and provision for two cyclic rates of fire, 700 or 1,000 rounds per minute. The MG87 can also be mounted in armoured vehicles other than the Pz 87. The MG87 is still produced at the Waffenfabrik Bern and some weapons are expected to be installed in fortifications; production of the MG51, however, appears to have been terminated.

The MG51 and MG87 will no doubt remain in Swiss service for years to come, as both are robust and well-made weapons that seem destined to last for a very long time. Their one drawback seems to be that they are much heavier weapons than their counterparts produced elsewhere, but that is the price that has to be paid for carving

machine guns 'from the solid'.

At one stage during the 1950s numbers of MG51s were sold to Denmark, chambered for the American 0.30-06 cartridge (7.62 mm × 63), but few, if any, remain in service there today as that nation later decided to standardise on the German MG3 and its 7.62 mm NATO ammunition.

SIG 710

The series of machine guns known under the general designation of SIG 710 were developed by SIG for export sales since the Swiss Army was already well enough equipped with the MG51. The series was based on a gas-based operating mechanism derived from some of the German small arms development work in progress as the Second World War ended and later used as the basis for the 7.5 mm Stg 57 assault rifle, produced by SIG to act as the standard Swiss assault rifle for many years.

On the SIG 710 series a chambered cartridge is seated in a partially fluted chamber. As the cartridge is fired, some of the propellant gases seep backwards along the grooves of the fluted chamber and push the spent case to the rear; it is this backwards pressure which provides the propulsion energy for the system, involving rollers, ramps and a bolt all interacting to lock the breech at the point of highest internal pressure yet release it to carry out the ejection and loading functions once that pressure drops to a safe level.

The first of the SIG 710 series, the 710-1, used a barrel-change system very like that of the German MG42. The next model, the 710-2, used a carrying-handle-actuated method to change barrels. The 710-3 reverts to the MG42 barrel-changing method but also has several significant differences from the earlier two models – the SIG 710-1 and 710-2 were offered in several calibres (6.5, 7.62 and 7.92 mm) to suit prospective purchasers, while the 710-3 is available only in 7.62 mm NATO. The latter model also uses a generally simpler and lighter method of construction which is also less expensive

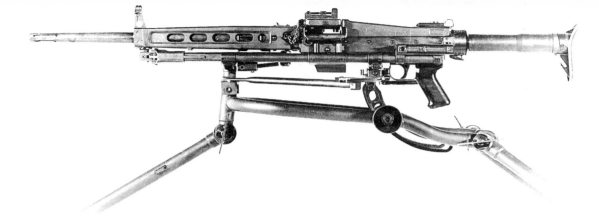

The SIG-710 general-purpose machine gun.

than the earlier two versions. All three make use of steel stampings and other modern manufacturing procedures, but the 710-3 makes more use of plastics and has a generally simpler outline.

Mention of steel stampings should not give the impression that the SIG 710 series are poor-quality weapons. The opposite is the truth for, as with any SIG-produced weapon, the overall standards of manufacture and finish are superlative.

Various accessories were developed for the SIG 710 series, including a blank-firing barrel, a dial sight and a soft-mount tripod.

At one time a device for automatically dispersing fire either in elevation or traverse (or both at once) was offered.

For all that, sales of the SIG 710 series were disappointing. As already mentioned, none were delivered to the Swiss armed forces and the only known customers were Bolivia and Brunei; for the latter a soft-mount twin mounting was developed for use on light patrol craft. Some reports mention sales to one of the various Chilean gendarmeries but this cannot be confirmed, even if SIG SG510-4 7.62 mm assault rifles are licence-produced in Chile.

DATA

Model	MG51	MG87
Calibre	7.5 mm	7.62 mm
Weight (gun only)	16 kg	30 kg*
Length	1.27 m	1.174 m
Length of barrel	564 mm	475 mm
Rate of fire	1,000 rpm	700 or 1,000 rpm
Feed	belt	belt
Muzzle velocity	780 m/s	approx 840 m/s
		*with mount

Model	SIG 710-3
Calibre	7.62 mm
Weight (gun only)	9.25 kg
Length	1.143 m
Length of barrel	559 mm
Rate of fire	800-950 rpm
Feed	belt
Muzzle velocity	790 m/s

CHAPTER 18

ITALIAN EFFORTS

ITALY has always been a nation with a tradition of sound engineering and a definite talent for design. It therefore comes as something of a surprise to discover that, as far as machine guns are concerned, the Italians have all too often in the past allowed their talents to run away with them. Most of the machine guns produced in Italy before the Second World War were usually marked by many undesirable design features that more thorough development and forethought could have eliminated.

The pre-war Italian machine gun scene was populated by several different models with design assets of doubtful value, such as oiling cartridges as they were fed into the chamber to assist extraction, the use of ammunition feed trays from which cartridges had to be stripped for feeding, and the half-cocked introduction of a new ammunition calibre which had to be abandoned at the outbreak of war. In short, most Italian machine guns were user-unfriendly and awkward to handle as well.

When Italy started to re-arm after 1945, virtually all the old models were abandoned. For some years the new Italian armed forces used a mixture of American and British weapons before it was decided to licence produce the German MG42/59 to provide them with a general-purpose machine gun. The licence production is carried out by various manufacturers within Italy to the extent that exports have been made to nations such as Chile, Denmark, Mozambique, Nigeria and Portugal.

With the main requirements of the Italian armed forces thus met for the time being, there was no need for the local small arms industry to devote much time to machine guns. They therefore concentrated on rifles, sub-machine guns and pistols, with the name of Pietro Beretta SpA much to the fore. Within a very few years Beretta had emerged from the upheavals of the war years to become once more one of the world leaders in the design and development of small arms, and especially automatic pistols.

Beretta pistols are highly respected throughout the small arms fraternity, a respect crowned by the US Army's adoption of a Beretta pistol to become its current service side-arm (the 9 mm M9), an adoption by a nation that regards the automatic pistol as its own invention. Such achievements tend to shroud the fact that Beretta have also been producing a range of assault rifles for years.

Off-shoots from the array of Beretta as-

The Beretta 5.56 mm 70/78 light machine gun, complete with a quick-change barrel – this model did not, however, attract sales.

sault rifles have been heavy-barrelled variants intended for use as squad light fire support weapons. As such, all the various Beretta models have suffered the same drawbacks as every other type of 'machine rifle' in the same class. Beretta did produce some models with quick-change barrel systems such as the 5.56 mm Beretta Model 70/78, an off-shoot of the AR 70 assault rifle family, but apart from limited exports to Malaysia, sales were few.

During the late 1980s the Italian Army decided to adopt a new family of 5.56 mm combat weapons, including a heavy-barrelled assault rifle to act as a light fire support weapon. The Beretta entry for the resulting competition was based on their AR 70 assault rifle family, but updated to take advantage of the experience gained during the production of the earlier weapon. Known as the Beretta AR 70/90, the new weapon family consists of an assault rifle, a carbine for special forces, a specialised shortened carbine version for armoured troops, and a so-called light machine gun, the AS 70/90.

AS 70/90

In early 1991 it was revealed that, following the usual series of intensive trials, the Beretta 5.56 mm AR 70/90 family had been selected for adoption by the Italian armed forces, so the AS 70/90 is now entering large-scale production.

The AS 70/90 is really little more than an AR 70/90 assault rifle with the addition of a slightly longer and heavier fixed barrel, an adjustable bipod, an enlarged metal handguard and a revision of the trigger mechanism to allow firing from an open bolt. The locking system is the same as that used on the AR 70/90 and uses the now widely adopted rotating bolt system. Ammunition feed comes from an M16 rifle-type 30-round box magazine. Rifle grenades can also be fired from a fixture at the muzzle.

The AS 70/90 has a futuristic appearance, partially provided by the unusual outline of the butt stock. The outline was selected for the ability of the shape to provide a good 'spare hand' grip when firing bursts. Another visual feature is the

The 5.56 mm AS 70/90 light machine gun.

prominent fixed carrying handle over the receiver – it is fixed so as to provide a sighting channel for the fixed 'iron' sights, but it can also be removed to reveal a mounting base for optical or night vision sights.

The AS 70/90 would appear to be more than capable of providing the required automatic fire support for an infantry squad, but the bursts involved will have to be short as the limitations of the fixed barrel and the magazine capacity will prevent any notion of sustained fire. The AS 70/90 will thus suffer from all the usual drawbacks of the 'machine rifle' concept.

DATA	
Model	AS 70/90
Calibre	5.56 mm
Weight (gun only)	5.34 kg
Length	1 m
Length of barrel	465 mm
Rate of fire	approx 800 rpm
Feed	30-round box
Muzzle velocity	approx 950 m/s

CHAPTER 19

THE ORDINARY AMERICANS

MACHINE gun development proceeds apace, and one of the main centres of the technology involved in the next generation of machine guns is the United States. Indeed, so much is happening there that two chapters will be devoted to the subject; this first one will deal with the more conventional approaches to recent machine gun development.

Machine gun development in the United States is a joint effort with both commercial concerns and the various ordnance departments and research institutes attached to the US Army or the other armed forces being involved. This dual approach has led to a great deal of confusion in the past, even amongst those actually involved in the development processes, and will no doubt continue to do so in the future.

During the various stages of an American machine gun's path from the drawing-board to introduction into service the project may pass from commercial hands to the military and back again, the process often being repeated several times and sometimes with the realm of the academics being introduced as well. Added to this is the propensity for the military authorities to alter, add or subtract features or requirements at odd unexpected intervals or even terminate or suspend a project altogether without apparent reason.

As a not unexpected result, American small arms development projects often seem to get bogged down or even founder altogether as development marks and sub-marks appear and disappear (occasionally only to re-emerge later) with bewildering frequency. Considerable pains are taken to ensure that a weapon will operate under every conceivable (and often unlikely) situation, even if it is intended for use in just one environment or role. All too often the end result is far from what was originally proposed. Another noticeable feature of the American small arms development 'system' appears to be that whatever is on hand often has to be adapted and altered to meet new and far-removed performance or role targets, no matter how unsuitable the starting material might appear to be. In this manner huge amounts of money and resources have been lavished (and often wasted) attempting to make a project deliver unrealistic performances and end results that a more objective approach could have prevented.

Anyone who has doubts as to the veracity of the above statements has only to wade through just a few of the reports and other documentation published by the various American ordnance authorities to get just an inkling of the scale of the hazards that can arise once any weapon development is undertaken for the US armed forces. It is apparently all too easy to become enmeshed in a sea of detail and limited objectives that prevent any researcher from being able to determine what is actually going on at any one time. Actually being involved in the process must be equally frustrating for all those concerned.

Added to this is the sheer volume of weapons development work actually being carried out in the United States at any one time. Universities, military commands, individuals and industry all attempt to produce their own innovations, all adding to the efforts of the various US Army ordnance authorities to determine and meet future weapons requirements and to ensure that existing in-service weapons are capable of meeting their user's needs to the best of their ability.

A book of this nature cannot possibly cover every machine gun development of recent years for the simple reason that there have been so many of them, and all too many of what seemed to be promising and advanced projects have simply been terminated or held in abeyance for one reason or another, with their present and future fates uncertain. What this chapter will attempt is to pick out a few of the more significant developments of recent years.

To demonstrate the possible pitfalls and unexpected end results of recent American machine gun development we will commence with the tale of the M60.

M60

As late as the Korean War the US Army was largely equipped with machine guns that dated back to the Great War. Good as most of these weapons were, a change of ammunition standards to meet the requirements of NATO was about to take place, so the early to mid-1950s was deemed a suitable time to convert to the concept of the general-purpose machine gun, in common with most of the other NATO nations.

Also in common with many others, the American small arms establishment had been greatly interested in German innovations such as the MG42. They had also been greatly influenced by a German Second World War automatic weapon that has not been mentioned thus far in this book. This was the 7.92 mm *Fallschirmjagergewehr 42*, or FG42, a remarkable assault rifle design produced for the Luftwaffe, who disliked the notion of using the lower-powered 'intermediate' 7.92 mm × 33 cartridge introduced by the German Army and requested a light automatic assault rifle firing the standard full-power 7.92 mm × 57 rifle cartridge. The mechanism devised by Krieghoff to put the proverbial quart into a pint pot was much admired by those in a position to appreciate the technicalities involved.

The FG42 attracted so much attention that during the period immediately after 1945 the Springfield Armoury produced a trial machine gun known as the T44. This design was really an FG42 converted to accommodate an MG42 belt feed in place of the awkwardly placed box magazine of the original. The original 7.92 mm calibre of the German FG42 was carried over, as was the 'all-in-line' layout, which latter feature allowed the recoil spring housing to be carried right through to the butt plate and thus reduce the overall length of the weapon.

The T44 used a gas-operated system which did not require the use of a gas regulator. Gas regulators have been mentioned throughout the earlier part of this book and are an important component in any gas-operated machine gun mechanism. They are nearly all adjustable to alter the amount of gas tapped off from the gun barrel to drive the system pistons and thus the locking, extraction and loading mechanisms under varying environmental and other conditions. When rifle grenade launchers are involved, the regulator can be switched off altogether to allow as much propellant gas as possible to reach the launcher attachment located at the muzzle.

On the T44 and FG42 some of the propellant gases were tapped from the barrel and directed through a series of holes around the sides of a piston to push the piston to the rear, but as it moved the piston automatically cut off its own gas supply, thereby creating what is known as a 'constant volume' gas operation.

The T44 gas system and bolt, combined with the MG42 feed, offered much, but it was considered that further development would be required. The result was the T52 series, with some changes made to the gas system; the opportunity was also taken to re-locate the feed system from the side to the top of the receiver. From that evolved the T161 series, originally chambered for the 0.30-06 cartridge. Alterations such as re-placing the wooden furniture by plastics and adapting the weapon to fire the 7.62 mm × 51 NATO cartridge eventually re-sulted in the T161E3, and it was this version that was adopted to become the US Army's new general-purpose machine gun, the 7.62 mm Machine Gun M60.

The above account is a much simplified rendering of the transition from post-1945 concept to late 1950s production model. In between came many time-consuming and expensive hitches and changes of require-ments to the extent that the end result ended up satisfying few. It was an early and classic case of too many fingers in the pie.

For all its dignified antecedents and all the trouble taken by the US Army auth-orities involved, the M60 is an awkward and bulky machine gun with several unde-sirable features. Although described as a 'lightweight' weapon, the gun alone weighs 10.51 kg. Add to that a belt of ammunition and the weapon becomes something of a load to handle as a light machine gun. The load is not helped by the dangling ammuni-tion belt which looks good on 'Rambo' Hollywood epics but in more practical terms is prone to catch on anything in the vicinity or to drag through dirt or water. Although there is provision for supporting an ammunition box on the side of the receiver, it appears to be little used. Extra ammunition belts were usually carried over the shoulder by every man in a section during the Vietnam conflict, with one man in each section being responsible for organ-ising and carrying the extra belts to the two-man team handling the gun.

Being an air-cooled weapon the M60's barrel has to be changed at intervals – but not just the barrel is changed. As it is removed the bipod and the forward part of the gas cylinder come away as well. To add to this there is no barrel handle, as there is

The 7.62 mm M60 general-purpose machine gun.

Above *A US Army military policeman manning a 7.62 mm M60 machine gun on a vehicle mounting.*

Below *An Australian soldier manning a 7.62 mm M60 machine gun – note the special blank-firing barrel.*

Debussing from an Australian Army M113 armoured personnel carrier - the soldier in the hatchway is carrying a 7.62 mm M60 machine gun while the one on the right is armed with a 9 mm F1 sub-machine gun.

on just about every other similar weapon's barrel-change system (the M60's carrying handle was secured to the receiver and proved to be too light and flimsy for the purpose of carrying the weapon under combat conditions), so the M60 gunner (or his assistant) has to carry and use an asbestos glove to handle a hot barrel during the changing procedure. At the same time he has somehow to keep the forward part of the weapon off the ground. There is also the problem that the second man of the usual two- or three-man M60 team has the added burden of carrying around the extra weight of the bipod and gas cylinder for no useful reason. This factor, among others, was one of the main reasons why within many US Army units the M60 was often known simply as the 'pig'. It should, however, be said that the term was also used as one of approval as well as derision, for many soldiers came to rely upon the potential firepower of the M60 during the Vietnam campaigns.

Many designers have criticised other detail design aspects of the M60, the rear sights being one item that is usually mentioned (due to the small size of the figures used for the range settings); the sighting system also comes under criticism as all zeroing has to be carried out on the rear sight alone.

To counter all these negative points, there are some good features on the M60. For a start, most US Army troops will not hear a word against their M60s, although those who have handled the machine guns used by NATO or other nations usually express some grudging reservations. The gun is sturdy and the barrels, being stellite-lined, have a long life. The overall construction is good and makes use of some metal stampings and plastics. Handling as a portable weapon is regarded as adequate, as the large forestock provides a good grip. When carried the folded bipod legs are also well shaped to provide a good hand purchase. Neither of these handling points detracts from the basic point that the M60 is awkward and bulky compared to many of its contemporaries.

Nearly all the criticisms highlighted here

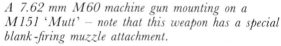

A 7.62 mm M60 machine gun mounting on a M151 'Mutt' – note that this weapon has a special blank-firing muzzle attachment.

An M60 machine gun team covering troops landing from a UH-1D Huey helicopter.

are of little importance when the M60 is mounted as a fire support weapon on the Machine Gun Tripod Mount M122. Barrel changing has to be carried out at regular intervals; each M60 team usually carries three barrels. Even when using a glove, barrel changing on a tripod is much less of a problem than when the M60 is used as a portable weapon. The ammunition belts can be more readily controlled and the bulk of the weapon becomes immaterial.

Many of the M60's drawbacks came to prominence during the weapon's first real trial under combat conditions. Vietnam experiences rammed home all the points mentioned above and many others as well, so

the M60 once again entered the American development maze for yet more trials, experimentation and the subsequent modifications. The end result had no fewer than 12 major modifications incorporated, plus more minor changes as well.

To the soldier the most obvious and welcome change was to the barrel change system, which did away with the need to remove the bipod and gas cylinder as well as the barrel. The whole front end of the M60 was altered to achieve this and the gas cylinder was itself the subject of many modifications, usually directed to making the components simpler and more durable. The ammunition feed system was also much modified and simplified, while minor modifications extended to such topics as the sling swivel locations.

With all the modifications incorporated the M60 became the M60E1, but arriving at that stage took considerable effort and a great deal of money. Then once again the quirks of the American weapon development establishment intruded. Despite the fact that all the M60E1 changes were approved, the M60E1 was not in the end adopted for service. Thus the M60 soldiers on in its original form.

The M60E1 was not adopted by the US Army mainly because by the time it was ready the provision of two different ammunition calibres, 5.56 and 7.62 mm, within each infantry unit and sub-unit was seen to be an unnecessary logistical complication. It would be far better to standardise on the 5.56 mm and for this an entirely new Squad Automatic Weapon (SAW) would be required. After the usual series of lengthy and intensive trials that lasted even longer than usual, even for the American way of doing things, the SAW eventually adopted was the M249, the FN Minimi (see chapter 6). Thus the demise of the M60 as a portable light machine gun was seen to be imminent and all the effort lavished to produce the M60E1 had apparently been for nothing. The M60 is now employed mainly in the tripod-mounted fire support role by the US Army.

However, some of the M60E1 work was incorporated into an M60 variant known as the M60E3. This was largely developed by SACO Defence Inc, now a subsidiary of the Chamberlain Manufacturing Corporation but for long a subsidiary of the Maremont Corporation, the organisation responsible for the bulk of the M60 production run. With demand for the M60 largely met, they decided to produce a lighter version incorporating all the modifications intended for the M60E1, and thus turn the M60 into something like a 7.62 mm Squad Automatic Weapon.

The M60E3 is marginally lighter and shorter than the M60, but the main recognition feature is the foregrip under the barrel and the less prominent bipod located much further back. The carrying handle has been beefed up and can now be used to remove the barrel. There are many other detail changes to the trigger mechanism, the sights and the gas system, which has been simplified. Apart from these changes the M60 and M60E3 are much the same and any soldier familiar with the M60 will be able to cope with the M60E3.

So far only the US Navy and Marine Corps have adopted the M60E3 and it was observed in action during the 1991 Gulf conflict. The US Marine Corps refer to the M60E3 as the 'Echo 3' and intend to convert their existing M60E3s to the Echo 3 HB (Heavy Barrel) configuration using their own workshop facilities and kits supplied by SACO. Apart from the new heavy barrel, which will enable the M60E3 to be fired over longer periods before a barrel change is necessary, the kits include a revised foregrip and some other changes intended to make the M60E3 easier to carry and use in action.

At one stage SACO intended to produce a lightweight 'Universal Machine Gun'

The 7.62 mm M60E3 lightweight machine gun, known to the US Marine Corps as the 'Echo 3'.

based on the M60E3 and involving possible employment as a co-axial weapon, but that project was terminated.

Apart from the M60E3 there are other variants of the M60. In common with the general practice of making any general-purpose machine gun fulfil as many roles as possible, the M60 has been adapted to act as a combat vehicle co-axial machine gun. This variant is known as the M60E2 and differs from the basic M60 in many respects. Starting at the muzzle, the barrel is lengthened by an extension tube and contains a flash suppressor. Modifications to the gas cylinder prevent any possible escape of propellant gases to pollute the atmosphere inside an armoured vehicle turret, and there is no provision for a bipod. The trigger mechanism is replaced by a remote control fixture and there is no butt. The M60E2 has been mounted on the US Marine Corps's M60A1 main battle tank since 1977; its configuration varies according to the vehicle involved.

There are two further M60 variants, the M60C and the M60D. The former is intended for fixed mountings on helicopters,

has no butt and is equipped with a electrical solenoid-actuated remote firing system; there was a similar M60CA1 intended for use on light aircraft but it appears to have been withdrawn. The M60D has the butt removed and replaced with a spade grip trigger system for use on pintle or pedestal mountings, possibly on vehicles but mainly for firing through helicopter side hatches. The M60D has been extensively deployed on helicopters such as the UH-1D and UH-1H 'Huey', the UH-60 and the CH-47D Chinook. Other applications include light naval patrol craft and vessels used for 'riverine' operations. If required, the M60D can be dismounted and fired from its bipod as a normal field weapon.

The M60 series of machine guns have evolved into reliable and sturdy weapons, but the old undesirable features still persist. Australia, Taiwan and South Korea are among the main overseas users although smaller quantities have been delivered to the Cameroons, Egypt, El Salvador and Ecuador. The latter has a few M60Ds mounted on UH-1D helicopters while the Cameroons use their small number of M60s

An early helicopter mounting for a 7.62 mm M60C machine gun.

The M60D version of the basic M60 machine gun, intended to be pintle-mounted on helicopters or ground vehicles.

as armament for light patrol vessels. Taiwan has been licence-producing the M60 since 1968, using machinery imported from the United States; it is used by the Taiwanese armed forces as the Type 57.

M73

Following on from the saga of the M60, the M73 machine gun story provides yet another example of a convoluted development and service history. The M73 is not a field weapon but was designed from the outset to be a co-axial machine gun nestling in the restricted space between the breech ring and mantlet of the then new M60 main battle tank. The restricted area necessarily dictated the compact dimensions of what was to become the M73 but there were other considerations involved.

Most armoured vehicle co-axial weapons are usually adaptations of ground-use machine guns, and as such they either have to incorporate substantial modifications for their specialised role or they lack some requirement or other that is unique to the co-axial machine gun. One of the most important of these requirements is that no propellant gases should leak into the confined atmosphere of the armoured vehicle interior; the gases normally released when firing a ground-use machine gun are seldom detectable in the open air but the

same volume of gas released into a closed-down turret could rapidly disable the crew. Another requirement for a co-axial weapon is that it should take up as little room inside the turret as possible, where space is at a premium. Other requirements are the ability to feed ammunition from the right or left and the ability to change barrels without having to remove the machine gun from its position to any great extent or having to dismantle the turret in the process.

The US Army requirement for a purpose-built co-axial machine gun was first put forward in 1950. Research and development work on the project proceeded until 1953 when one of the usual American development system hazards arose and work was suspended until 1956. Once work resumed, hardware was ready by early 1958.

Four different proposals were put forward by the Springfield Armoury, one of which, known as the T197, was selected for further development. This weapon owed its origins to an Australian designer who had worked on the basic design concept at the Royal Small Arms Factory at Enfield, in the United Kingdom, before taking it to the United States, where the design was further developed to become the T197.

Unlike many of its contemporaries, the T197 was recoil-operated in order to keep down gas emissions, and had a fire rate reduction unit producing a relatively low rate of fire to again ensure that fumes were removed from the barrel and chamber before the breech lock was opened. One important feature of the T197 was that the body could be rotated on a hinge to left or right to replace the barrel when necessary.

The T197 proved to be a complex device that required a great deal of further work before it could be accepted for service. One source of concern was the sideways-operating breech block which complicated the ramming of a cartridge for loading. Spent case extraction and ejection after firing was another source of development delay, but by the middle of May 1959 the T197, which by then had reached the T197E2 stage, was accepted for service as the 7.62 mm Tank Machine Gun M73. Production began during 1960.

Even then the M73 proved to be not completely satisfactory and a revised extraction system was developed to produce the M73E1, subsequently the M73A1. Other changes added at the M73E1 stage included a revised mounting and an extended stellite liner for the barrel. Existing M73s were partially retrofitted to convert them to near M73E1 standard but even then the ejection system had to be revised yet further to produce an entirely new 'M' number, the M219. Externally the M73 and M219 are identical and differ only in detail internally.

There was one further M73 variant, the XM161, proposed in 1966 and having the M73A1's fire rate control system removed to improve reliability under Arctic conditions. It was not, however, accepted for service.

The M73/M219 series were used as the co-axial machine guns for the initial versions of the US Army's M60 tank series, and with production proceeding for the intended purpose, the quirks of the American small arms development establishment once again intruded to produce one of the odder side-shows of the American machine gun scene. Having spent a great deal of time and money developing and producing this purpose-built co-axial machine gun for armoured vehicles, it was then proposed to produce a flexible variant of the M73 for ground use only. The result was the M73C, an M73 modified by adding sights and a spade grip trigger mechanism. There was even a special tripod developed for the new variant, the XM132. Fortunately reason appears to have prevailed and only a few M73Cs were manufactured, although those few did see action in Vietnam.

Production of the M73/M219 ceased some years ago, and those in service will gradually be replaced by either the M60E2 (see under M60 above) or the M240 version of the Belgian FN MAG (see chapter 6). Thus there is currently a period when the US armed forces have not just one standard 7.62 mm co-axial machine gun in service, but three or even four if the dwindling numbers of old 0.30 M37 co-axial weapons are taken into account.

The 7.62 mm M73 co-axial machine gun – the M73A1 and M219 are visually identical.

More Brownings

The story of the Browning machine guns was outlined in chapter 2, but the history of one example from the Browning range is far from over. While the earlier 0.30/7.62 mm Browning machine guns have largely faded from the scene or are at best serving out their old age with dignity, the story of the 0.50/12.7 mm M2 HB heavy machine gun continues with no apparent sign of any halt to its long and distinguished history.

The explanation for this continuing state of affairs was provided in chapter 2, but there have been attempts over recent years to somehow 'improve' the M2 HB. The reasons are not all that hard to discover, for the Browning machine guns have always been complex pieces of machinery that can require some looking after by skilled armourers, and with a few features, such as weight and bulk, that are now considered undesirable. Hence the constant attempts to 'gild the lily'. Unfortunately for all those concerned, all the various gilding projects have largely come to naught.

The Second World War years saw many trial projects based on the Browning M2, mainly directed towards making the weapon more suitable for the demands of modern air warfare. Numerous trials models with increased rates of fire, different barrel lengths and weights, improved mechanisms, and so on, came and went, but the end results were few, other than the AN-M2 and AN-M3, both of which were aircraft weapons with increased rates of fire.

Development projects involving the M2 continued after 1945. The T42 was yet another aircraft gun that came to naught, while the M85, mentioned in chapter 2, was a more successful project that produced a co-axial and cupola gun for armoured vehicles.

However, a more novel approach to the M2 was undertaken by industry. At one point during the early 1980s it was thought that a lightened version of the M2 would prove attractive to many potential customers, including the US Marine Corps,

and the commercial designers got to work, with two concerns, SACO and RAMO, producing actual hardware.

SACO Defense Inc produced their new lightweight M2 under two names, the 'Fifty/.50' or the General Purpose Heavy Machine Gun (GPHMG, not to be confused with the project covered in the following entry). The project took three years to complete but at the end of it all SACO's 'M2' weighed nearly 15 kg less than the original and had several new features added. One obvious place from where weight had been pared was the barrel, which appears to be much thinner than on the M2 HB. It has a muzzle brake added and the bore is chrome lined to reduce wear and thus reduce the heat produced when firing. To assist cooling, the SACO GPHMG barrel has a quick-change feature involving a bayonet type fitting that also does away with the perennial need for cartridge head space adjustment. A carrying handle has also been added. Much of the weight reduction has been achieved by liberal use of light high-strength alloys in place of the heavier steel used on the original. Many of the components used in the SACO GPHMG can be interchanged with standard M2 HB parts, although some of them will introduce a weight penalty.

The RAMO lightweight M2 follows much the same general lines as the SACO model. Lightweight alloys have been introduced where possible, the barrel has a quick-change feature and is also stellite-lined, and a flash suppressor has been added to the muzzle. One added feature is an adjustable buffer that allows the rate of fire to be varied.

The SACO and RAMO lightweight M2s can fire all the usual 0.50/12.7 mm ammunition, including the saboted SLAP, and can utilise all the usual tripods and other mountings employed by the standard M2 HB. However, although both designs are stated to be in production, neither appears to have met with much sales success so far. Instead, both concerns continue to manufacture the standard M2 HB along with

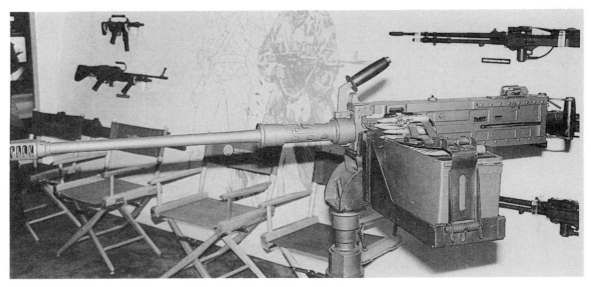

The SACO GPHMG lightweight version of the Browning 0.50/12.7 mm M2.

parts, mountings and special kits such as quick-change barrel conversions for retrofitting to existing M2 HBs.

GPHMG

During the late 1970s a series of US Army ordnance authority meetings drew up a possible requirement for a new 0.50/12.7 mm heavy machine gun which would eventually replace the in-service M2 and M85 models. The resultant development programme became known as the General Purpose Heavy Machine Gun (GPHMG) project.

Two design approaches emerged. The early stages of the project were confused, with at least one design being based on the M60, and produced in at least two forms, one having the same general layout as the M60, complete with pistol trigger group, and the other used spade grips. Much of the original work was carried out by the US Army Armament Research and Development Command (AARADCOM) based at Dover, New Jersey, and the AAI Corporation of Baltimore. The original M60-based work was eventually by-passed by a completely new approach known as the 'Dover Devil'.

The Dover Devil was an air-cooled gas-operated weapon with a modular design to assist maintenance and featuring a dual-feed mechanism that allowed two belts to be fed into the weapon, one from the right, the other from the left. The feed was so arranged that two different ammunition natures could be held ready for use, eg ball or armour-piercing, and the gunner could select which ammunition to fire by the flick of a selection switch. This concept was not original, having already been used on many previous experimental machine guns and cannon, some dating back to wartime German developments. Maremont had attempted to produce a similarly-equipped 7.62 mm co-axial weapon for armoured vehicles back in the early 1970s, but that project had faded away by the end of that decade.

The Dover Devil was originally a 20 mm cannon project scaled down to 0.50/12.7 mm for the GPHMG programme. The modular design was based on a receiver formed basically around two tubes inside which were two gas pistons to operate all the various mechanisms. Compared to the Browning M2, the weight of the Dover Devil was almost halved, the number of parts was much reduced and it was considered that the

The original 0.50/12.7 mm 'Dover Devil' heavy machine gun.

gun had considerable potential.

Then the whole project was suspended, apparently for lack of funds and for the reason that the M2 HB, and its stable-mate the M85, were still carrying out their tasks perfectly satisfactorily. The advantages offered by the Dover Devil were not considered to be all that significant to warrant any drastic change of procurement, so the project faded although the overall concept lasted a little while longer.

The AAI Corporation carried on further development work on the GPHMG and some changes were introduced, noticeably around the receiver module which was altered to be formed around three tubular units to add strength and reduce manufacturing costs. Alterations were also made to the feed to improve reliability, and some components were simplified.

It was all to no avail. The AAI GPHMG is theoretically still available but all further

The AAI version of the 0.50/12.7 mm General Purpose Heavy Machine Gun.

Above *A close-up of the dual feed system used on the AA1 0.50/12.7 mm GPHMG.*

Below *The final version of the 0.50/12.7 mm General Purpose Heavy Machine Gun.*

development and marketing appears to have been suspended, although the 0.50/12.7 mm 50MG heavy machine gun produced by Chartered Industries of Singapore appears to owe much to work carried out on the GPHMG project (see chapter 12).

M16 off-shoots

The 5.56 mm AR-15/M16 rifle series has for long had heavy-barrelled variants in one form or another. Most of them have been little more than the basic rifle with a heavier barrel and the addition of a light bipod. Typical of these was the Colt CAR-15 HBAR (heavy barrel assault rifle) M1, which fired from an open bolt and could be fitted with two- or three-round burst control devices. A few of these were purchased by the US Army for trials but no major adoption resulted. The HBAR M2 was an experimental version with a belt feed, but that project did not proceed far either.

The main drawback with these ultra-light machine guns was, as ever, that their automatic firing capability was severely limited by their ammunition feed capacity (other than on the HBAR M2) and the limited ability of their fixed barrels to absorb heat. Once again they were little more than machine rifles.

A late 1960s attempt to overcome the drawbacks of the machine rifle approach involved the Colt 5.56 mm CMG-1 and CMG-2. The latter featured a 150-round drum magazine, a quick-change barrel system and some interesting detail design features. However, the CMG proposals met with little interest and the whole project was quietly shelved.

Nevertheless the notion of a heavy-barrelled M16 variant persisted. By the late 1980s another approach was attempted with Colt's HBAR M16 which was a much more drastic re-modelling of the basic M16 rifle. This time the main change was to the foregrip which was made much larger and

The Colt 5.56 mm M16 HBAR (Heavy Barrel Assault Rifle).

square in cross-section to improve heat dissipation from the barrel. An M60 bipod was attached under the muzzle and a foregrip added. With the arrival on the scene of the M16A2 series of assault rifles the weapon was revised slightly to become the Colt M16A2 Light Machine Gun, or M16A2 LMG.

The M16A2 LMG has a heavier barrel than the standard M16A2 rifle and fires from an open bolt. The M60-type bipod originally used on the HBAR M16 has been replaced by a smaller and lighter equivalent, the foregrip is now a rudimentary post, and a carrying handle is located over the prominent hand guard. Internally a hydraulic buffer has been added to reduce the recoil forces and maintain the cyclic rate of fire at between 600 and 750 rounds per minute when firing bursts.

Despite its designation, the M16A2 LMG

The complete Stoner 63 family formed from a few basic components.

is still a machine rifle. It does not have a barrel-change system and its ammunition capacity is limited to the standard 30-round M16 box magazine. To some extent the latter situation can be overcome by the use of one or other of the commercially available high-capacity magazines specifically developed for use with 5.56 mm weapons; these include designs such as the American C-MAG, with its twin-drum arrangement that can hold 100 rounds, and the MWG 90-round drum magazine. Other such magazines have been proposed by commercial concerns.

To date sales of the M16A2 LMG appear to have been few. A semi-automatic (single shot only) version intended for possible use by police and para-military organisations has also been developed.

ARES

Eugene Stoner was one of the principals involved in the design and development of the series of rifles that led to the revolutionary 5.56 mm AR-15 rifle and thence to the M16 that was adopted by the US armed forces. Following the experience gained, and wishing to develop some of his ideas further, Stoner established a link with Cadillac Gage and, working within this organisation, he led a team that developed what was to become the Stoner 63 System.

Stoner was once a Marine and has his own ideas as to what weapons front-line soldiers should use in combat. One of his most dramatic ideas has been to create a whole series of weapons based on only a few basic components. By adding to these components the basics could be used to create almost any type of automatic small arm that might be required. Originally produced to fire the 7.62 mm × 51 cartridge, the Stoner 63 System fired the 5.56 mm × 45 round.

Stoner's basic components were a receiver (mainly manufactured from steel pressings), a bolt and piston assembly, a return spring and a trigger group. To these could be added various lengths and weights of barrel, box magazine or belt feed mech-

The Stoner 5.56 mm belt-fed machine gun, part of the Stoner 63 System.

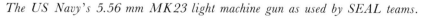

anisms, and butts to create a whole family of weapons. The Stoner 63 System originally encompassed an assault rifle, a shorter assault carbine, a light machine gun with magazine feed (referred to as an automatic rifle), a light machine gun with belt feed, a medium machine gun and a fixed (or co-axial) machine gun. The System was later split into two groups, the rifle group and the machine gun group.

All these weapons used the same rotary bolt mechanism as the AR-15/M16 rifle series. The light machine guns operated using a conventional gas-operated system and could use either a top-mounted 30-round M16-type box magazine or a belt feed from a box holding up to 150 rounds. A quick-change barrel system was incorporated. To convert the light machine gun for the medium role, the belt-fed version was placed on a tripod with the butt removed. The fixed, or co-axial, version was placed on a vehicle mounting, also with the butt removed.

The most advanced weapon in the Stoner machine gun group was the light machine gun which was developed into a version on which the belt-fed version was rearranged

The US Navy's 5.56 mm MK23 light machine gun as used by SEAL teams.

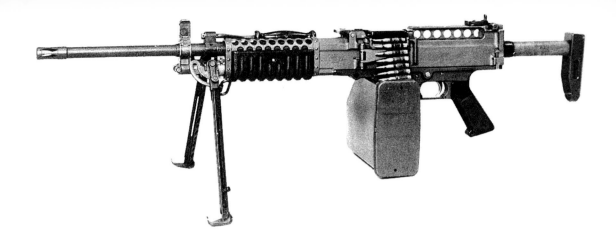

The standard version of the ARES light machine gun fitted with a 200-round belt box.

so that the feed mechanism, and the associated ammunition box secured under the receiver, could feed from the right instead of the left. It was this component of the Stoner 63 System that achieved most success, small numbers being acquired by the US Marine Corps as the XM207 and by the US Navy as their MK 23, both in 5.56 mm. The US Navy MK 23s were used by SEAL special forces teams in Vietnam, yet despite the good reports passed back by the SEALs, no more of these weapons were acquired by the US armed forces and, despite considerable efforts to create interest within Europe, the Stoner 63 System appears to have quietly passed from view.

Following a series of corporate moves, the Stoner designs passed into the hands of ARES Inc of Port Clinton, Ohio, who are still promoting a light machine gun based on the Stoner designs but considerably up-

dated. ARES refer to their model simply as the ARES 5.56 mm Light Machine Gun. It visually resembles the earlier Stoner weapons and retains the same modular construction techniques but has a number of updates, mainly involving the introduction of corrosion-proofed materials, including stainless steel and aluminium. To make use of as many existing accessories as possible, the ARES gun can accommodate items originally intended for the M16 rifle, the M60 machine gun and the M249 co-axial machine gun.

The ARES Light Machine Gun is fed by a 100- or 200-round belt held in an ammunition container (also used by the M73/M219 co-axial machine guns) slung under the receiver, as on the Stoner original. One feature of the ARES weapon is that the butt can be removed and a shorter barrel fitted (by making use of the barrel

A lightweight version of the ARES light machine gun fitted with a box magazine feed and with a muzzle compensator installed.

quick-change system) to convert the weapon into a hip-fired light assault machine gun. In this form, and with a 200-round ammunition belt loaded, the weapon weighs only 7.02 kg.

The ARES Light Machine Gun can be supplied to fire either SS 109 or M193 5.56 mm ammunition. It can also be converted to box magazine feed.

The exact present-day status of the ARES Light Machine Gun is uncertain. Reports mention low-rate production but for whom is not known.

DATA

Model	M60	M60E3
Calibre	7.62 mm	7.62 mm
Weight (gun only)	10.51 kg	8.61 kg
Length	1.105 m	1.067 m
Length of barrel	560 mm	560 mm
Rate of fire	550 rpm	550 rpm
Feed	belt	belt
Muzzle velocity	855 m/s	855 m/s
Model	M73/219	SACO Fifty/.50
Calibre	7.62 mm	12.7 mm
Weight (gun only)	14 kg	25 kg
Length	889 mm	1.56 m
Length of barrel	559 mm	914 mm
Rate of fire	500-625 rpm	500-725 rpm
Feed	belt	belt
Muzzle velocity	855 m/s	850 m/s
Model	RAMO M2 Lightweight	AAI GPHMG
Calibre	12.7 mm	12.7 mm
Weight (gun only)	26.72 kg	24.95 kg
Length	1.524 m	1.549 m
Length of barrel	914 mm	n/a
Rate of fire	550-750 rpm	400 rpm
Feed	belt	dual belt
Muzzle velocity	866 m/s	865 m/s
Model	M16A2 LMG	ARES
Calibre	5.56 mm	5.56 mm
Weight (gun only)	5.78 kg	5.37 kg*
Length	1 m	810 mm*
Length of barrel	510 mm	550 mm*
Rate of fire	600-750 rpm	600 rpm
Feed	30-round box	belt
Muzzle velocity	990 m/s	945 m/s
		*standard model

CHAPTER 20

ROTARIES, CHAINS AND OPEN CHAMBERS

WHEN the machine gun first appeared on the battlefield it was sufficient that the weapon should simply go on firing for as long as the trigger mechanism was engaged. The actual rate of fire in rounds per minute was secondary, although some of the early machine guns, and even the contemporary manually powered Gatling guns, could achieve cyclic rates of fire of approaching 1,000 rounds per minute.

However, some perceptive soldiers noted that very high rates of fire were seldom needed; too high a rate often meant that too many bullets were being directed towards a target when one or two would suffice. Therefore too high a rate of fire from a machine gun would simply waste ammunition against most of the battlefield targets likely to be engaged. In fact, some theorists calculated that an ideal cyclic rate of fire for the infantry machine gun was between 400 and 550 rounds per minute (almost exactly the rate of fire of most of the 'classic' machine guns such as the Browning 0.50/12.7 mm M2 HB and the British 0.303 Vickers gun).

These 'ideal' fire rates applied only when the machine gun was employed against ground targets. Once the aeroplane became a viable war machine everything changed.

Early fighter pilots noted to their cost that in air-to-air (and even air-to-ground) engagements, targets were captured in their sights only for fleeting seconds, during which period there was little chance to loose off more than a few rounds, which all too often involved rifle or small-calibre projectiles, so the chances of inflicting any significant damage on the target were remote unless a lucky shot hit a vulnerable area.

One immediate and simple solution was to increase the number of weapons involved. Twin-gun aircraft mountings, with two machine guns placed side-by-side on a common frame, became commonplace and doubled the available firepower. By the Second World War some fighters used massed batteries of up to eight rifle-calibre machine guns mounted in the aircraft's wings (such as on the immortal Spitfire and Hurricane of 1940) or nose. In addition, the war witnessed a definite trend towards heavier aircraft machine gun calibres to the extent that 20 mm automatic cannon were widely used by 1945, and some advanced aircraft sported even heavier calibre automatic weapons.

However, the basic problem grew even more critical. Aircraft targets still remained in weapon sights for mere fractions of a second and even those instances grew shorter as aircraft performances increased by leaps and bounds with the introduction of the jet engine. The problem still remained that automatic weapons somehow had to increase the number of rounds that could be fired once a target appeared in the sights if there was to be any chance of inflicting worthwhile damage to an enemy.

Designers had for long been attempting to increase the rate of fire of their progeny for aircraft installations. To quote but one example, throughout the Second World War the Browning 0.50/12.7 mm M2 was the subject of numerous attempts to somehow increase the rate of fire. Among the few end results of these costly exercises were the Browning AN-M2 and AN-M3, with the latter attaining up to 1,250 rounds per minute. These increases were, however, purchased at a cost, for at these fire rates the mechanical stresses involved were such that key components were constantly operating at or near a critical load and could break or malfunction at the slightest excuse.

Designers also strove to produce entirely new aircraft weapons with high rates of fire but almost always had to revert to attempts to somehow enhance existing machine gun mechanisms and concepts. After 1945 their researches became increasingly frustrated as the existing recoil, muzzle-energy and gas-operated machine gun systems proved to be inherently unable to meet the ever-increasing demands for higher and yet higher rates of fire.

It was time for a drastically new approach to machine gun design.

Paradoxically, one of the first successful attempts to produce a quantum leap in machine gun fire rates involved one of the very first viable sustained fire weapons ever developed. That weapon was the Gatling gun.

Project Vulcan

The Gatling gun had seemingly been relegated to the dustbin of history by the advent of the Maxim gun. At the time of its introduction the latter was much smaller and lighter than the Gatlings of the time and required no manual effort to make it operate. Despite some sterling sales efforts to prolong its commercial life the Gatling gun was soon relegated either to the scrap heap or to the storeroom; nearly all had vanished as military weapons by 1914.

There it seemed the Gatling gun story ended. However, it was really about to start all over again on a scale never envisaged by its originator, for after 1945 the Gatling principle was taken down from the shelf and re-examined to determine its potential as a means of providing automatic weapons with high cyclic rates of fire for aircraft use. The main change to the Gatling methods of old was that the post-1945 designers were thinking in terms of using external power sources to drive the Gatling mechanism.

As happens so often in mechanical engineering history, the notion of harnessing an external power source to the Gatling gun was not new. As early as 1893 an electric motor had been harnessed to a Gatling gun with the result that a surprising 3,000 rounds per minute was achieved. The fact was duly recorded but nothing further came of the project.

However, in 1945 it seems that the 1893 results came to light once more, for in that year the US Army funded a research project to determine if the Gatling principle could be adapted to meet modern high fire rate requirements for aircraft guns. The project demonstrated that the notion looked very promising so the next stage involved actually combining an old Model 1883 0.45-inch Gatling gun with an electric motor driving the normally manually operated crank. During tests the gun and electric motor combination developed a theoretical cyclic rate of fire of no less than 5,800 rounds per minute, even though bursts of no more than 50 rounds were involved at any one time.

In June 1945 General Electric were given the task of developing an externally powered 20 mm aircraft gun using the Gatling principle. The programme was known as 'Project Vulcan' and, via the developmental T45 and T171 series of guns, the resultant weapon became known as the M61 Vulcan.

For all its modernity, the Vulcan embodied exactly the same mechanical principles as the original manually operated Gatling guns. On the Vulcan gun a cluster of 20 mm barrels, usually six, were arranged to revolve horizontally around a central pivot using power from an electric motor. Rounds were fed one at a time from a magazine into the feed mechanism and from thence into a position behind one of the barrels. As that barrel rotated a cam and cam follower system ensured that the cartridge was pushed into the barrel chamber, fired, and the empty case extracted ready for the re-loading process to start again as the barrel was driven round to its original position. The system allowed time for the barrels and chambers to cool to a safe level between each firing, even at the high rates of fire involved on the Vulcan guns, although prolonged bursts would have resulted in barrel overheating.

One great advantage of the Gatling gun principle is that the mechanism is not dependent on the ammunition for its operation. On any conventional machine gun, if a round fails to fire for some reason or another the mechanism ceases to function further and the malfunctioning round has to be cleared by hand, usually by manually re-cocking (re-charging) the weapon. On the Gatling gun any malfunctioning cartridge is simply driven out of the gun and it continues to operate.

Modern rotary guns can be powered either electrically or, in a few cases, hydraulically. Most installations use drives provided by compact high-technology electric motors that derive their power from the carrier aircraft's or helicopter's own systems. The motors involved are sealed to retain their inherent reliability. Using electricity also means that varying the drive motor speed will also vary the gun's rate of fire. Most rotary guns have a control device

to vary the fire rate infinitely as required, while some have a switch that will automatically select a pre-determined rate, eg 3,000 or 6,000 rounds per minute.

Using electrical power for the gun often means that the same power source can be utilised to drive the often highly complex ammunition systems involved with rotary guns. However, the mechanical loads involved are considerable and are such that, as a rotary gun trigger is pressed, it can take a finite amount of time before the gun is operating at its full firing rate – the same applies when the trigger is released. In theory the gun will continue to fire until the system brakes to a halt. In practice, however, the times involved are minimal and are measured in fractions of a second.

Early Project Vulcan guns were able to attain the projected 6,000 rounds per minute, and subsequent development was directed mainly to reducing weight and improving the reliability of the components. By 1957 the M61 was in production, and production of the improved version, the M61A1 still continues.

Throughout its service life the six-barrelled M61A1 has proved to be a thoroughly reliable and efficient weapon, and has been deployed on many aircraft types involving pod, fixed internal and flexible tail mountings. Adaptations have also been introduced to enable the Vulcan gun to become a naval weapon, as on the autonomous Phalanx anti-ship missile close-in defence weapon system. There are also Vulcan-based towed and vehicle-mounted air defence weapons; for the latter role the basic M61A1 was adapted to become the 20 mm M168 gun mounted on the towed M167A1 Vulcan Air Defense System, or VADS – there is also a self-propelled version carried on M113 armoured personnel carriers. The latest versions of the VADS involve laser rangefinders and modern tracking radars. In addition, Vulcan guns have been mounted on helicopters and gunships. There is also a three-barrelled version known as the M197E1.

The high rate of fire of the 20 mm Vulcan

guns, typically 6,000 rounds per minute (ie 100 rounds every second), has been such that special and highly-advanced methods of getting ammunition into the gun have had to be devised. These feed systems are a subject of study in themselves as the ingenuity and technical accomplishments of the mechanisms involved have to be seen to be believed. For most Vulcan gun installations some form of drum is involved, inside which linkless rounds are driven towards the gun via 'Archimedes screw' helical slots. These drum systems can hold thousands of rounds ready to fire but, such is the power of the Vulcan gun, most of these drums can be emptied in only a few bursts.

The Vulcan guns are 20 mm weapons, and from them have originated a whole family of rotary weapons, some of which were nothing more than trial weapons in odd calibres. Other rotary guns have been produced with calibres of 20, 25 and 30 mm, but they are really outside the scope of this book and deserve a study of their own. The first of the rotary machine guns that falls within the calibre confines of this book is the 7.62 mm Minigun.

Minigun

Once the 20 mm Vulcan gun was in full-scale production development attentions were diverted towards producing a rifle calibre variant. The first studies, funded by the US Air Force and conducted by General Electric, commenced during 1960, and by late 1962 the first hardware was undergoing firing tests. By 1964 the new weapon was used in combat for the first time as the 7.62 mm GAU-2B/A Minigun, firing the NATO 7.62 mm × 51 round. The same weapon is known to the US Army as

Head-on view of a 7.62 mm Minigun.

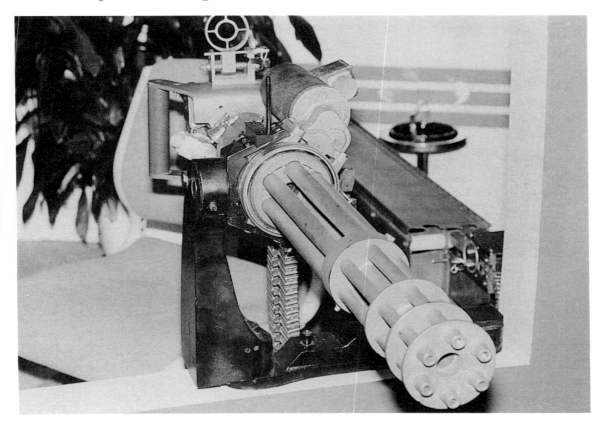

the 7.62 mm M134 Minigun.

The six-barrelled Minigun is a scaled-down version of the 20 mm Vulcan gun and differs mainly, apart from the dimensions, in using mechanical firing pins to fire the 7.62 mm cartridges instead of the electrical ignition used for the 20 mm rounds. The cyclic rate of fire produced is 6,000 rounds a minute, the same as that of the 20 mm Vulcan, although on some installations this is variable or can be reduced to an optional 3,000 rounds a minute by simply operating a switch. The Minigun can use either linked or linkless ammunition feed systems according to the installation involved.

The first Minigun installation was in

An early (1971) development mounting intended to suspend a flexible 7.62 mm Minigun under a helicopter.

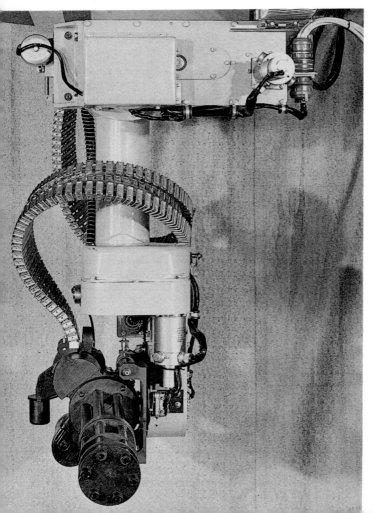

SUU-11/A aircraft pods that could be slung under aircraft wings or on helicopters. However, the first real combat applications for these Minigun pods was actually inside aircraft, having been adapted to be carried inside the rear cabin of the AC-47 on its now-famous 'Puff the Magic Dragon' gunship operations in Vietnam. One AC-47 could carry up to three SUU-11/A pods firing out from one side of the aircraft ('side fire') as it wheeled around a fixed spot on the ground. The combined fire of the three Miniguns proved to be devastating to ground targets, so much so that the gunship concept was later developed to involve larger and heavier aircraft carrying more powerful weapons such as the 20 mm Vulcan and 40 mm Bofors guns. On the AC-47 the early installations, involving the Minigun pod, were found to take up too much space inside the fuselage, so more compact MXU-470/A 'Modules' were developed with vertical drum magazines, each having an increased linkless ammunition capacity of 2,000 rounds.

Fixed internal versions of the Minigun were developed for aircraft use but perhaps the most widespread airborne application of the Minigun (apart from the AC-47s) has been on flexible side-firing mounts on helicopters such as the UH-1B, UH-1H and UH-1N 'Hueys'; for most of these applications the Minigun's rate of fire is reduced to 4,000 rounds per minute. In Vietnam they proved to be highly effective as landing area clearing weapons during airborne assaults. The most extreme of the helicopter-mounted Miniguns was the XM28 chin-mounted turret intended for the UH-1D. This installation contained two Miniguns fed from a single ammunition drum, but it was not approved for service. Rather more prosaic was the XM27E1 Helicopter Weapon System, also known as the HGS-5. This was a Hughes Helicopter mounting carried by an OH-6A light helicopter involving a single Minigun and a box magazine holding 2,000 rounds, the gun having been adapted to fire at rates of either 2,000 or 4,000 rounds a minute; over 1,000

Preparing one of the three SUU-11A pods, each containing one 7.62 mm Minigun, on an AC-47 gunship.

systems were manufactured. Despite the experimental 'X' designation, the XM27E1 system was used in action in Vietnam. Similar installations are still carried by the AH-6 and MH-6 helicopters operated by one of the US Army's Special Operations Groups.

Various ground mountings for the Minigun, including tripods, have been developed and demonstrated, and pintle mountings for light naval vessels and 'riverine' operations craft have been proposed, although to date none appear to have been adopted. The main problem for ground or naval Minigun applications is that some form of power, usually a large battery, has to be involved along with some sort of suitable ammunition storage and feed system. All these extras are likely to be heavy and bulky, probably weighing more than the weapon itself.

Apart from use by the US armed forces, the Minigun is in service with Australia, Canada, Ecuador, El Salvador, Honduras (15), Israel, South Korea, Morocco, Singapore, Spain (at least 20) and Turkey (368).

One odd off-shoot of the Minigun story was a gas-operated version, the XM133. As each barrel was fired, gas was tapped off from one central source to power the usual piston which in turn rotated the central cam system to actuate the mechanism. However, the XM133 proved to be unable to produce the required 6,000 rounds per minute fire rate and also proved to be unreliable, so was abandoned. When one considers the efficiency and reliability of the electrically driven Vulcan, Minigun and other similarly powered rotary guns, one wonders why the XM133 was even considered for investigation unless it was for some unstated ground-based role where the usual drawbacks of electrical power requirements could be overcome.

The Six Pack

Having reduced the 20 mm Vulcan gun design down to 7.62 mm to produce the Minigun, General Electric decided that the next step would be to develop a 5.56 mm version. Using their own funding for the project they did just that, and christened the result the Microgun, although it is widely known as the 'Six Pack', from the number of barrels involved.

The Six Pack is virtually a miniature

Vulcan gun that fires linked or linkless 5.56 mm × 45 ammunition fed from 500-round factory-packed cassettes held in position in pairs by an ammunition rack. The cassettes are so arranged that as the last round from the first cassette is fired it automatically joins up with the first round from the next cassette to maintain a burst uninterrupted.

On the Six Pack the rate of fire is infinitely variable from 400 up to 10,000 rounds per minute, although for most applications the weapon is limited at the top end to 4,000 rounds per minute. It has been demonstrated firing bursts of up to 2,500 rounds at a time. To prevent 'cook-offs' resulting from the heating after-effects of such bursts, the Six Pack loading system automatically clears all rounds from the barrels after each firing. As the Six Pack is intended for use on infantry mountings such as tripods, it can be broken down into two loads for carrying. The length overall is only 686 mm.

The US armed forces trialled the Six Pack and gave it the designation of XM214 Microgun, but to date none have been procured by them or any other armed service. Proposals have been made to place the Six Pack inside an aircraft or helicopter pod, or to mount the weapon on light vessels, but neither of these projects appears to have reached the hardware stage as yet.

The Six Pack appears to have been an example of a weapon produced to meet a tactical requirement that has yet to emerge. At the time of writing it no longer features in current General Electric sales literature.

GECAL 50

The first rotary gun produced to fire the 0.50/12.7 mm round was a six-barrelled test weapon produced in 1970 and known as the GAU-6. At that time the intention was to produce an externally powered rotary weapon for internal installation on tactical strike aircraft that would fire a special 10 mm round – the 0.50/12.7 mm cartridge was used simply for testing until development of the experimental 10 mm round was completed. In the event the requirement for the special 10 mm ammunition was withdrawn and only one GAU-6 gun was manufactured and tested. It was intended that a fully developed 10 mm seven-barrelled gun would have a variable fire rate of up to 10,000 rounds per minute, but the only 0.50/12.7 mm example manufactured had six barrels and was limited to 4,500 rounds per minute by the strength of the ammunition links involved.

During the early 1980s the desirability of producing a 0.50/12.7 mm rotary gun was raised in order to overcome what were seen as shortcomings regarding the 7.62 mm Minigun. Good as the Minigun was (and still is) for many tactical applications, it was felt that more range would be an asset and the ability to have an anti-armour capability would also be an advantage. While the ordinary Browning M2 HB could meet these requirements, it was thought that for the roles envisaged a new weapon with an increased rate of fire and less complexity would be required. The proposal was given extra urgency when nine American helicopters were lost during the 1983 invasion of Grenada, losses that were at least partially attributed to the fact that the helicopters concerned were under-gunned and could not neutralise the opposing ground defences at the ranges involved.

General Electric had been involved in the early stages of developing a 0.50/12.7 mm rotary gun since mid-1982, and the eventual result was the General Electric GECAL 50, an electrically powered rotary gun firing standard 0.50/12.7 mm ammunition (including armour-piercing rounds) and produced in two main forms. Since the GECAL 50 was developed to arm aircraft and helicopters it was felt that a high fire rate was needed, but for less exacting installations a lighter version with fewer barrels and a lower rate of fire would be developed in tandem. The result is that there are two types of GECAL 50: a six-barrelled version delivering up to 8,000 rounds per minute, and a three-barrelled version with its fire

An early three-barrelled version of the General Electric 0.50/12.7 mm GECAL 50.

rate halved to 4,000 rounds per minute. To complicate matters somewhat there are also versions with rates of fire limited to 2,000 and 4,000 rounds per minute (six-barrels), or 1,000 and 2,000 rounds per minute (three barrels). It is intended that the three-bar-relled version is for use mainly on light helicopters and ground-based or naval mountings. Yet more variation is introduced to the GECAL 50 family when barrels of differing lengths become involved.

A later three-barrelled 0.50/12.7 mm GECAL 50 rotary machine gun, now known as the GAU-19.

The first GECAL 50 was produced during 1983 and began an intensive development programme the following year. The first examples were six-barrelled models – the lightweight three-barrel version appeared later.

At one stage it was intended that one of the most important uses of the GECAL 50 would be in a flexible chin-mounted turret fitted to the V-22 Osprey tilt-wing transport aircraft under development for the US Marine Corps. Unfortunately for General Electric this requirement was withdrawn during 1985 after cuts in the defence budget. The long-term chances of reviving the Osprey installation grew even more remote with the withdrawal of funding for the entire V-22 Osprey programme in 1990. An alternative plan to mount the GECAL 50 on the UH-60 Black Hawk helicopter also failed to materialise, leaving General Electric with a still partially developed weapon system on their books and no prospective customers.

The GECAL 50 follows the same general lines as the other General Electric rotary guns. Ammunition is fed into the gun from an ammunition container holding a 750-round belt, the links of which are removed prior to actually feeding the rounds into the gun. The stresses involved in transporting the belt are partially overcome by the use of a booster assembly which helps to drive the ammunition along a flexible metal ammunition chute and into the de-linker assembly.

The easily changed barrels used on the GECAL 50 are chrome-lined but, even so, firing a 200-round burst from a six-barrelled gun at the maximum rate of fire will result in the barrels glowing to red heat. On an airborne installation this will be at least partially overcome by the cooling effect of a slipstream, but on ground or naval mountings some form of burst limiter may well be an advantage.

Examples of the GECAL 50 seen to date rarely have any form of sighting system installed although it seems certain that some form of optical system will have to be developed for ground or naval mountings. An optical reflex sight has been observed on GECAL 50s demonstrated in the United Kingdom.

A three-barrelled GECAL 50 mounted to fire from a side hatch on a Westland/Sikorsky UH-60 Black Hawk helocopter.

A GECAL 50 being fired from a British Longline light strike vehicle.

The development of the GECAL 50 does not appear to have been rewarded by many sales as yet, but the alliance of the well-tried 0.50/12.7 mm ammunition and the rotary gun concept does have its attractions. It could yet emerge that the GECAL 50 will meet with all the sales and tactical success of the 7.62 mm Minigun and the 20 mm Vulcan gun.

Chain Guns

All the rotary guns described above were developed specifically to produce high rates of fire, primarily for aircraft installations, and their main design feature is that they all use an external power source in the form of an electric motor to actually drive their mechanisms. However, they are not the only forms of machine gun to employ exter-

A vehicle-mounted version of the three-barrelled 0.50/12.7 mm GECAL 50 – note the reflex sight.

nal power, for an entirely separate group of automatic weapons are also driven by external power sources. These are collectively known as Chain Guns.

The term Chain Gun is actually a registered trademark, originally belonging to Hughes Helicopters Inc who were taken over to become the McDonnell Douglas Helicopter Company, shortened to MDHC for the purposes of this account.

During 1970 a part of the old Hughes concern, the Hughes Tool Company, commenced the development of an externally driven 7.62 mm co-axial machine gun with approximately the same dimensions as the 7.62 mm M73/M219 tank machine gun. Only one piece of hardware was actually produced, a test bed prototype known as the Externally Powered Armoured Vehicle Machine gun, or EPAM. The intention was that every stage of the EPAM's operation would be precisely driven and timed by an external motor via a gearbox and a cam. The involvement of an external drive system removed the need for the gun's mechanism to rely upon the ammunition to provide the energy to drive everything, so the external motor had much the same function as on the rotary guns. But whereas the rotary guns used the external power to create speed, on the EPAM the intention was to produce exact timings and reliability through the use of a minimal number of components; the rate of fire of the EPAM was planned at around only 550 rounds per minute.

Test firings of the EPAM were conducted and the system was seen to be viable but over-complex. It was therefore decided to dispense with the gearbox and cam mechanism and employ a far simpler drive chain instead. Thus the next stage was the Chain Gun proper.

On all Chain Guns every part of the operating mechanism is driven from a length of industrial standard roller chain looped into a 'race-track' configuration. The chain is directed around four sprockets, one of which actually drives the chain while another uses the drive to power and time the ammunition feed system; the other two sprockets are idlers. Within the chain is a single master link which carries a cam follower to drive a slider acting in a transverse slot on the underside of a bolt carrier. The bolt carrier thus slides backwards and forwards on a rod and guide rail arrangement as the chain cycles around the sprockets. In this manner the actions and locking action of the bolt on the carrier can be smoothly generated and precisely and positively timed and driven, as can the other operations such as the ammunition feed, ramming and spent case ejection. The rate of fire can also be precisely controlled. Other advantages inherent in the Chain Gun system compared to self-powered systems are a very high state of reliability, the employment of fewer and lighter components and a generally more compact mechanism.

The first weapon to utilise the Chain Gun principle was produced during 1972. It was a 30 mm weapon which had been accepted into US Army service as the M230 by 1976 and is now carried in a swivelling chin mounting under the AH-64A Apache attack helicopter. During the same period, a second programme concentrated on a 25 mm Chain Gun that evolved into the highly successful M252 Bushmaster mounted on the M2/M3 Bradley infantry fighting vehicles and the wheeled Light Armoured Vehicle (LAV) series; other M242 Bushmaster applications include naval mountings. Both variations are still in production.

There is also a third member of the Chain Gun family that fits within the calibre confines of this book, and that is the MDHC 7.62 mm EX-34.

EX-34

Development of the EX-34 was completed by 1974, following on directly from the experimental EPAM project; from the outset the EX-34 was intended to be a co-axial machine gun for armoured combat vehicles. It was therefore configured to fit directly on to the mounting brackets originally intended for the M73/M219 machine guns in

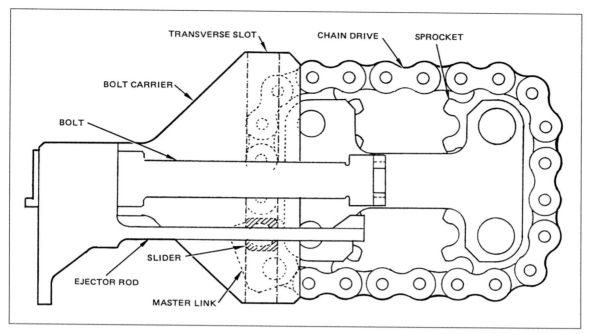

The general operating principle of the Chain Gun. As the chain is driven around, a slider on the master link slides within a transverse slot on a bolt carrier, thus moving the bolt carrier backwards and forwards. On this drawing the chamber and barrel are on the left.

M60 tanks, although the EX-34 has not yet been adopted by the US Army.

The chain drive system employed in the EX-34 is exactly the same as that used on the larger M230 and M242, but is scaled down to suit the size of the weapon and its 7.62 mm × 51 NATO ammunition. To minimise the amount of gas escaping into a turret interior the EX-34 has a long bolt dwell time (ie the length of time the bolt remains closed) to allow propellant gases inside the barrel to escape forward. Another desirable requirement of a co-axial machine gun is met by the ejection of spent cartridge cases forward from the gun and out of the turret entirely (forward case ejection is a feature of all the Chain Guns). Another positive point for the EX-34 is that the entire receiver body can be hinged upwards or downwards to gain access to the barrel for easy changing; the entire barrel change sequence takes less than 10 seconds, during which time there is no need to unload the gun.

Field stripping the EX-34 involves only seven assemblies.

There are two barrel lengths. For co-axial installations a longer 703 mm barrel is involved, which has an unperforated barrel jacket extending to the muzzle and incorporating a venturi system that draws air forward for cooling and doubles as a fume extractor. The shorter barrel is only 580 mm long and lacks the barrel jacket; it is intended for vehicle installations other than turret interiors.

Ammunition is fed into the EX-34 in disintegrating link belts, and the same 0.3 horsepower electric motor that drives the chain system is also used to drive the feed system via one of the four internal sprockets. The rate of fire is a steady 520 to 550 rounds per minute, although an experimental model was under development to fire 1,000 rounds per minute.

Both the US Army and Navy have tested the EX-34 extensively but despite the glowing reports that were circulated after the trials no orders have yet resulted. In the meantime MDHC have arranged an EX-34

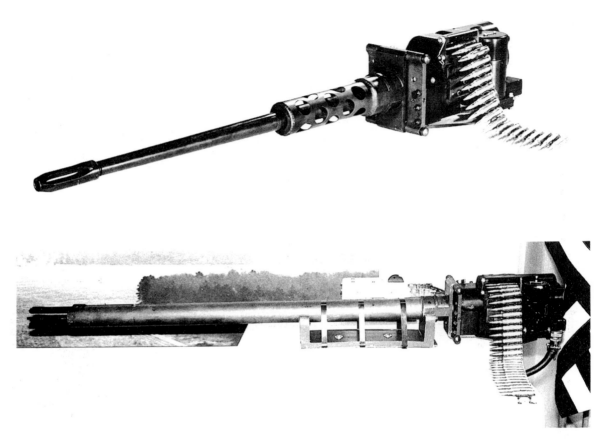

The 7.62 mm EX-34 Chain Gun and its long-barrelled version.

licence production agreement with Royal Ordnance of the United Kingdom. This agreement followed extensive tests using a small number of EX-34s purchased from the United States during 1978 and 1979. The 'British' EX-34 is now in production as the long barrelled L94A1 (the short barrelled version is the L95A1) to form the co-axial armament of the Warrior infantry fighting vehicle and possibly for the Challenger II tank. Other applications will follow as it is understood that the EX-34 will be employed on all future British Army combat vehicles.

Although originally developed as an armoured vehicle co-axial machine gun, the EX-34 has in addition been employed as a light helicopter weapon. Mounted on an MDHC Model 500 or 530 Defender light

helicopter, the EX-34 forms part of the HGS-55 Helicopter Weapon System; each forward-firing EX-34 is flexible in elevation only on this system, the ammunition is carried in a 2,000-round box magazine, and the EX-34 fires at 570 rounds per minute.

ARES Again

The MDHC Chain Guns are not the only externally powered machine guns to be driven by an electric motor. Apart from the General Electric rotary guns there is another weapon known as the 7.62 mm ARES Externally Powered Machine gun, or EPG. It would appear that this weapon was developed as a parallel to the EX-34 component of the Chain Gun family, and functions using a cam drive in place of the

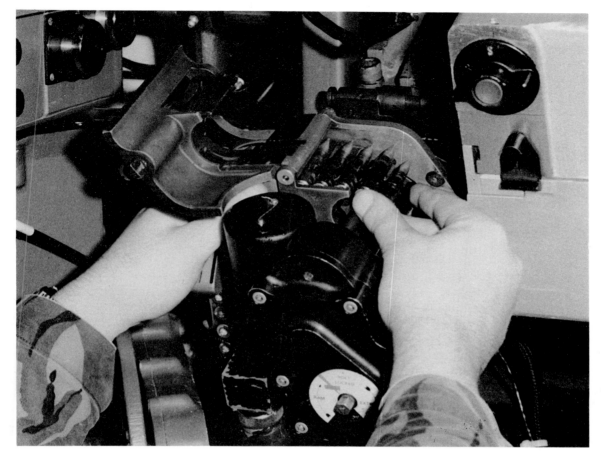

Practice-loading a 7.62 mm EX-34 Chain Gun with inert ammunition inside a British Army Warrior infantry combat vehicle; in British Army service the EX-34 is known as the L95A1.

chain of the EX-34. The rate of fire is variable up to 650 rounds per minute and in the event of a power failure the EPG can be driven by a hand crank. Apparently development of the ARES EPG has been completed but little more has been heard of it during the last few years.

Open Chambers

All the machine guns mentioned in this book so far, whether self- or externally-powered, all employ a chamber into which a cartridge is rammed to be fired. The chamber walls contain the resultant firing stresses, heat and pressures, and the spent case then has to be removed and ejected before a fresh cartridge can be rammed into

the chamber for the next shot.

All this reciprocating action plus the need to ensure that the chamber area walls are thick (and heavy) enough to contain the firing stresses are two inherent but time- and energy-consuming features of all chemically powered small arms and artillery weapons produced to date. There is, however, one further form of projectile weapon that does not need a chamber to allow it to operate. These types of weapon are known as 'lockless' or 'open chamber' weapons.

On these weapons the ammunition acts as its own firing chamber – it is simply aligned with the bore of the barrel and fired while still maintained in position in the ammunition feed mechanism. There are no ramming and extraction movements as each round is fed in from the side to be fired, after which the spent case is removed for ejection, again with a sideways motion.

Early open chamber experiments using conventionally cased ammunition all led to failure since, not surprisingly, the cartridge cases simply burst when ignited. Reinforced cases showed more promise but the conventional circular cross-sectioned cases were still prone to distortion or rupture away from the areas where they were held secured in the feed system.

The answer to these problems was gradually realised to be an entirely new form of ammunition that became known as a Tround. The Tround is roughly triangular in cross-section but with all angles and sides rounded off to produce a shape that can be loaded into a hopper or magazines and which will not produce harsh angles to snag either on side walls or on other Trounds; the triangular cross-section also demands less stowage volume than the circular outline of conventional rounds. One further distinguishing aspect of the Tround is that the projectile does not protrude from the case as it does on an orthodox piece of ammunition. Instead, the projectile, either a conventionally shaped bullet or a dart-like flechette, can be telescoped into the body of the Tround. To make the Tround even more different from other types of ammunition, its body is not metal but a strong polycarbonate-based plastic.

The Hughes Tool Company were involved in much of the early development of open chamber automatic weapons under contract to the US Army and Air Force, and during the early to mid-1950s were involved in a research and development programme involving the T154 30 mm cannon intended for use as a tail-mounted defence weapon for bomber aircraft. This programme evolved into a series of firing test beds with no real weapons produced and involving both single- and double-barrelled guns as objectives.

The general principle was that Trounds were fed into the gun from a hopper and into a revolving drum assembly. The revolving drum used lateral slots machined to accept the incoming Trounds and into which the Trounds readily fitted for rotation to align with a barrel for firing. At the instant of firing the stresses produced were contained by the Tround carrier and the external walls of the revolving drum housing. After firing, the continued rotation of the drum assembly moved the spent Tround case out of the gun. Designs were produced whereby one drum assembly could service two barrels, one on either side, and thereby double the firepower produced.

The T154 and Tround concepts were demonstrated to be viable but the programme had lapsed by the end of the 1950s. Various reasons were cited, including excessive ammunition weight, excessive loads on some gun components and other reasons which no doubt included the adoption of a unique type of ammunition for one specialised application. For all that, demonstrator models produced theoretical rates of fire of up to 2,000 rounds per minute. Apart from the Hughes Tool Company, also involved in the Tround programme were Pachmayr, AAI, the Armour Research Foundation, the Olin Mathieson Chemical Corporation and TRW.

With the demise of the T154 programme it seemed as though the Tround would also pass away – but that was not to be. One David Dardick, who had been involved in the early design and development work for the Tround, developed a small arms variation firing 0.38 projectiles from pistols and rifles. The resultant weapons attracted a great deal of attention in small arms circles but few sales resulted.

Undeterred, Dardick employed some lateral thinking and converted the Tround concept for rock drilling. Using Trounds, Dardick devised a system whereby they were used to fire short bursts of small ceramic projectiles at cyclic rates of up to a quoted 30,000 times a second and at velocities of up to 1,370 metres a second. The ceramic 'bullets' did not penetrate the rock but as they shattered into dust they created shock waves within the rock surface and numerous tiny cracks resulted. Thus when a drill bit was applied to the rock face the drilling was made that much easier.

By the mid-1980s interest in using the Tround in high fire rate aircraft automatic weapons had again revived. Dardick, using his Tround International Company, once again produced an automatic gun involving Trounds.

This time the Trounds used 12.7 mm projectiles encased in plastic and with percussion primers in the base. First shown in 1986, the Tround International gun was intended to act as a test bed for a 20 or 25 mm aircraft cannon; it was externally powered and fed Trounds from a large drum-like magazine, which was also externally powered by an electric motor. No performance figures were released regarding this gun since it was intended to act as a test bed only, but it is understood that it achieved fire rates of up to 5,000 rounds per minute.

During the early 1970s the Hughes Tool Company once again revived the notion of encapsulated ammunition for their so-called 30 mm Lockless Automatic Gun System. On this test weapon the ammunition used a flattened octagonal cross-section with the projectile telescoped within the body of the case. Only one of these weapons was produced, in 1972.

Interest in the open chamber principle for automatic weapons is not completely dormant but any serious research and development interest is barely perceptible. However, it seems certain that the Tround, or something very like it, will emerge again one day for use in high fire rate automatic weapons and that some form of open chamber gun will one day be accepted for operational service.

The experimental 0.50/12.7 mm Tround International machine gun.

DATA

Model	M134 Minigun	Six Pack
Calibre	7.62 mm	5.56 mm
Number of barrels	6	6
Weight (gun only)	15.9 kg	12.3 kg
Length	800 mm	686 mm
Length of barrel	559 mm	n/a
Rate of fire	6,000 rpm	up to 10,000 rpm
Feed	belt	belt
Muzzle velocity	869 m/s	990 m/s

Model	GECAL 50	EX-34
Calibre	12.7 mm	7.62 mm
Number of barrels	3 or 6	1
Weight (gun only)	30 or 43.6 kg	13.7 or 17.86 kg
Length	1.181 m	660 mm or 1.25 m
Length of barrel	886 mm	580 or 703 mm
Rate of fire	4,000 or 8,000 rpm	520-550 rpm
Feed	belt	belt
Muzzle velocity	884 m/s	862 m/s

CHAPTER 21

THE FUTURE

AT the end of the previous chapter it was speculated that some form of open chamber machine gun, together with its associated ammunition, will one day be accepted for service as an operational weapon. This will probably be as an aircraft gun where the high fire rates made possible by the omission of reciprocating bolt movements and subsequent ease of ammunition handling can be used to the best advantage.

The use of the Tround in some of the open chamber experiments of the last few decades leads one to speculate that further innovations in the automatic weapon field will also be introduced. One innovation that is already looming on the small arms horizon is the introduction of caseless ammunition of the type developed to be fired from the German Heckler & Koch 4.7 mm G11 assault rifle. The 4.7 mm × 33 caseless ammunition involved does not require the usual metal cartridge case, as the propellant charge acts as its own container and is entirely consumed at the instant of firing. On the G11 rifle a three-round burst limiter device enables the rifle to operate at cyclic rates of fire of up to 2,000 rounds per minute – normal automatic fire rates are around 600 rounds per minute.

Some consideration has already been

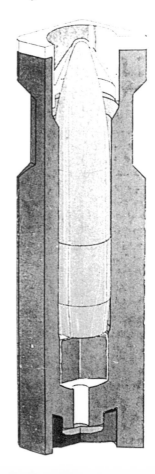

Things to come – a cross-section of an experimental 4.92 mm × 33 caseless round developed by Dynamit Nobel of Germany.

given to producing a light support weapon equivalent of the G11. During late 1988 illustrations were shown of a mock-up involving what appeared to be an enlarged G11 assault rifle but was in fact an entirely new portable light support weapon firing the caseless 4.7 mm × 33 ammunition. The entire project was again a Heckler & Koch proposal.

The futuristic-looking proposed weapon had some very unusual features, not the least of which was a pre-packed 300-round container in the butt from which the caseless rounds were fed sideways one at a time – only just before firing was each round turned to face the barrel. As an ammunition container was emptied the entire butt hinged open, the spent container was removed for disposal and a fresh container inserted. The operating mechanism involved three chambers in a revolver assembly to reduce the risk of 'cook-off' and the entire recoil-powered mechanism was intended to provide a smooth 'floating' system with a low recoil impulse.

It was proposed that a fully loaded weapon would weigh approximately 7 kg; length overall would be approximately 940

mm. No mention was made of the rate of fire but it was doubtless similar to that of the G11 rifle.

The Heckler & Koch light support weapon got as far as hardware models but there the project has remained, for the time being at least. It is a virtual certainty that one day something like the proposed light support weapon will appear in working hardware form, but that day might be postponed following the lack of orders for the G11 rifle, a situation imposed by the need to transfer funding to the politically attractive measures that are uniting the old East and West Germanys.

A prospect with far more attractive long-term ramifications would seem to be the introduction of liquid propellants. These are already well advanced down the development path for field and tank artillery pieces and continued development is bound to result in some form of utility in the small arms sphere. The prospect of troops going into action carrying automatic fire weapons together with a small tank topped up with liquid propellant and a magazine full of separate projectiles may seem outlandish, but the time when such an occurrence

An outline drawing of the proposed Heckler & Koch light support weapon firing caseless ammunition.

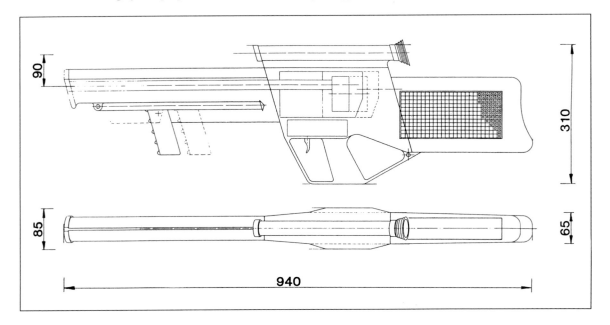

might become reality is not all that distant and some form of automatic fire support weapon might well be one of the first applications for liquid propellants.

However, neither the caseless nor the liquid propellant approach to ammunition innovation will mean the end of conventional ammunition as we know it. All over the world large ammunition manufacturing plants are established and in production, and to make any drastic changes to such a well-entrenched infrastructure would demand something really revolutionary; even then there would remain a market for the orthodox products for decades to come. We will not see the demise of the metallic cartridge-cased piece of ammunition in our lifetimes, nor will we see the replacement of all the present types of automatic weapon that fire them.

Of course the types of projectile fired from machine guns might well alter dramatically. The decades since 1945 have witnessed repeated attempts to introduce the lethal little flechette in place of the conventional bullet, but for one reason or another the former has yet to gain acceptance as a rifle-fired projectile, let alone for machine guns. The coming years will probably see more and more employment of saboted projectiles (or armour-piercing discarding sabot – APDS) in attempts to provide machine guns with improved anti-armour capabilities, or even the introduction of small-calibre armour-piercing fin-stabilised discarding sabot (APFSDS) kinetic energy projectiles. The latter are already in service for calibres as small as 35 mm so the time will soon come when they intrude into the small arms field; heavy machine guns will then be among the first to make use of them.

One aspect of technology that has yet to make its large-scale appearance to the small arms scene, and thence to machine guns, is electronics. Microchips and miniature computers have already been introduced in the workings of computerised sights such as MUGS (see chapter 2) for heavy support weapons, and the increasing introduction of such devices for all types of small arms must

be anticipated, along with night vision capabilities integrated into standard optical sights. However, there is one area where electronic devices are already beginning to appear and that is gun control.

By gun control it is meant that many aspects of machine gun and other weapon operation which are currently controlled by mechanical devices will be converted to electronic control. Aspects that could become involved with electronic gun control include rates of fire, gas regulation, ammunition counting and burst limitation systems. For example, no matter what variations in the rate of fire might be introduced by performance fluctuations in the power or batch of ammunition being used, a constant rate of fire could be readily attained by using some form of microprocessor-based control circuitry, possibly to match the best performance of a buffered mounting to maintain accurate fire at long ranges, or whatever. Other local variables such as temperature, humidity and altitude could also be introduced to gun control operations to the extent that fire control as well as gun control could be considerably enhanced. Despite their capabilities, modern microprocessors and their power sources are minute and could be easily concealed in a machine gun butt or pistol grip with no significant weight or space penalties being introduced, and it is only a matter of time before the first of them appears on machine guns.

Other innovations the years will bring to machine guns will include reduced weights caused by the introduction of lighter yet stronger materials. The employment of light alloys has already made a considerable difference to the weights of the current generation of machine guns compared to their forebears. Modern materials such as reinforced plastics or ceramics seem about to introduce yet another downward trend in small arms weights as they are applied to areas of weapon design that were once the exclusive premise of heavy metals. Whether really ultra-lightweight machine guns beyond an as yet undefined weight limit are a viable proposition is something that will no doubt be argued over long and late, but the soldiers who have to carry the things will no doubt be grateful.

Armchair speculation of the above sort can be indulged in for hours, the result being that more and more seemingly unlikely future prospects will no doubt come to mind. This summary is an outline of innovations involving machine guns that can be confidently anticipated – we will see about the others.

One unfortunate fact is, regrettably, deemed to be virtually a cast iron certainty. Machine guns of every type of shape will continue to be devised and produced for as long as men set out to kill each other in an organised manner.

Despite all the horrors of nuclear, chemical and other aspects of modern warfare that the years might bring, weapons such as machine guns will remain important man-killers for as long as we can foresee.

Firepower will go on killing. Would that it were not so.

INDEX